The Nazi Party and the German Foreign Office

Routledge Studies in Modern European History

The Nazi Party and the German Foreign Office

Hans-Adolf Jacobsen
and Arthur L. Smith, Jr.

Routledge
Taylor & Francis Group
New York   London

Routledge
Taylor & Francis Group
711 Third Avenue
New York, NY 10017

Routledge
Taylor & Francis Group
2 Park Square
Milton Park, Abingdon
Oxon OX14 4RN

First issued in paperback 2012

International Standard Book Number-13: 978-0-415-95771-7 (hbk)
International Standard Book Number-13: 978-0-415-54320-0 (pbk)

Library of Congress Cataloging-in-Publication Data

Jacobsen, Hans Adolf.
  The Nazi Party and the German Foreign Office / Hans-Adolf Jacobsen and Arthur L. Smith, Jr.
      p. cm. -- (Routledge studies in modern European history ; 11)
  Includes bibliographical references and index.

  1. Bohle, Ernst Wilhelm, 1903-1960. 2. Auslands-Organisation der NSDAP. 3. Germany. Auswärtiges Amt--History--20th century. 4. Ribbentrop, Joachim von, 1893-1946. 5. Germany--Politics and government--1933-1945. 6. Germany--Foreign relations--1933-1945. I. Smith, Arthur Lee, 1927- II. Title.

DD256.7.J336 2007
327.1243009'043--dc22   2007000117

Visit the Taylor & Francis Web site at
http://www.taylorandfrancis.com

and the Routledge Web site at
http://www.routledge.com

Contents

Foreword

This is the story of a young, ambitious German who wanted to become Adolf Hitler's foreign minister. His name was Ernst Wilhelm Bohle, and by the age of thirty he already occupied an important position within the Nazi hierarchy as the leader (Gauleiter) of the Nazi Party's foreign section (Auslandsorganisation der NSDAP, or AO). As originally conceived, the office was responsible for members of the party who resided abroad, and, after Hitler's assumption of power, distributed National Socialist propaganda materials via Germany's commercial shipping. The primary focus of the study is the examination of a period in the 1930s, when the AO, under Bohle's leadership, sought to expand its role beyond its original mission by seeking direct participation in the conduct of German foreign policy. It illuminates a dimension of Nazi state history often neglected in accounts of the Third Reich by emphasizing the internal battles that erupted over the question of Party authority versus established state institutions. To this extent, it is a revisionist work.

In attempting to ultimately transform the AO into a real Nazi Party foreign office for a German nation under National Socialism, Bohle fully intended to supplant the traditional diplomatic body that historically had functioned as the Foreign Office (Auswärtiges Amt, or AA). While Hitler did not actually endorse Bohle's encroachment upon the duties of the Foreign Office, neither did he expressly forbid it. There was also a certain amount of support for Bohle from some old line party members who not only harbored resentment against the entrenched diplomatic clique that had managed foreign policy before Hitler, but viewed the replacement of all federal institutions of the Weimar Republic with National Socialist creations as the logical result of instituting the new regime.

In not too many years, the history of the Hitler movement will be nearing the century mark, and with the elapse of time there will be the inevitable revision of certain aspects of that era based upon new interpretations made by a fresh generation of historians. This does not necessarily mean any radical departures from currently held views, but perhaps a re-examination aimed at providing more balance in understanding the workings of the

National Socialist German Workers Party against a background not entirely dominated by World War II and the Holocaust.

In examining the career of Ernst Wilhelm Bohle and the history of the Auslandsorganisation der NSDAP, the intent is not to suggest a departure from the generally held interpretations of Nazi foreign policy during the 1930s, but to point out the very bitter fight for control of implementing that policy. Bohle's goal was to make the Foreign Office and its highly trained diplomatic personnel clearly subordinate to the aims of Adolf Hitler and the Nazi Party. Hopefully, he and the AO, as the designated party foreign office, would play a central role in the process. The precise history of how Bohle tried to accomplish this and the reasons he did no succeed, even though he had strong support at times from powerful party leaders, provides a look at one of the early battles for power in the Third Reich that is relatively unknown.

This work is based upon three large collections of unpublished materials, each encompassing a different time-frame. The collections are: records of Bohle's life and career found in party files; Allied court trial materials, and interrogations between 1945 and 1948; and, numerous personal interviews and correspondence of persons who worked with Bohle (including his wife, Gertrud). The fact that some of the documents relating to the same subject were recorded many years apart is very relevant to the overall theme. In some instances, documentary descriptions of the same events are separated by more than thirty years. This does not necessarily mean that a more accurate account emerged in the process of examining them, but an opportunity was provided to make a comparison and develop a new perspective.[1]

NOTE

1. The most important published studies of the AO are Hans-Adolf Jascobsen, Nationalsozialistische Aussenpolitik, 1933–1938 (Frankfurt/M.: Alfred Metzner Verlag, 1968), and Donald McKale, The Swastika Outside (Kent, Ohio: Kent State University Press, 1977).

Introduction

The study of Hitler's Germany occupies a unique place in the historiography of contemporary history simply by virtue of the huge quantity of published materials (over 100,000 books since 1945) that continually appear. With the exception of some apologists or neo-Nazi publications, the vast majority of the works, whether woven around individuals or events, have usually agreed upon certain basic themes: National Socialist Germany was a totalitarian regime. Absolute power was concentrated in the hands of a Nazi leadership, which exerted total control over the German people, as well as the populations of states that were annexed or conquered in war. Expansionist actions at the expense of peaceful neighboring states were a mainstay of Hitler's foreign policy. Genocidal and euthanasia programs were initiated against people regarded as racially or physically inferior beings.

To understand how a liberal republican state surrendered itself to such complete dictatorship, certain events between the years of 1918 and 1933, must be noted. Obviously, the single most import factor in determining the course of German history before Hitler was the defeat in the First World War, and the punitive peace settlement that followed. Later, despite some successes in establishing a democratic state, the Weimar Republic was confronted with economic and political failure, and became more and more vulnerable to pressures from the extremes of left and right. At first, the National Socialist Party was simply one of a number of these extremist movements, but from the very beginning, the political platform stressed the unfairness of the Versailles Treaty as the major source of Germany's ills. It was a message that found a broad receptivity with the German voters as the republic foundered.

Emerging as the leader of this National Socialist German Workers' Party (NSDAP), Adolf Hitler clearly understood the appeal these complaints had with the German public. He knew that when the arguments against the Versailles settlement were presented, no matter how simplistically, they were eagerly accepted as the explanation for the country's woes. With unrelenting attacks upon the communists, the Jews, and the "November criminals" who had accepted the treaty in Germany's name, Hitler ably articulated the sentiments of the masses.

With an uncanny ability to assess the public mood, he eventually succeeded in persuading the Germans that patriotism and love of the fatherland were synonymous with National Socialism.

Assisted by a cadre of faithful followers like Rudolf Hess, Hermann Göring, Joseph Goebbels, and Heinrich Himmler, Hitler insisted that if Germany was to regain her place among nations, she had to be strong, and could never again be vulnerable to the forces that had brought about the collapse of 1918. Only German dominance of vital resources could insure against such a repeat. This meant the control of certain areas beyond Germany's borders was absolutely necessary to its long term survival.

On January 30, 1933, Adolf Hitler, as leader of the most powerful party in the Reichstag, was named the chancellor of Germany by the elderly President von Hindenburg. In the following weeks it became clear that the aim of the NSDAP was to destroy all opposition and assume total control of the state. The process began with a decree (Verordung) to "protect" the German people by restricting public meetings, publications, and demonstrations. After a fire destroyed the Reichstag on February 27, the Nazis secured the authority to arrest the communists as the perpetrators who were plotting to overthrow the government.

Many of Germany's political leaders from the conservative ranks still labored under the illusion that they could exert some control over the ambitions of Hitler and the Nazi Party. However, with their tightly organized structure and military auxiliary, the National Socialists pushed their program forward, and dissenters and opponents found themselves in "re-training camps," which later became concentration camps.

The spring and summer of 1933, witnessed a powerful Nazi propaganda effort focused upon the "new Germany." It consisted of massive public displays aimed at awakening strong patriotic emotions with slogans that merged the identity of the NSDAP with the state. A period of adjustment (Gleichschaltung) to the new order was announced, permitting the citizens to absorb the changes and acquire the proper attitude toward the National Socialist government. At the same time, all positions of civil authority were in the process of being occupied by members of the party.

On March 24 a fateful step was taken when the Reichstag passed the Enabling Act, which basically ended the power of Germany's legislature. The Reichstag became totally subordinate to the NSDAP, and served as a backdrop for many of Hitler's speeches. The same was true for the cabinet. Soon, with the appearance of the German Labor Front (Deutsche Arbeitsfront) led by Robert Ley, trade unions were dissolved, and some twenty million workers and employers were joined in a membership hailed as the resolution to class warfare. Similar integration was applied to the variety of agrarian organizations composed of producers and distributors of food stuffs.

In a final consolidation of Hitler's power, every vestige of discordance within party ranks was quelled. In the process, several prominent NS leaders were murdered in the infamous "night of the long knives" in June 1934.

Among them was the leader of the Brown Shirts (SA or Sturmabteilung) Ernst Röhm, Gregor Strasser, and General Kurt von Schleicher.

Although the dictatorship was closing around them, the German people were accepting of the new order in exchange for the dramatic upsurge in employment initiated by the introduction of massive public works projects. Little attention was focused upon the fact that significant numbers of the new projects were aimed at rearmament. Utilizing the plebiscite as a measure of public opinion, the Nazis could rightly claim that the German people were exhibiting a new pride and confidence in their fledgling government.

Outside observers of the Hitler experiment were awed by the early successes and were prone to exaggerate the ease with which a dictatorial regime had been introduced. It is true that the takeover of state and local institutions occurred with surprising speed, but rivalries continued to exist not only between the pre-Hitler employees and the new National Socialist arrivals, but also in the sharp competition among the Hitler followers themselves. Despite the constant friction among the party leaders to establish their own exclusive areas of administrative control, there was never any doubt that the major foreign policy aims remained Hitler's domain.

Although Hitler's leadership of party affairs was never seriously challenged after 1934, older NS members, impatient to fully initiate the state they had envisioned in the nineteen-twenties, sometimes found Hitler's contradictory actions to be frustrating. His tactics of delay and compromise, as well as an abandonment of some of the ideas put forth in 1924, in *Mein Kampf,* proved for some of his supporters a serious disappointment, although much of this was diluted by Hitler's impressive successes in both foreign and domestic affairs during the first several years of the regime.

Despite the beginnings of economic programs that contained disturbing rearmament dimensions, there were steps taken in the direction of searching for peaceful solutions to certain problems in foreign affairs. For example, the first important treaty that Hitler agreed to with Poland in 1934 was a ten year non-aggression pact that added diplomatic prestige for both nations, although it did not address the smoldering German resentment toward the existence of the Polish Corridor that had been created as a result of the 1919 peace settlement. In the following year, an Anglo-German Naval Agreement established a ratio between the navies of England and Germany, and, presumably, averted naval competition by eventually agreeing upon a proportion of one-hundred to thirty-five. Thus, these first steps toward introducing Germany's new government into the world of international diplomacy through peaceful treaty negotiations somewhat softened the initial concerns of neighboring states.

In spite of what appeared to be a smooth-working diplomatic German Foreign Ministry (Auswärtiges Amt), there was a scramble from various sources eager to have a voice in affairs abroad. This resulted in a certain amount of confusion at times, especially when it conflicted with a policy or negotiations that the AA traditionally conducted. In addition, it was not unusual for Hitler to occasionally commission an individual to undertake a special mission without regard to diplomatic protocol. Sometimes, actions of Nazi Party leaders like Hess or Göring also complicated matters by issuing a statement or giving a speech that contradicted established policy.

While Bohle no doubt regarded the AO as the logical office to have a share in the conduct of foreign policy (after all, its title was the Foreign Section of the Nazi Party), there were other contenders. Potentially, the most threatening to Bohle was an office directed by Joachim von Ribbentrop, called the Dienststelle Ribbentrop, which acted in an advisory capacity to Hitler. Although this was well before he assumed the Foreign Minister's post in 1938, it meant that he was familiar with Bohle's ambitions, and was alert to any real or imagined encroachments upon the territory that traditionally belonged to the Auswärtiges Amt. Thus, the stage was set for the rivalry that developed between the two men as Ribbentrop continually tried to reduce the importance of the AO, and Bohle persisted in his attempts to increase his organization's role in Germany's foreign affairs.

Another party leader who had thoughts about dabbling in foreign policy was long-time Hitler associate Alfred Rosenberg, the acknowledged philosopher of National Socialism. In earlier times, he had also acted in the capacity of advising Hitler on foreign affairs, and had entertained the possibility of becoming Germany's foreign minister. When this did not happen, Rosenberg took over the party's foreign affairs department (Aussenpolitisches Amt, or APA), which further blurred the territorial divisions between the Foreign Office and the party offices, and added to the confusion about who was making foreign policy. In reality, however, Rosenberg's office had very little influence on policy, and never emerged as an active force to challenge the AA.[1] However, the Nazi state was a Machiavellian world that did not function according to the rules of good management. Bohle fully understood this, and knew that he had to avoid stepping on the toes of certain party elite, but at the same time continue to advance his own ambitions.

The AO leader was acutely aware that his relative youth and newcomer status to the Nazi ranks fed the prejudice that some older party members harbored. It did not help that he was also a foreign born German, or Auslandsdeutsche, which meant to the German who had remained at home, such people did not have quite the same love of the fatherland. The Auslandsdeutsche had also acquired a certain cosmopolitan air that was often regarded with suspicion. These views were reflected in the German concept of citizenship with its multiple subdefinitions.[2] Contrary to some of these negative opinions, Germans who had lived abroad viewed their overseas experience as an enriching one that gave them a much wider knowledge of the world, and a perspective that their counterparts at home did not possess.

Ernst Wilhelm Bohle was born in England in 1903, and spent his first years in Bradford, Yorkshire, where his father was employed as a professor of engineering. Later, the family moved to Capetown, South Africa, and young Bohle attended an English secondary school there before departing for Germany in 1919. Supported by his father, Bohle began his studies at universities in Cologne and Berlin, and eventually graduated from the Berlin Handelshochschule in 1923 with a diploma in business. He now found that his background as an Auslandsdeutsche was a very positive asset, and he found employment with a number of English and American firms that conducted business with Germany and Holland. Soon, he was able to open a small business that specialized in automobile accessories, but with the onset of the Great Depression, he was forced to look for employment elsewhere. It was at this juncture, in response to a newspaper add, that he applied for and was accepted for a job with the Foreign Department (Auslandsabteilung) of the National Socialist Party office in Hamburg. In his application, Bohle listed his areas of expertise as England, South Africa, and the United States. He emphasized not only his English fluency, but a "...solid understanding of the English mentality."[3] It was November 1931, and Bohle was not yet thirty years old.

It is not clear just when Bohle began to see a future in his new job of expert adviser (Referent) in this obscure little office of a political party that many predicted would soon disappear for lack of voter support. At some point he must have decided that there could be a more positive connection between German foreign policy and Germans who lived or worked abroad that went beyond just registering party members and collecting dues. Of course, just how this could be developed depended upon the success of the NSDAP in national politics. He probably could not have predicted when he joined the party in 1931, that in less than two short years, Hitler would assume the chancellorship of Germany, and open the way for his followers to exercise their ambitions. There was no reason for Bohle, who had always been interested in foreign affairs, not to think that the future was virtually unlimited for a young man with ideas. He was also aware that with the assumption of power came responsibilities that some of the older and less well educated party members could not handle easily, and that younger, more capable men would receive recognition from party leaders. For Ernst Bohle that party leader was Deputy Führer Rudolf Hess, with whom he formed an early bond.

Like Bohle, Hess was born abroad, in Egypt, and was a strong supporter of the Auslandsdeutsche, whatever their status. Hess also envisioned an important role for the Auslands-Organisation, and it was no doubt through his influence that Bohle, after participating in a Führer conference, was raised to the rank of Gauleiter[4] in October 1933, a very prestigious party position with broad powers. Considering that Bohle had only joined the party two years earlier, and many loyal members were still waiting for their rewards, his appointment was extraordinary.

When literally interpreted, Bohle's position as head of the Auslands-Organisation made him the leader of all German citizens who were living abroad, and while he often denied any direct involvement with the millions of Germans residing around the world who were not citizens, the potential implications were obvious. He was enough of a diplomat to try and remain aloof from the interminable squabbles that characterized the politics in many of the German foreign communities, but at the same time to provide support for his resident representative (Landesgruppenleiter). Bohle was fully aware that most of these local arguments had little relevance for Berlin, nor for what his own office was trying to promote. He also understood his own limitations in attempting to resolve them. More often than not, he left these problems to his Landesgruppenleitern, some of whom had lengthy personal histories in the communities, and intimate knowledge of what might be involved in a specific dispute. Since a number of these men held early party membership, and the privileges pertaining thereto, Bohle knew that he had to walk softly, and at times, simply take a hands-off policy and hope that an explanation for Hess or some other leading Nazi, would not be necessary.

Unlike some of his party colleagues, who focused their energies upon the petty issues that characterized much of Nazi bureaucracy, the AO leader recognized the importance of certain priorities that Hitler pursued at the time. He knew that the questions involving the border Germans played a far more significant role in Hitler's planning than the fate of the Germans who had formerly live in South West Africa, for example. The vital issues of the day were the politics surrounding those Germans who lived in the Polish Corridor, Austria and Czechoslovakia, and Bohle oriented the work of the AO accordingly.

While there is no single key to understanding the true nature of the Hitler state, a major step is achieved by an examination of the lives of those persons who faithfully supported him. A dictator requires a loyal military force and obedient civil service. Bohle never appears to have seriously questioned the wisdom of National Socialist rule, and yet, as an intelligent individual familiar with the world outside of Germany, and, unlike most of the German leadership, in touch with a wide spectrum of public opinion from every corner of the globe, he followed Hitler to the bitter end. Like many others in the Hitler state, his ambitions caused him to turn a blind eye to the evils of Nazism. Hopefully, the story of his life as the Gauleiter of the Auslands-Organisation, and his efforts to ultimately supplant the Foreign Office, provide a fresh insight into why Hitler received such loyal support from people who knew better.

1   A Source of Funding

Nineteen-twenty-five was an interesting year for postwar Germany. The Weimar Republic was beginning to reap some of the rewards of economic recovery, and the nation was once again assuming a more meaningful role in world affairs. The "spirit of Locarno," with its arbitration treaties guaranteeing the frontiers of France, Belgium, Poland, and Czechoslovakia, opened the way for Germany's membership in the League of Nations.

The death of Social Democratic President Friedrich Ebert in February, and the election of the elderly Field Marshal Paul von Hindenburg in April, did not dampen the optimism among Germany's leading statesmen, and the crippling reparations and disastrous inflation seemed headed for some resolution. In foreign policy the reins were in the skillful hands of Gustav Stresemann, whose name had become synonymous with the rising tide of good will among nations.

It was also the year that an Austrian immigrant named Adolf Hitler began the process of re-building a relatively obscure political party in Germany called the National Socialist German Workers' Party (Nationalsozialistische Deutsche Arbeiterpartei, or Nazi Party).[1] Released from prison after attempting to overthrow the Weimar Republic in 1923, Hitler's efforts at resurrecting his political movement were thought by most observers to be futile. It is unlikely if many German voters even remembered his name.

It looked like an almost hopeless task for Hitler, and while he had been all but forgotten at home, a tiny group of Germans in faraway America calling themselves the "Freie Vereingung Teutonia" (Free Association of Teutonia), sent him a birthday greeting (he turned 36) and twenty-five dollars. Obviously, touched by the note from the groups' leader, Friedrich Gissibl, the future Führer replied: "If the well-off among the Germans here and abroad would offer as much in comparison for the movement, the situation would be quite different in Germany."[2]

The financial situation for the Nazi Party was a desperate one at the time, and every possible source of funding was exploited, no matter how insignificant. Actually, the idea of seeking money from members abroad through dues and contributions, was not a new one. Gissibl had sent money to Hitler before, and after founding the Teutonia with some Germans in

Detroit and Chicago, in 1926 he requested that his little group be recognized as a branch of the NSDAP.[3]

Definitely interested in the prospect of enlisting some new dues-paying members, the Nazi Party's office in Munich (Hauptgeschäftsstelle der Parteileitung der NSADP), quickly responded, and informed Gissibl that registration cost one mark per member, with monthly dues of fifty Pfennings, and additional donations would be gratefully accepted. No mention was made of granting the Teutonia a branch status of the NSDAP. Later, a letter from Gregor Strasser, an early rival of Hitler's for leadership and a leading organizer of party affairs, to Gissibl read: "I have discussed the entire situation with Herr Hitler, and we've come to the following decision: It is with the utmost pleasure that we welcome the National Socialist position of the Teutonia, and recognize a kindred organization in our circle of friends.... We do not wish, however, to officially designate you as representative of the Party, and then experience the same difficulties as before because of the use of the name itself."[4]

Strasser made it clear that the party had not yet formulated a foreign policy in regard to the Germans who lived abroad, but that a great deal of interest was coming from those communities. The party certainly wanted to accept those Germans who wished to be affiliated with the Nazi movement, but there were problems if such groups were actually regarded by their host state as being integrated into the NSDAP, Strasser pointed out. When possible, the best way was to take the same name and work closely with Munich, but have their own organization, like the Germans in Czechoslovakia, he concluded.[5]

Actually, organizing fragmented pockets of Germans abroad who showed some initial enthusiasm for the Nazi Party was not a high priority during this period, although there were individuals who were persistent in pursuing the idea. Gissibl had a counterpart in South America named Bruno Fricke, who had contacted Munich in March 1929 with the suggestion that the party needed an office devoted to the Auslandsdeutsche. In fact, he requested a hundred party membership applications in order to enroll Germans he had organized in Paraguay. He was notified that instructions would be forthcoming, and in the meantime, he was to continue to act as the leader of the "Gruppe Paraguay."[6]

This was not what Fricke had in mind, however. When he had suggested that the party create an office for the Auslandsdeutsche, he was already preparing to return to Germany, and was thinking of himself as heading such an office. Despite being told that he was more useful to the party abroad by raising funds for the movement at home, he was not to be put off, and returned to Germany.[7] His plan was to approach party leaders, such as Alfred Rosenberg, who were sympathetic to the idea, and propose that such an office could oversee the creation of small National Socialist groups (Ortsgruppen) abroad. In the event of any objections by the host country, a group could simply adopt another name, and continue to function.[8]

While no one among the party leadership voiced any objections to Fricke's idea, it came at a time of deepening economic depression in 1930, and the nation was overwhelmed with a multitude of problems. Unemployment was soaring and the NSDAP was focused on the domestic situation with little concern at the moment for the Auslandsdeutsche. Fricke knew this, and in return for appointment as head of a Party Auslandsdeutsche office he offered to pay his own expenses: "I am not asking for anything, only the permission to do what my Ausland compatriots are asking: To create a National Socialist organization abroad."[9]

In the event an Auslands office was created, it fell within the responsibilities of Gregor Strasser, with whom Fricke had been negotiating. There was a problem, however. When Fricke returned to Germany he had taken a position in his hometown of Danzig as head of the Party's Sturmabteilung (SA, or Brown Shirts), and had become involved in some local intrigue concerning street tactics that was displeasing to Hitler. In addition, Strasser was not impressed with Fricke, and described his ambition to head an Auslands office as " illusionary."[10] In fact, Strasser already had another candidate in mind. A party member named Martin Löpelmann, who was a member of the Reichstag. He did not have any special expertise in the situation of the Auslandsdeutsche, but he did participate in committee work that touched on the subject. In November 1930, Strasser promised to discuss the matter with him before Christmas.[11]

The meeting never took place, however, and many years after the Second World War Löpelmann denied any knowledge of the proposed meeting, and denied that he had ever heard of anyone named Bruno Fricke. He admitted that as a Reichstag member he had had some contact with Germans living abroad, but it was of a very minor nature, mostly answering their letters about something or other. Löpelmann said that no one in the party had ever asked him about his work, and certainly not Strasser. He claimed that because he had participated in an earlier protest against Goebbels in Berlin when he was in the SA, Strasser would never have picked him for the job.[12]

There was really no shortage of people like Fricke, who saw an opportunity in heading a party office for the interested Germans who lived abroad. This was especially true if, according to party policy, the position could pay for itself in dues, and bring in some money to Munich. It helped to secure consideration for the job if one had a personal contact with Hitler, and could perhaps convince the Führer of the potential importance of organizing the Auslandsdeutsche into a support group for the party. There was an individual who fit this description. His name was Kurt G. W. Lüdecke.[13]

He had become acquainted with Hitler in the summer of 1922, and greatly impressed with the future Führer, volunteered his services to the party. He was not exactly the typical recruit for he had traveled extensively, and had made some money in the post-war period selling surplus German army supplies. At loose ends and searching for something that expressed his feelings about Germany's situation, he was immediately attracted to the Hitler movement: "I had found myself, my leader, and my cause," he later wrote.[14]

To those who knew him, Lüdecke already had a reputation as an individual not to be trusted in business dealings, and had, in fact, a police record for swindling. Evidently none of this really mattered to Hitler and his followers for Lüdecke had some money to pledge to the party cause as well as his own enterprising personality. He quickly ingratiated himself with Hitler, and was soon advising the Nazi leader on party strategy. He suggested that a study of Benito Mussolini's success in Italy could provide helpful ideas, and offered to go there as the party emissary. Lüdecke's request was strengthened by his boast that in his many travels he had actually met Mussolini, and was prepared to explain the importance of the Nazi movement to the Italian dictator.[15]

Considering that Mussolini was already a figure of world stature, it would appear a bit incongruous at this date for Hitler to dispatch anyone to brief him on the politics of an unimportant Germany political party, but perhaps Lüdecke's persuasive powers and the boast of having met Mussolini were decisive factors, for Hitler provided him with a note authorizing him as the representative of the National Socialist German Workers' Party in Italy.[16] Lüdecke actually did see Mussolini, but there is no evidence that the Italian leader was impressed by the visit or agreed to any form of cooperation. Matters were probably not helped by the subsequent failure of the Hitler putsch in November, and the collapse of the party, with many members arrested or fleeing the country.

By Lüdecke's account, he was chosen by some of the party members who had taken refuge in Vienna, to go to the United States, which he had already visited once, to solicit funds to help rebuild the movement. Armed with a letter of introduction from the Vienna group, as well as a similar letter from Hitler, now serving his time in Landsberg prison after being convicted for his participation in the failed putsch in Munich, Lüdecke set off for the United States in January 1924. Hitler had given instructions that Lüdecke was to take charge of all funds gathered, and, when possible, to personally return them to Germany.[17]

Whether Lüdecke saw a future for himself in party work at this time or not, is difficult to say, but the fact that he was agreeable to the idea of going to America, and making contact with the German communities there to seek contributions to a rebuilding of the Hitler movement, does indicate he saw a potential source of income from Germans who lived abroad. It was certainly premature to consider any plan for the distribution of National Socialist propaganda among the Auslandsdeutsche, or the formation of Nazi Party cells outside of Europe.

In any event, Lüdecke's trip to the United States was a total failure. He did inform Hitler that he had succeeded in getting the American automobile manufacturer Henry Ford to make a modest contribution to the cause, but essentially, the German Americans he encountered were not interested.

They were largely social organizations interested in music, exercise groups, or regional in nature such as Bavarian, Swabian, and so forth. They were not much interested in the political situation in Germany, and not ready to give money to something they had never heard about.[18]

Obviously disappointed, Lüdecke returned to Germany, but soon the Nazis were making news again, and Hitler was receiving more attention. Heartened by this quick change of events, Lüdecke decided to return to the United States with the hope that the German Americans would now be better informed and willing to offer some financial support. He was also beginning to see his traveling past as a kind of preparation for his role as the man to spread the party word among the Auslandsdeutsche. Promoting himself as the expert on current politics in Germany, and especially the Hitler movement, he met with German American groups in New York, Chicago, Detroit, Cincinnati, Milwaukee, and St. Louis. While he was able to generate a little interest here and there, it was not enough to provide him with support or return any funds to the party. He did brag in his messages home that he had become an expert on the United States and Canada, and had driven a quarter of a million miles.[19]

Meanwhile, the fortunes of the party had improved significantly, and, to Lüdecke's surprise, several young men who called themselves Nazis had surfaced in New York, and claimed to have formed a branch of the party there. Although Lüdecke made contact with the New York group, he was disturbed that such a thing could happen without his knowledge. He insisted that he, and he alone, had been personally commissioned by Hitler to direct any such development, although he admitted that he had not been in close touch with Munich of late, nor had his 'commission' been a direct order from the Führer. [20]

Clearly, Lüdecke was jealous that some young Nazi had appeared on the American scene, and now claimed to have enough followers to establish a branch of the party on American soil. As Nazi strength grew at home, and more and more Auslandsdeutsche exhibited an interest in the Hitler movement, the possibility of establishing branches abroad no longer seemed so unrealistic, but Lüdecke ridiculed the idea that just any interested German who resided abroad was qualified to act as the leader. He said that he had encountered many of these would-be leaders in German communities during his travels, and "...they're no credit to the Party. They strut through the streets of German neighborhoods puffed up and loudmouthed....As propaganda, they're pretty bad."[21]

It was, no doubt, with considerable disappointment that Lüdecke got word that Strasser had appointed a Nazi Reichstag member named Hans Nieland to the post of leader of the Auslandsabteilung der NSDAP, as of May 1, 1931. Counting too much on his past association to insure him the leadership, Lüdecke appealed to Strasser, pointing out that Nieland was not the right person because he lacked the proper experience for such a job, and had never even been out of Germany. Strasser rejected Lüdecke's appeal, and told him that "...if you had only stayed here instead of leaving us after Hitler came back from Landsberg...you'd have your own foreign bureau by this time and wouldn't have to worry about Nieland."[22] The message here was that keeping up your party contacts was more important than your qualifications, however, this was not end of Lüdecke's association with the Nazi Party

It was also a time of tumultuous and rapid changes in German politics as the Nazis gained a major presence in the 1930 Reichstag elections. There was increasing civil disorder , and in May 1931, the failure of the Austrian Kredit-Anstalt signaled the beginning of bank closures in Germany, and the end of the flow of capital from abroad. Unemployment was escalating rapidly and the German government, under the leadership of Centerist Heinrich Brüning, was ready to institute emergency decrees in the name of the aging President von Hindenburg in an attempt to cope with an increasingly desperate situation. As the nation edged ever closer to chaos, Hitler recognized that the time was quickly approaching when power would soon be within the grasp of the National Socialists.

Meanwhile, of less national importance, but significant to the continuing story of the Nazi Party and the Auslandsdeutsche, Hans Nieland proceeded to open an office in Hamburg, and began enrolling interested Germans who lived abroad in the Auslandsabteilung der NSDAP. At this point, little attention was given the question of citizenship or residence status of the interested individuals who applied for membership.

Nieland was still not yet thirty years old, and as a party member, had been elected to the German Reichstag in the 1930 landslide. He never exhibited much interest in the subject of foreign affairs, and was grateful for securing a position that enabled him to employ his out-of-work father and sister in the Hamburg office. His appointment to the job had probably been influenced by the fact that several party friends had approached Strasser about creating a position that would indicate to the Auslandsdeutsche that the party cared about them. Again, an example of the rule that contacts counted more than qualifications in the Nazi hierarchy. Actually, not everyone in the party leadership favored such an office, and did not regard the Auslandsdeutsche situation as one that required early attention. Ernst Wilhelm Bohle, who later headed the office, wrote that not many party members wanted to take on the thankless work of dealing with the Germans who lived outside Germany's borders, or deal with the task of trying to recruit them for the movement. There was also the question of finding the necessary funds to do these things and build an organization.[23]

After the NSDAP became the ruling party of Germany in 1933, many of these earlier concerns often took on a significance that was not commensurate with their importance at the time, but for a political movement that appeared to be totally finished in 1923, the 1930 election triumph sent hopes soaring. In April 1931, Strasser directed that all Ortsgruppen (local groups), Stützpunkte (NS cell abroad), and single party members living outside Germany were now under the administrative authority of the Auslandsabteilung der NSDAP. The Saarland, Danzig, and Austria were not included. Dr. Hans Nieland was named as the leader of this Hamburg office.[24] A city selected primarily because it was a port city that provided an easy avenue for shipping propaganda literature via German seamen who were party members; it was also Nieland's home.

With Strasser's endorsement, Nieland composed his first message (Rundverfügung Nr. 1) to his new charges: "Our Führer, Adolf Hitler, has confirmed the proposal of Reichsorganisationleiter Gregor Strasser to establish a foreign office, illustrating the interest in you and your welfare. Now, it is up to you to demonstrate to the Führer that you are not going to stand by in the fight for German freedom...so this call goes out to you today to join with the German people in this battle with all of your strength."[25]

After this brief but forceful introduction, Nieland outlined the organizational structure of his new department, and on paper, at least, it was one of grandiose proportions and literally covered the world. Answerable to Strasser's Organisationsleitung I der Reichsleitung, the Auslandsabteilung consisted of Nieland, his office staff(father and sister), and the individuals responsible for the various geographical divisions.[26] However, Nieland noted, there were no funds available to his office from the party treasury (Reichsschatzmeister) because every pfennig was being used for the struggle now unfolding at home. Therefore, the Auslandsabteilung must support itself from members' dues payable in advance, a sum of three marks monthly beginning 1 May 1931(this was one mark higher than in Germany, but conditions were worse there), and an entrance fee of two marks. Do not avoid your duty, Nieland wrote, because the party is fighting for its life, and must be given all your support.[27]

The next step, Nieland continued, was to stimulate the growth of party units abroad. Germans everywhere must be encouraged to create Ortsgruppen and Stützpunkten, and this can be done as soon as fifteen or more people in small towns, or fifty people in larger cities, can be organized into an Ortsgruppe, and their names forwarded to Hamburg for authorization. In accord with NSDAP rules, the group will elect its own leader, who will be responsible to the Auslandsabteilung for a monthly report and the collection and submission of dues. The Ortsgruppenleiter will also have the task of distributing propaganda materials that are sent from Germany, soliciting subscriptions to NS publications, and sending articles to the local press. On the question of supplying the press with articles, Nieland explained that the fact that they originated with the party information office should not be mentioned, and the authors would appear to be neutral individuals. In closing, he wrote that "your job is to work hard in order that at year's end we can tell the Führer that the Organisation Ausland exists!"[28]

Anxious to succeed, and enlist as many Germans as possible, it is significant that Nieland never mentioned anything in his message about a citizenship requirement. The failure to clearly state that only German citizens were qualified to become members of the Auslandsabteilung, left the question open for many Germans living abroad who no longer held German citizenship. It was an omission that would divide many German communities abroad and create unpleasant relations with host countries.

Armed with lists of possible members and office stationary with his own letterhead, Nieland soon began receiving inquiries from Germans worldwide, eager to know what this new office was all about. Sorting out the correspondence that seemed to have the most promise for contacts and influence, Nieland answered personally. He recognized the fact that if the office was to be a success, he had to work fast to establish some kind of wide network of party units. Almost immediately, he knew that avoidance of the citizenship requirement meant problems with the host countries, however, at the same time he was aware that there were many influential Germans living abroad who no longer held German citizenship but showed a strong interest in the Hitler movement. The problem would be to encourage participation from all interested Germans, but avoid running afoul of the law in those nations with German communities.[29]

Nieland's practice in dealing with the citizenship question at first was to follow the lead that had been used by Strasser's office. For example, when Gissibl had requested Ortsgruupe status for the Teutonia, he was informed that as soon as he could verify fifty members it would be granted, but no mention was made about a citizenship requirement. Now, however, as the prospective members began to rapidly increase, Nieland had to adopt a more positive policy. The matter was referred to the party lawyer and Hitler's personal attorney, Dr. Hans Frank. Nieland was summoned to Munich for discussions, and the decision was made that only a German citizen (Reichsdeutsche) could hold party membership.[30]

The decision seemed clear enough, as far as it went. There does not appear to have been any further discussion on the matter of membership requirements. However, despite acknowledging a certain sensitivity to what other governments might regard as an intrusion, there was no reluctance to see front organizations as an alternative in enlisting non-German citizens. Apparently, Nieland and the Reichsleitung did not anticipate that the arousal of hostile feelings would be equally as strong toward a thinly veiled Nazi organization. The very tactic meant the infiltration of hundreds of German clubs and organizations by party members determined to infuse the communities with National Socialist propaganda. Either Nieland failed to see what would happen, or he saw the additional source of funds as worth the risks.

It was his argument that front organizations allowed many interested Germans who no longer held German citizenship, to participate in National Socialist activities when properly led by party members. He cited the Teutonia in Chicago, as an example. It had over two-hundred members and some fifty of them were not German citizens. It had qualified as an NSDAP Ortsgruppe, and maintained separate records on the two groups. The leader of the Teutonia can, at the same time be the leader of the Ortsgruppe, and, of course, a party member, Nieland wrote: "The Teutonia is the cover organization, and the Ortsgruppe the center piece."[31]

He did admit that the circumstances were not the same in every country where the German communities were located, but they did have some things in common. It is well known that every nation guards its sovereignty with laws that permit expulsion for certain violations, and it is very important that every effort be made to avoid breaking these laws. This means, the admission of non-German citizens to party membership can not be allowed, no matter how friendly party presence may be received in a community abroad. Of course, it will not always be the case that party members will be greeted with open arms, Nieland continued. He cited a recent report he had received from Spain where a group of German citizens had attempted to form an Ortsgruppe and had instead aroused the wrath of the other Germans living there because they feared that the Spanish government would force them all out.[32]

The large number of non-German citizens who wanted to partake in the Hitler success exceeded even Nieland's early estimates, and they were proving a far too valuable as a propaganda tool, as well as a source of money, for the Auslandsabteilung to enforce its ban against their participation in a Ortsgruppe. However, the front organization strategy that he had devised met early and strong opposition abroad, and he decided that it could be revised to the extent that the sharp criticisms directed at the party could be ameliorated somewhat. His proposal was, that instead of clandestinely mixing the affairs of a front organization with the Ortsgruppe, and keeping two sets of books, it would be better to simply encourage the creation of National Socialist organizations abroad that would enroll anyone, but have no legal connection to the party's Ortsgruppen. An informal arrangement could then be established between such organizations and the Auslandsabteilung der NSDAP. [33]

At this point in time, October 1931, the activities of Nieland's office were but a very minor part of party concern, but he was convinced that the Nazis were on the road to victory, and this meant the potential expansion of the Auslandsabteilung into an important arm of overseas propaganda. In this anticipation, he drafted a vastly expanded plan for an office consisting of eleven departments, which he submitted to the party's Reichsleitung. It was a fortunate moment for the NS Reichstag member, for Strasser was considering placing all German seamen who were party members into the Auslandsabteilung. This meant not only a substantial increase in membership(about five-hundred seamen), but the transfer of their party dues to Nieland's Hamburg office.[34]

This was not an action that was met with everybody's support, however. Party members jealously guarded their areas of authority, and when it meant a loss of some of the rank and file (and money) to another member, it often meant that a bitter fight ensued. The brief history of the NSDAP was already rife with instances of deadly infighting as members struggled for position and authority, a practice that Hitler encouraged. Party files are filled with records and correspondence of numerous cases of charges and countercharges brought to the Reichsleitung and party court for resolution. In this instance, many of the seamen had been enrolled in other Gaue controlling port cities (Hamburg, Ost-Hannover, Pommern, Danzig, and Königsberg), and the respective Gauleitern were definitely not in accord with the transfer, especially since it entailed the loss of funds. Each of the Gaue in question had a Seefahrt Sektion that enrolled seamen party members, and the suggestion was made to Strasser that matters remain as they were, but that the seamen be responsible to Nieland's office only for carrying propaganda materials to spread abroad.

Nieland's leading opponent was the Gauleiter of Hamburg, Karl Kaufmann, a man not be taken lightly. He had a long and faithful record of service to the party, having joined the movement in 1921. Kaufmann had done early party organizing in the Rhine-Ruhr, and was well acquainted with Hitler, who had selected him as a possible Reichstag candidate in 1928, and was appointed Hamburg Gauleiter in 1930. He objected to the transfer of the seamen out of his Gau to the Auslandsabteilung on the grounds that Nieland knew nothing about ships and shipping companies, and was a poor leader for the seamen. However, Nieland was successful in persuading Strasser that under his direction the Nazi seamen would soon drive all the Communist and Social Democratic seamen off the ships, and Kaufmann was forced to retreat.[35]

Nieland's personal dossier at the Reichsleitung revealed, however, that Kaufmann had good cause to complain. The main charges against him were incompetence and nepotism. The German community in Rome complained to Munich about the very poor impression Nieland had made on a recent visit, and Rudolf Hess was informed that men in Nazi Party uniform, presumably members, were appearing on the street of that city and soliciting money. While Hess thought the men in question might be Communists who were trying to embarrass Hitler, he did direct Nieland to notify all members abroad that any such activity would bring expulsion from the party.[36]

When Strasser removed the party branches in Switzerland and Italy from Nieland's jurisdiction, the Auslandsabteilung leader, regarding the action as a penalty, hurried to Munich to defend his position, but found himself instead facing the charge of nepotism. Specifically, he was accused of excluding qualified party members from jobs in his office in order to employ less competent relatives. His father was chief clerk and his sister office cashier, and neither had joined the party until Nieland hired them. Nieland insisted that his sister had left a higher paying position to take the job in his office, and that until very recently, his father had worked without pay. He implied his relatives were important in the running of the office because he needed people in whom he could place the utmost trust as some of his work was highly confidential.[37]

It is impossible to say whether Nieland's defense helped him survive various charges, or whether the far larger arguments raging within party ranks simply reduced his activities to a matter of no real importance. Gregor Strasser, the most important party leader next to Hitler, was pushing for more focus upon the socialist aspects of National Socialism, which he regarded as essential if the party was to become a serious voice in government. Hitler's demands for all or nothing, and his rejection of all provisions of the Versailles Treaty, and the reparations bill was, however, receiving a strong endorsement from the German voter as unemployment soared over six million people by the end of 1931.

Meanwhile, the government led by Centerist Heinich Brüning was struggling to keep the coalition functioning. Brüning hoped to strengthen his position in the coming March elections by backing a proposal to form a customs union with Austria. The idea was strongly opposed by Germany's neighbors, France, Poland, and Czechoslovakia, and rejected by the Hague Court. As the economic crisis deepened, Brüning was finally forced to announce that Germany could no longer meet the reduced reparations payments arrived at by the 1929 Young Plan.

Just how thoroughly all of this influenced the German electorate is impossible to calculate, but there is no denying the dramatic impact of the terror in the streets of Germany's major cities as the Nazis and Communists fought for control, and the government was no longer capable of maintaining public order without resorting to emergency decrees(permissible under Article 48 of the Weimar Constitution). By the end of 1931, the German Republic, born with such hopes during the miseries of defeat, was on the verge of disintegration.

2 The Gau Ausland (AO) and Ernst Wilhelm Bohle

By the beginning of 1932, it was obvious that the authority of the Reichstag had weakened so badly as to be almost meaningless. Chancellor Brüning was convinced that a new election would bring the National Socialists to power, and he attempted to extend Hindenburg's presidency to 1934. To do this, however, required the cooperation of Adolf Hitler and Alfred Hugenberg, chairman of the rightist Deutschnationale Volkspartei (German Nationalist Peoples' Party), and Brüning could not secure it. This forced the elderly Hindenburg to stand for re-election in March, but he fell short of the needed majority, and had to face Hitler again in April. The Nazi Führer did not defeat the old marshal, but the NSDAP garnered well over thirteen million votes, almost double that received in the 1930 election.

Brüning, now governing largely by presidential decrees, and in strong disagreement with Hindenburg about the alarming growth of unemployment and land policies in East Prussia, submitted his resignation in May. Another important factor in his decision to resign was the insidious political intrigue led by Reichswehr Minister General Kurt von Schleicher, who succeeded in replacing Brüning with Franz von Papen, a conservative Catholic with little understanding of Germany's problems. With Constantin von Neurath as foreign minister and von Schleicher as defense minister, Germany's newly formed cabinet was quickly dubbed the "ministry of barons."

In the interval between von Papen's appointment on June 1, 1932, and Hitler's assumption of the office on January 30, 1933, Germany seethed with civil disorder as Nazis, Communists, Socialists, and Catholics battled for control of the cities. The July 1932 Reichstag elections returned 230 National Socialists, and when Hitler refused Hindenburg's proposal that he accept the position as von Papen's vice chancellor, a deadlock ensued. Although the November elections witnessed a drop in Nazi support and the resignation of von Papen, nothing was resolved. In the midst of this political turmoil, General von Schleicher assumed the post of chancellor, but the move only aggravated the already desperate situation, and the year came to a close with a growing confidence by Hitler that power would soon be his.

This confidence was widely shared by members, who must have sensed that they were in the forefront of a momentous wave of change about to sweep over Germany. When this was translated into individual action, it meant that Nazi Party members began to see opportunities for improving their own situations. Control of the state would obviously mean many state positions would become available to those who had a record of faithful service to the party, in many instances, regardless of qualifications.

Dr. Hans Nieland, now a Gauleiter, was no exception to the job fever sweeping over the Nazi Party. Meanwhile, he had notified all members abroad that every party identification card had to have the new Auslands-Ausweis Hülle (cover) with the stamp and his signature as of the first of March, 1932. The cost was sixty pfennigs plus postage.[1] This was only one of numerous efforts Nieland engaged in to extend his authority and make his position important in anticipation of a Hitler victory.

The year was unfolding as a crisis for Reichsleiter Strasser, and he did not always regard Nieland and his concerns as matters of priority. Often, Nieland's pressures were ignored and correspondence went unanswered. Aware of the internal conflicts that were raging between Hitler and Strasser, Nieland tried to convince the Reichsleiter that his ambitions for the Gau Ausland were synonymous with the larger picture of the future of National Socialism: "I understand," he wrote, "that the current internal political questions are far more important than the activities of the Auslandsabteilung....However, I regard it as my duty as the Leiter of the Auslandsabteilung not to slack off from the work, but to press on. As the time draws nearer for the seizure of power (Machtübernahme), the more important it is to have a reliable, working party apparatus abroad that can provide propaganda and clarity."[2]

While such a statement could well be interpreted as coming from someone truly interested in suggesting how the role of the Auslandsdeutsche might represent a true asset to a Hitler government, Nieland had neither the background nor the ability to provide such leadership. His past utterances and interests did not indicate any abiding interest in the world of the German abroad, but instead a persistent drive to make his office a self-paying unit of the Nazi Party. Within this same letter to Strasser, he complained about the loss of funds from those members in Italy and Switzerland, who had been removed from the Auslandsabteilung, and asked that at least some portion of their dues be assigned his office. [3] While Nieland's request to share in the dues of members from Italy and Switzerland was denied, Strasser did assign him authority for the membership of all party people residing in the Baltic and Scandinavian regions, and agreed to a temporary payment of five hundred marks monthly.[4]

These petty details of party finance have little significance in themselves beyond illustrating the intense and never ending squabbles over money that characterized the Hitler movement. The intensity was just as fierce when it involved questions of authority and jurisdiction. Every ounce of territory was jealously guarded, and even the slightest hint from any quarter that one party member had designs on another's area of control, could result in a battle that left bitter resentments and promises of revenge. Sometimes the threat of encroachment was based on rumor, but the possibility of falling out of favor with Hitler was a constant fear, and no one was immune.

Of course, Nieland was well aware of the risks and gains involved in the politics of the party, but the status and the structure of the Gau Ausland were quite different from the other Gaue. Most of the membership was not in Germany, and certain vital administrative functions were entirely dependent upon a staff hundreds, or even thousands, of miles distant from Germany's borders. This arrangement made the Gau more vulnerable than usual to any ambitious party member who saw Nieland's leadership as weak. He did have influential party friends, but his position was being constantly assailed by members who had lived abroad for years, and resided in German communities where they had already assumed leadership roles. Many times such individuals had a far better grasp of world affairs outside of Germany than Nieland did, and a more realistic view of what function the Auslandsdeutschen could fulfill, if and when Hitler became chancellor.

This was especially a problem for Nieland when his instructions regarding a program or policy formulated in Hamburg, were resisted at the local level by a party member who wielded influence in a foreign community. It was not unusual for such an individual interested in organizing a party unit to seek his authority directly from Munich, and Nieland only found out about it after the fact. Such actions were regarded as acceptable in accord with the leadership principle (Führerprinzip) that Hitler had outlined in *Mein Kampf,* that endorsed the power of the individual to exert his will over the majority.[5] While the leadership principle prevailed in many instances, it did not insure competence, and often resulted in aggressive and ambitious party members attaining positions that required skills and background that they did not possess.

Nieland was regularly confronted with such challenges to his jurisdiction from party members who sought to bypass his authority, or even ignore it. In March 1932, for example, Nieland sent a sharp complaint to Strasser regarding a party member in Holland who was causing a disturbance among other members there, and claiming that he had Munich's support. Nieland wrote that he suspected further intrigue and was certain that someone in the Munich Brown House headquarters was behind it all. Whoever was doing this, he continued, was well acquainted with party politics, and in the interest of the Gau Ausland must be strictly dealt with: " I will not tolerate this any longer."[6]

Despite the tough sounding talk, Nieland's complaint did not seem to make much of an impression on the Reichsleitung, in fact, Strasser did not even reply. This is not too surprising considering the inner struggles that were consuming the party leadership at this point, and no doubt to many of the major figures involved, the Gau Ausland was the least of their concerns.

Without question, Nieland understood the Machiavellian world of Nazism, and he knew that he had to make his modest undertaking meaningful to the party leadership if it was to survive. Plagued by the constant lack of money to do more, he sought schemes that would bring in some revenue and at the same time be compatible with party policy. One such, was the launching of a newsletter ("Confidential National Socialist Foreign Letter," one mark, fifty pfennigs) to the Auslandsdeutsche, extolling the virtues of National Socialism, and charting the gains that were being made toward securing power. In the initial offering, he praised the Auslandsdeutsche as representatives of the finest that Germany had to give(efficient, strong, intelligent, etc.), however, in the past they had not been able to play a significant role in world events because they did not have a cause and a leader, but it was different now: "Our Leader is determined to provide you with the opportunity to integrate into the National Socialist movement, and it was for this reason that the Auslandsabteilung was created."[7] He exhorted his readers not to forget that the United States would have never entered the First World War if the millions of Germans living there had been an organized force. This fact illustrated the importance of the role of the party members abroad in the new German foreign policy, he concluded.[8]

It was almost inevitable, considering the volume of propaganda that accompanied news about Hitler's movement in Germany, that foreign governments regarded Nieland's office as a cover for spy activities. This was especially true after the Nazis came to power. It appeared to be a logical assumption, and was so pervasive in the news media that it created a picture that greatly distorted the actual functions of the Gau Ausland (later called the Auslands-Organisation, or AO). This does not mean that there was no cooperation with Germany's intelligence apparatus later, but spying and espionage were not functions of the Gau.

Nieland's dilemma was that he had to officially disclaim any attempt at recruiting non-German citizens, but at the same time he wanted their support. Not only were they helpful in determining the receptivity of a German community to National Socialist propaganda, but were a potential source of funds. The ruse of creating front organizations that cooperated closely with a Nazi Landesgruppe may have avoided some legal problems, but it did not fool local authorities, and often aroused open hostility. The early organizations adopted names like "Friends of the Hitler Movement" or "Friends of National Socialism", and hoped to enlist those people who had begun to find the rise of the Nazi Party attractive and interesting. Nieland insisted that the organizations offered the Germans who no longer held German citizenship the opportunity to join with their brothers in the Fatherland in the support of National Socialism.[9] Despite the growing hostility in various foreign states, however, there was no denying that the NSDAP was on the verge of engulfing Germany, and a number of Nazi Party members recognized the potential value of cultivating a closer relationship with the Germans who resided abroad. For Nieland, this recognition had already translated into his elevation to Gauleiter.

When placed into the proper perspective, however, this early role of the Auslandsabteilung, and later Gau Ausland or Auslandsorganisation, started with an idea of some party members to create an office that would enroll all NSDAP members who lived abroad into a special unit, supply them with the news of what was happening in Germany as the National Socialists fought for power, collect enough dues that would pay for the office, and send a bit to Munich. Since this was still the period before Hitler became chancellor, there was not too much concern that a party office with the word "Ausland" or "foreign" in its title, implied a definite interest in foreign affairs. No one in the party leadership seems to have raised the question of a potential conflict with Germany's traditional foreign office (Auswärtiges Amt, or AA), when the Nazis came to power.

A reason for the apparent disinterest in the Gau Ausland before 1933, was that it was not a policy-making arm of the Hitler movement, and was not charged with conducting any foreign affairs beyond the distribution of propaganda in the name of the NSDAP. Considering the turmoil that characterized German politics, and the desperate fight the Nazis were involved in as they struggled to gain political dominance, the trials and tribulations of the Gau Ausland were totally unimportant to the party leadership, as well as to the rank and file membership. Those individuals most interested in making the welfare of the Auslandsdeutsche a concern in party affairs, were a few men, mostly unemployed, who saw the possibility of winning a job in a depression world, and at the same time serving a political movement that promised a future.

It was the speed with which the NSDAP came to major prominence on the German political stages that changed the picture. What had been at times a distant possibility, now appeared within arm's reach, and the entire party structure was suddenly imbued with a new significance. The Gau Ausland was no exception. Nieland's office was reorganized into six, later eight, separate administrative sections, each responsible for a different part of the world where party members lived. Hundreds of newly enrolled German seamen carried a party identity card issued by the Gau Ausland (NSDAP Ausland-Ausweis).[10] By September of 1932, the Gau Ausland had managed to take in some 3,832 marks (well over 10,000 dollars) in dues. When Nieland made his report, the tone was quite optimistic. In a clue to his own thinking at the time about the possible future role of the Gau Ausland, he wrote that while his office had developed strong contacts with Germans abroad, there had been an avoidance of foreign officials and the foreign press, because a party foreign policy office still did not yet exist.[11]

Although there were those in the party who had reservations about Nieland's work, his report was impressive. He could boast that his organization literally stretched around the world. It had grown from 486 members in May of 1931 to 2,720 members by September1932. There were 10 Landesgruppen (national), 34 Ortsgruppen (regional), 43 Stützpunkte (local), plus 214 individual party members without local connections (2,720 party members living in Switzerland and Italy were not included). Party members and units could be found in fifty-one countries.[12]

Of course, the degree of involvement and connection to Hamburg varied considerably from place to place. Significant factors were the number of Germans who resided in a community, how sympathetic they were to National Socialism, how many party members lived among them, where the community was located, and how receptive the host country was to Nazi agitation. In his report Nieland spelled out some of the situations that existed. For example, in Norway there were three party members, two of whom later returned to Germany, and contact was lost with the third; in Poland there were seventeen party members, but no organization for they were scattered over the country; in Czechoslovakia sixteen party members worked 'underground', because the situation was very "delicate"; Rumania had an Ortsgruppe in Bucharest and the outlook was very positive; neither Greece (twenty-eight party members) nor Turkey (sixteen party members) had yet qualified for an Ortsgruppe.[13]

Although the Gau Ausland had six party members living in Palestine, Nieland described it as one of the more difficult places he dealt with in attempting to broaden the National Socialist base. However, Shanghai, China had over one hundred party members, and an Ortsgruppe, and it was even more promising in Holland with one-hundred-fifty party members in two Ortsgruppen, and a Landesgruppe. London, which had an Ortsgruppe since December 1931, had seventy-six party members, but most of them were there to study English, and were not permanent residents. Canada and the United States, reported together, had one-hundred-ninety-seven party members. While the United States looked like fertile ground with interest coming from the "Teutonia" and the "Friends of the Hitler Movement," Canada was a different problem with party members living in quite isolated places.[14]

Nieland's report contained an interesting reference to Ernst W. Bohle's father, Professor Dr. Hermann Bohle, who was teaching at the University of Cape Town in South Africa. The elder Bohle had assumed a leading role in organizing a group of party members there, and Nieland had high praise for his efforts, but pointed out a problem: "The majority of German citizens living there are very dependent upon Jews," he wrote, "and therefore can not endanger their livelihood by joining the party. South Africa is without a doubt, a country with the strongest Jewish population in the world."[15]

One area of the world with quite strong party membership was Latin America, although Nieland did not emphasize this in his report. For example, Brazil had five-hundred-four members, Argentina two-hundred-seventy-eight, Chile over two-hundred-fifty, and Paraguay seventy-seven members.[16] A possible reason for Nieland's omission may have been the fact that another party member, Bruno Fricke, had organized the earliest group of members in Paraguay in 1929, and had urged party leaders to consider the creation of a foreign office at that time.

Only a few months after his lengthy report, the Nazi Party gained its awaited victory and assumed control of Germany, Nieland was relieved of his position as head of the Gau Ausland and appointed chief of police of the city of Hamburg. While this may have been a more suitable career move for a man who had held membership in the NSDAP since 1926, a party number under the fifty-thousand mark, and a World War I veteran, Nieland did not exactly see it that way.

When asked about the details thirty-five years later, Nieland was still convinced that his removal had been the result of some convoluted party intrigue. First of all, he said, Hitler had been influenced by Kurt Lüdecke, who had a very negative opinion of the Auslandsdeutsche at the time because of his own failure to organize them behind National Socialism. Then, he continued, Josef Goebbels wanted to control all propaganda efforts both in Germany and abroad, and did not want the Gau Ausland to be involved beyond arranging the shipping of the materials. Finally, the overall situation within the party with Strasser's resignation and Robert Ley as his replacement, meant that many of the people who had worked for Strasser were marked for dismissal, Nieland included.[17]

When Ernst Wilhelm Bohle was named to head the Gau Ausland, the office was almost on the verge of extinction. Ley had plans to reorganize the office, and transfer certain functions (like the seamen membership) to other Gaue. Although Bohle wished to remain employed in some aspect connected with the Auslandsdeutsche, he recognized that he also faced the possibility of unemployment if the Gau Ausland disappeared. Fortunately, when working for Nieland, he had become acquainted with Alfred Hess, the brother of the Deputy Führer of the party, Rudolf Hess, so Bohle decided to go directly to Hess, and make his case for the continuance of the Gau Ausland.[18]

Bohle knew that the Deputy Führer had a strong interest in the Auslandsdeutsche, because of having lived a number of years in Egypt as a youth, and often referred to himself as a "foreign German." Bohle said he told Hess that if the Gau Ausland was dissolved "...there would be a lot of trouble and the Germans outside would start their own organizations...it would be better to have a well-disciplined organization than to allow organizations in other countries to work on their own. It took me sometime to persuade him."[19]

The meeting with Rudolf Hess was a turning point in Bohle's career, and became a very important influence in his life. He was still a young, and relatively unimportant Nazi functionary to have made such a close and personal contact with the man that Hitler had appointed as his deputy. It gave Bohle a powerful mentor and protector in the party. Shortly after the meeting with Hess, Bohle received news that he had been appointed to head the party office for Germans abroad, and although he felt that Rudolf Schmeer, director of the party personnel office (Leiter des Personalamtes), had been instrumental in the appointment, it was clear that it could not have happened without the contact he had established with Hess. Bohle claimed later that he was totally surprised by it all: "I hadn't the faintest idea that I would be appointed because I was absolutely unknown at that time, absolutely a new party member, didn't belong to the old group; I only joined in March 1932 — of course, I wanted to make a job of it."[20]

Bohle had another meeting with Hess after the confirmation of his appointment on July 4, 1933. He said that Hess never had any specific complaints about the work that Nieland had been doing with the Auslands-deutsche, but emphasized that it was important that they received a good, positive image of National Socialism. "He said he wanted no troubles out-side...and the general directions he gave me were not to have any trouble with foreign states....That was the standing rule he gave me."[21]

There was no question but that Bohle's elevation to such a high position (Gauleiter) at his age and brief party tenure, was very unusual. This was the year of taking power, and thousands of Nazi Party faithfuls who had paid their dues through the lean years, as well as hundreds of thousands of ordinary unemployed Germans, were clamoring for jobs of any kind with the new regime. While Bohle was not exactly unprepared for the position, and was better qualified than Nieland had been, there were hundreds of party members with a far more impressive record of service to the cause who were just as well prepared. In fact, it would not be too far from the truth to say that Bohle was not even a thoroughly committed National Socialist at the time of his appointment, although his family background was one of strong German nationalism and bitter opposition to the Treaty of Versailles. The only logical explanation for his good fortune in 1933 had to be the support he received from Rudolf Hess.

Like many of the German families who lived and worked abroad for a number of years, the Bohle family did plan to return to Germany some-day.[22] Ernst was born in Bradford, England, on July 28, 1903. In a postwar statement that betrayed neither pride nor regret, Bohle said: "I simultane-ously derived German nationality from my father, who had been natural-ized with the stipulation in his naturalization papers that he could retain his German citizenship when in Germany. I therefore had dual nationality."[23]

Originally from the Rhineland, Hermann Bohle took a position as a col-lege instructor in mechanical engineering in Bradford, however, a few years after Ernst's birth he accepted a professorship at South Africa College, later the University of Capetown. The five Bohle children, two boys and three girls, were raised in a home atmosphere that placed a strong emphasis upon German nationalism. The father was very active in the German communi-ties in South Africa and South West Africa, and forbade his children to speak English during the First World War.[24]

It is probable that many of Ernst Bohle's ideas and views about Germany's defeat in the war, and the problems that followed, were strongly influenced by his father. The elder Bohle regularly wrote to his son before the Nazis came to power complaining about the absence of nationalistic fervor of the German diplomats serving in South Africa, and the increasing dominance of the Jews and the communists.[25] However, according to family acquaintances, the mother too, was very influential in Bohle's early life. A friend who knew the Bohles in South Africa, and later in Berlin, described the mother as a warm and loving presence in the family: "It was well known in Berlin, that the first thing Ernst Bohle did every day on his way to the office, was to stop and visit his mother."[26]

Bohle's early life was also strongly influenced by the fact that his elementary and high schools years were spent in English schools in Capetown. Although there is no evidence that he spoke extensively about this later, the fact that he was so conversant in the language and familiar with English customs and literature, made him somewhat unique among the higher Nazi officials. However, Bohle senior did not want his children to lose their Germandom while living abroad, and certainly not during the First World War, so it can be assumed that Ernst lived in a home atmosphere where there was a strong emphasis upon German culture and nationalism.

Bohle left Cape Town in 1919 for higher studies in Germany, and it was a period that brought home strongly to him what defeat meant for Germany. Although still a student, he witnessed the political and economic struggles that sharply divided the country in its efforts at recovery. He became familiar with all of truths and half-truths about the peace settlements, and was, no doubt, disturbed about the loss of colonies and border lands that now separated millions of German speaking people from their homeland. Considering the time he had lived abroad, this obviously had a greater meaning for him than for the average German.

He finished his formal education in 1923 at the Handelshochschule in Berlin, where he had studied business and economics, and graduated with the grade of "Good," and a diploma as a "Kaufmann." This was not the best year to enter the work world, however, for Germany was still reeling from the calamitous inflation that had decimated the economy, and shook the stability of the young Weimar Republic to its very foundations. He did manage to secure a number of part-time positions with import-export firms dealing mostly with imported car accessories. Between 1924 and 1931, he worked as a buyer for several foreign companies doing business in Germany and Holland. He briefly tried to establish his own import business, but it was not a success. With a wife and child to feed he searched for more steady employment, and answered an ad in a Hamburg newspaper that was seeking the services of an expert on Africa for the Foreign Department (Auslandsabteilung) of the Nazi Party. Although the position was only part-time, it promised full employment in the near future. Dr. Hans Nieland had placed the ad, and the date was November 1931.[27]

The arrangement did not last too long, and even with the impressive job description of "Foreign Expert on South Africa, England and the United States," Bohle complained that no compensation was forthcoming, and he had to work evenings because Nieland's relatives had the day jobs. After several months Bohle quit, but retained his party membership, and began a brief period of work at the Egyptian Consulate. In October 1932, he was asked to return to a full-time position in Nieland's office that had, in the meantime, been elevated to a Gau. Bohle's new title was Inspector and Adjutant to Gauleiter Nieland. No doubt, a word from Hess was responsible. Bohle said he accepted the job because of his long standing interest in a career in Germany's foreign service, and saw this as an opportunity to realize that ambition.[28]

Obviously, the relationship between Nieland and Bohle was not the most harmonious. Bohle regarded the Gauleiter as totally unfit for the position, and said that they never discussed anything related to Germany's foreign affairs because Nieland had little or no grasp of the life of the Germans who lived overseas. He regarded knowledge of a foreign language and residence abroad as essential requirements to lead the Gau Ausland, neither of which Nieland possessed.[29] Bohle probably did not know just how tenuous his position was at the time, for the future of the party was far from assured and there was no certainty that the Gau Ausland would be continued, but he had made his decision to cast his lot with the NSDAP. He was twenty-nine years old, and soon to be appointed the youngest Gauleiter in the Nazi hierarchy. Even at a time when it was not unusual for a new face to assume an important position in the new Germany, Bohle's quick advancement astonished many old party members, but for him it looked like the future unlimited as the leader of the Auslandsorganisation (AO) der NSDAP.

3 Internal Politics and the Germans Abroad

Ernst Wilhelm Bohle was a reasonably smart twenty-nine year old who now recognized that a way had been opened for him to possibly realize his dream of becoming involved in the foreign policy apparatus of a new Germany if the Nazis took power, and as the newly appointed Gauleiter of the Auslandsorganisation (AO) of the NSDAP, he had an important position within the party structure. However, the challenge he faced was maneuvering through the labyrinth that surrounded German foreign affairs. Not only would there be a resistant and entrenched pre-Hitler diplomatic corps that was certain it could not be replaced, but a number of Nazi Party members, some with far more influence than Bohle commanded, anxious to have a say in foreign policy making and who would oppose any expansion of AO power.

While he had his admirers for having become a Gauleiter at such a young age, others viewed Bohle's meteoric rise more skeptically. Unlike his fellow Gauleiters, he had no background in party history. He had not been in the First World War, an important benchmark among older party members, nor had he participated in the legend-making street brawls of the nineteen-twenties. Even his party membership was of recent vintage. Rudolf Hess's adjutant, Alfred Leitgen, admitted that complaints had been received from other Gauleiters: "Some of them," he said, "told me that Herr Bohle, in their opinion, was not a Gauleiter. His duties could not be compared to theirs. They said he was an experiment, and regarded the Auslandsorganisation as out of the mainstream. In their judgment, Herr Bohle was an outsider...he was an Auslandsdeutscher, and served the Auslandsdeutsche."[1] This was a charge he was to hear his entire career during the Hitler regime.

Bohle's bulwark against his detractors was Rudolf Hess, who obviously saw in the young man a kindred Auslandsdeutscher. Bohle knew this was his strength, and was not reluctant to admit it, for he saw Hess as the only Nazi leader who understood the problems of the German citizens who lived abroad. He said that he and Hess talked about how these Auslandsdeutsche felt that the homeland often treated them as second class citizens, and that matters did not change even after Hitler became chancellor. As citizens of

Germany they wanted the right to vote and have decent jobs when they returned home.[2]

Hess clearly served as a mentor for Bohle, and it is significant that the Deputy Führer respected Bohle's attitude toward those employees in the AO office who did not wish to become party members. One long-time staff secretary to Bohle, Brigitta Reich, said that the Gauleiter never seemed concerned if anyone working in the office was a party member or not: "Some of my coworkers, including myself, were not party members, and there were no efforts made by Herr Bohle to pressure us into joining the NSDAP, even though we were all employed doing party business."[3] Bohle's wife, Gertrud confirmed this view and said that although her husband believed that the programs that Hitler introduced were beneficial for Germany, he was never obsessive about National Socialism as a political philosophy.[4]

He was, however, intensely interested in talk about party politics and personalities, she said. He was completely devoted to his work, and she expressed some disappointment that he had little time for cultural activities like music and literature. She felt that his success had come too easily to him, and he had little understanding for the people who had to struggle. As for women, she made no mention of any infidelities, but remarked that he definitely saw women as inferior to men.[5] The lifestyle of the Bohle's appears to have been conducted on a relatively modest scale, although as a Gauleiter he could have lived much more lavishly. Vicco Karl Alexander von Bülow-Schwante, who was chief of protocol in the German Foreign Office at the time, said that the Bohle's lived simply, in a small, ordinary house in a Berlin suburb, and that Frau Bohle did all of her own housework without any help.[6] The same observation was made by the Bohle secretary, Brigitta Reich: "His private life was always a modest one and within the norms of the average citizen... He did not own houses or have a villa or a private car; he drove the car supplied by his office. His trips outside of Berlin were always on business, and never for pleasure."[7]

Ernst Bohle does not seem to have been bothered by his contradictory behavior in promoting what he called a "wordly view", and at the same time informing those foreign critics of AO activities abroad that National Socialism was not for export. He praised the Germans who lived abroad for having a far better understanding of the world than those who remained at home. Their experience enhanced their value to the party, and should be recognized as such, but these must be persons who had retained their German citizenship and were eligible for membership in the NSDAP, he said. Bohle had sympathy for the plight of the ethnic German (Volksdeutsche) who was enthusiastic about National Socialism, but was not officially permitted to join the Nazi Party. Despite much evidence to the contrary, he insisted that as the Gauleiter of the Auslandsorganisation, he never offered them any recognition.[8]

Bohle defended his viewpoint by comparing his actions with those of the British. He was just trying to do for the Germans abroad what Great

Britain had been doing for many years with their people who lived abroad, he said, and that was instilling in them a patriotism and a love of country that was as vibrant and strong as that of the German who lived at home. To carry out this mission, it was essential that efficient lines of communication be established between Germany and the German communities overseas. Facilitated by the party people in the field, a steady flow of information bulletins, books and other reading materials, and personal correspondence, reflecting the National Socialist philosophy, had to be dispatched. In addition, a regular schedule of visitors who were prepared to speak in detail about the programs and plans in the Third Reich, was a necessary ingredient. Every effort must be made to convince the Auslandsdeutsche that the government of new Germany cared about them: "I know from my own experience after World War I," Bohle said, "most of the Germans outside were falling away because nobody was looking after them. We want to get them back, get back their loyalty to their country."[9]

Ernst Bohle was convinced that propaganda was the key to persuading the Auslandsdeutsche to embrace National Socialism. There is no indication, however, that the AO leader introduced anything of an innovative nature into the propaganda content. In fact, most of what was sent out from his office was simply reworked material supplied by Josef Goebbels's Propaganda Ministry (Reichsministerium für Volksaufklärung und Propaganda). Bohle did claim credit for coming forth with the suggestion that all German citizens living abroad receive "...the standard work of the movement, *Mein Kampf.* It was well illustrated thousands of times before the Machtergreifung{taking power} that knowledge of this incomparable work was sufficient to make the toughest skeptic an enthusiastic supporter of the movement."[10]

Indicative of Bohle's growing authority was a Hess order in early October 1933, that stated that Bohle's office now officially handled all party memberships for Germans who resided abroad except for Austria, Memel, and Danzig. Further, any party office in Germany that had occasion to conduct any affairs with German members abroad was instructed to do so through Bohle. The Deputy Führer also directed all Nazi Party members who traveled abroad to notify the Auslandsorganisation before departing Germany.[11]

The citizenship issue continued to remain a problem for Bohle, despite repeated denials that non-German citizens were not eligible to participate in party affairs. The major difficulty stemmed from the policy of the Hitler government that aimed its propaganda messages to all Germans, regardless of their citizenship. In trying to define the connection of Germans everywhere to Germany based on blood , language, and cultural heritage rather than legal status, the question was left open as to who could and could not lend their support to the activities of the National Socialist Party. Those nations with large German communities registered their complaints, going so far at times as to outlaw the Nazi Party, but the problem persisted. It may well have been difficult, if not impossible, for Germany to have altered the situation even if Hitler had decided to do so. In many instances, the

Reichsdeutsche and Volksdeutsche were inseparable in some of the communities where both belonged to the same clubs and organizations and a significant proportion of the contact between the two groups was of a cultural and social nature.

Ernst Bohle was fully aware of all of the nuances involved, and must have grown weary of having to endlessly repeat his denials that his organization was in the business of subverting foreign governments. However, he also knew that to function successfully he had to close his eyes to the intermingling of party people with the non-German citizens in the communities abroad. Bohle understood the importance of the peace settlements of World War I to those Germans who lived beyond Germany's borders, and while the flame of nationalism continued to burn, he recognized that their anger and frustration lacked a focus. Too much of their political activity was regional in nature, often involving issues that had little or no relevance to the fatherland. What was lacking was organization and leadership that would bring the Germans abroad a unifying message, and for Bohle that was Hitler and National Socialism. He could not be held responsible if the message appealed to both citizen and non-citizen alike, nor for the mixing of the two groups abroad.[12]

Bohle faced a daunting task in not only introducing his organization to those Germans living in far distant lands, but to those closer to home, as well. The Treaty of Versailles had placed millions of people who were formerly German citizens into the border territories of Denmark, Poland, Czechoslovakia, Belgium, and France, while other thousands were separated from their homeland in Danzig, Memel, and the Saar. Additional German-speaking minority communities could be found in Lithuania, Estonia, Latvia, and throughout the former Hapsburg Empire.

The job was massive, but the rewards looked unlimited to the young Gauleiter. He knew that he would be confronted by jealously and infighting and pettiness of an almost unbelievable nature, but he knew it had to be endured to succeed ("For instance, in Buenos Aires, I think there were about 64 German clubs who all fought each other in the good old German way"),[13] and by the summer of 1933, Bohle had a network of 230 Landesgruppen, Orts-und Stüpunkte in place around the world, with party membership numbering over three thousand, and on the increase.[14] In a speech at the Reichsparteitag in Nürnberg in August 1933, Bohle outlined the future plans for his organization, and proudly pointed out that while Italy's leader Benito Mussolini had not shown any concern for the Italian people who lived abroad until after his regime was established, the NSDAP's Auslands-Abteilung (the future Auslandsorganisation, or AO), had begun its work long before Hitler took power. He emphasized that Germany's concern was the welfare of the Auslandsdeutsche, and that there would be no effort made to suppress the activities of those clubs and groups that existed in the German communities abroad. On the contrary, he continued, his office stood ready to offer an array of services in areas that have been unavailable heretofore, such as legal assistance of various kinds, aid for youth programs and women's organizations.[15]

At this point, membership in Bohle's Auslands-Abteilung meant automatic party membership, however, there were German citizens who lived and traveled abroad who were not enrolled in the Auslands-Abteilung . This was especially true of many of the employees of the German Foreign Office. For their own reasons, a number of the career diplomats who pre-dated the Hitler regime often took a kind of wait-and-see approach to party membership, and in the early years, tended to ignore Bohle's organization whenever possible.[16] While party membership remained restricted in Germany, Bohle had permission to recruit some members from what he estimated as two million German citizens who lived abroad, but his assistant, Emil Ehrich, thought this figure too high, and set the number of German citizens abroad as closer to 500,000. He said that Bohle's office was dependent for many of its statistics on the Foreign Office, and this was a problem, because many of the diplomatic personnel simply did not cooperate when information was requested.[17]

Bohle tried to avoid having to give exact figures when dealing with Nazi colleagues from other offices, but he said that his office did keep accurate data on the number of all party members who were living abroad. Some did not belong to the Auslands-Abteilung, he admitted, but he did not think that every rank and file member had a place in his organization, and noted that his Gau was the smallest of all of them: "I didn't want to have such a big organization....I didn't see any use in it, having a big blown-up affair... in fact, there was such a big demand for membership that we had to turn them down."[18] This description, given after the war, is not exactly compatible with the documented profile of the growth of the office between 1933 and 1937. In 1933, his early headquarters in Hamburg employed about forty people, but by 1937, with the main office now in Berlin, there were over two hundred employees.. The 1933 membership was some 6,000 persons, which increased in the next four years to over 30,000 members, and this did not include the German seamen who were enrolled in the organization.[19]

When Bohle took over the leadership of the Auslands-Abteilung, there were approximately three thousand German seamen serving on several hundred ships who held Nazi Party membership. When they were transferred to the Auslands-Abteilung, Bohle made every effort to keep their numbers confidential from his fellow Gauleiters, especially those who formerly had the seamen under their jurisdiction. Part of the subterfuge he employed was to permit the seamen to carry party membership cards that made no reference to his office, the reasoning being that this made it more difficult for the inquisitive to determine just how many were enrolled in the Auslands-Abteilung.[20]

Almost from the very beginning Bohle understood that the German Foreign Office people regarded his Auslands-Abteilung as strictly a party office that had to be tolerated, but should not be allowed to usurp the duties or responsibilities of the diplomatic corps. He knew that Foreign Office challenges to his activities would not be overt for fear of incurring the anger of important party leaders, many who regarded the older diplomats with scorn, but Bohle also knew that bureaucracy and tradition were on the side of the diplomats, and these could be potent weapons in thwarting his plans.

One of the first moves of the Foreign Office was to try and prevent Bohle's office from exerting any jurisdiction over the personnel abroad who were party members. When Bohle heard that the Foreign Office was proposing to create an Ortsgruppe oversea for their own party people, he immediately protested to Robert Ley, Reichsorganisationsleiter, and Nazi Party treasurer Franz Xaver Schwarz. "It is my opinion", he said, "that the establishment of a special group especially for the diplomatic representatives of the Reich abroad calls into consideration the fact that the overwhelming majority of these Party members first joined the movement after 30.1.1933. I therefore respectfully request that such a group not be created." Both Ley and Schwarz supported Bohle's request and the Foreign Office was denied the permission to have their own Party Ortsgruppe abroad.[21] This victory for Bohle, together with the Hess order of October, greatly strengthened his position and added to the impression that Nazi leaders did not regard the traditional Foreign Office as untouchable when it involved party decisions.

Emboldened by this show of support, Bohle took his planning for the future to Rudolf Hess. What is desperately needed, he told the Deputy Führer, is the creation of a minister's post for Germandom abroad. Germany has approximately thirty-five million of her people living outside her borders, and from a foreign policy standpoint, he said, their care and concerns are extremely important. This is an area that has long been neglected by previous administrations, but has the potential to be a powerful force in foreign relations. The key to focusing this potential was bringing organization through the efforts of party members abroad, who could be carefully selected and politically schooled for the task: "The development of such a group would naturally begin to exert an influence that over time would become an instrument of power that we currently do not possess."[22]

The Foreign Office was not capable of offering the necessary leadership, Bohle continued, nor did it exhibit the adequate National Socialist spirit that was essential to the success of such a large undertaking. In a cleverly worded complaint, he described the professional diplomats as charming and educated people, but not the aggressive kind of representatives that Germany required in her present situation. With the creation of a new ministry, Bohle said, a body would emerge that truly spoke for the new Germany. He suggested that Hess could gain a fuller picture of these proposals by a visit to the offices of the Auslands-Abteilung in Hamburg, where leading members of the staff could provide more details.[23]

Although there is no indication that Hess took Bohle up on his invitation for further discussions, the ideas that the young Gauleiter outlined are significant in that they illuminate his thinking even at this early stage about what he thought should be the future course taken. The very fact that he informed Hess that he and his staff had been working for some time on the idea of a separate ministry for the Auslandsdeutsche, was rather astonishing considering his brief tenure in the party and his young age. Obviously, he envisioned a major role for himself if any of the suggestions were actually endorsed by Hess and approved by other party leaders. The importance of Bohle's proposals can not be exaggerated because his own ambitions are clearly revealed, as well as his deep animosity toward the old guard in the German Foreign Office. Rarely, in his later career and battles with the Foreign Office, did he so openly state his thoughts in this manner. Bohle knew that no matter how negative his suggestions were relative to the Foreign Office, he had a measure of protection because the party structure controlled the state and was not to be challenged by any of the existing institutions, including the Foreign Office.

From the very beginning of his tenure as Gauleiter of the Auslands-Abteilung, Bohle viewed his duties as quite different from those of the other Gauleiters. He saw his Gau as unique as compared to the other forty-two Gaue, and he required a staff of people who possessed an educational background that understood how to cope with the work and problems of the Auslandsdeutsche. This meant that, unlike his fellow Gauleiters, he could not fill the home office with old party cronies whose only qualification was a low membership number. Bohle favored young, well-educated people who had had some experience abroad, and was not overly concerned about their political views. Noting that he had selected his personal assistant Emil Ehrich, when he was just twenty-five years old, Bohle said that this was not unusual for there were several young men in his office that he had picked because they showed a potential and could make a good career.[24]

Ehrich later recalled that Bohle's actions did not go unnoticed, and he was constantly being visited by curious party leaders who wanted to meet him and view his operations. From notes he had saved, Ehrich was able to reconstruct a particularly interesting meeting with Foreign Minister Konstantin von Neurath in November 1933. It was at this meeting, which according to Ehrich was called presumably to create a more friendly understanding between the two offices, that the real war between the Foreign Office and Bohle began. It was obvious that during the hour-long talk between the two men neither made much effort to disguise his true feelings.[25]

While the Foreign Office remained the major challenge to Bohle's ambitions to move his organization, and himself, into a stronger role in the realm of foreign policy, there were numerous other German groups and organizations eager to participate in some aspect of Germandom abroad. Some of them pre-dated the Hitler movement, sometimes by many years, and had developed strong ties with German communities abroad. Their activities varied from group to group, much depending upon the particular community overseas and its connection to Germany. Thus, one group in Germany promoted student-teacher exchanges, another supported vacation and retirement facilities , while a third was in the business of supplying German-language publications. These services were often directed toward the same communities and were advertised and sponsored by existing clubs and other social organizations. Visiting German dignitaries and lecturers also helped maintain the bonds with the homeland.

Bohle was more than willing to work with those groups whose activities corresponded with his agenda, and did not pretend to challenge his authority. He was aware that his organization was resented in some quarters and that his overtures were often ignored. More of a problem was the decision of some individuals to go over Bohle's head by directly contacting an influential party member in Germany with a request to settle a matter in dispute, but for those agreeable, or even eager, to work with the Auslands-Abteilung, Bohle offered strong support through the Landesgruppe in the form of funds and personnel for locally staged programs. Bohle characterized the situation as follows: "The difficulties were too many fingers in the pie; there were any amount of organizations, all of no special importance, but all meddling around in this work which was essentially a work of my department. We wanted to consolidate all that and have one leadership."[26]

The Fichtebund was an example of a contentious group that regarded Bohle's office as an interference with their own activities. It was founded in 1914, and had a record of strong support for Hitler long before he became chancellor. The Fichtebund's speciality was the printing and distribution of nationalistic propaganda, and it had solid contacts with many leading party members. The Fichtebund's contacts were equally strong among many German communities abroad. Bohle was not only critical of what he saw as the Bund's heavy handed propaganda approach, but he coveted the group's wide range of connections with the overseas communities. In attempting to subordinate the Bund to his own office, Bohle faced the problem that many of the Germans abroad who received literature from the group were not citizens of Germany. The Bund's entrenched position with the party also presented a problem. However, in an attest to his own diplomatic skills and growing influence, Bohle managed to finally force the Fichtebund to acknowledge his leadership.[27]

Not all of his attempts to reconcile existing groups and organizations to the predominance of the Auslands-Abteilung in the field of tending the needs of the Auslandsdeutsche went that easily. He tried to minimize his squabbles with those who opposed his aggressive efforts to bring everyone under his direction, and he had to be especially careful with the groups that had roots deep into German society. One such that proved a real challenge for him was the Association for Germandom Abroad (Verein or Volkstum für das Deutschtum im Ausland, or VDA). It dated from the early 1880s, and had its origins as a German school league in the Austro-Hungarian Empire. The VDA focused on education in German communities abroad, and often provided teachers and books from Germany, as well as various printed materials with subjects of interest for the Auslandsdeutsche.

Bohle had been critical of the VDA right from the beginning of his administration because he said that it created a confusion in his own work by insisting on openly directing its appeal to all Germans abroad with no distinction between citizen and non-citizen. Considering that Bohle had a problem enforcing such distinctions in his own organization, this may not have been the only reason for his animosity toward the VDA. He had a definite dislike for the head of the VDA, a strong willed individual who was not easily intimidated, named Dr. Hans Steinacher. When Bohle first indicated that VDA activities might be doing more harm than good for Germany, he was met by Steinacher's reply that "...everybody who had German blood belonged to Germany and was German."[28]

After his first meeting with the young Gauleiter, Steinacher wrote in his personal notes his impressions: "The man has become too big, too fast. Immature and untrustworthy! Among other things, he said that the idea of a racial community [Volkstum] was foreign to him. 'I was born and raised in England. My service is aimed at the practical.' My answer after this private talk was: 'Mr. Gauleiter, you are at the wrong place here.' Bohle made a wry face and turned wordlessly away. Too bad!"[29]

For the moment, Bohle had to accept the situation because Steinacher and the VDA had powerful friends. Rudolf Hess attempted to act as mediator between the two men by appointing an advisory committee to work with them, but the hostility did not disappear. At one point, in describing the situation, Bohle said: "He [Steinacher] hates me like poison because I disrupted his whole theory of 100 million Germans."[30] However, for one so young, Bohle had great patience and knew that the VDA enjoyed a prestige that he could not simply ignore. The right moment had not yet arrived for him to make his stand, but it would come.

The VDA was not Bohle's only competitor in the game of trying to win the favor of the Auslandsdeutsche. Another organization almost as deeply entrenched with the overseas Germans was the German Foreign Institute, or Deutsche Ausland-Institut (DAI). It had been organized in 1917, largely in response to wartime conditions, and was located in the city of Stuttgart. The honorary president, and mayor of the city, was Dr. Karl Strölin. Its activities were similar to those of the VDA, and overlapped in some areas with Bohle's organization as well. It had no branches abroad, and Strölin insisted that the major concern of the DAI was archival in nature with the collection and storage of data on the Auslandsdeutsche and their history.[31]

The DAI holdings often proved useful to Bohle and his staff when searching for information regarding a German community abroad, and it was probably for this reason that the two organizations, DAI and AO, were linked in the press from time to time. Bohle denied that there was any official connection between their organizations, and Strölin said that he was never invited to any of the policy meetings that the Gauleiter held.[32] The existing records indicate otherwise, however, and since Strölin's statement was made after World War II, he was obviously trying to distance himself from any connection to Nazi organizations.

It appears that Bohle initiated the first contact with Strölin in January 1934, when he requested the DAI leader to let him know of any irregular conduct by personnel in the Foreign Office, by which he meant, not showing sufficient support and respect toward the Nazi Party, and its members. The Gauleiter also utilized DAI files when compiling a complaint against a German diplomat whom he wanted removed from the Foreign Office. Strölin's office showed no reluctance in complying with such requests. The materials usually consisted of letters of complaint that had been sent to the DAI from Germans living abroad with the names of German consular officials who had behaved badly toward them. [33] When receiving some of the requested materials, Bohle appeared to make no distinction between German citizens and non-citizens as reporting sources in making his case against the German diplomat in question.

The VDA and the DAI were not the only challenges to Bohle's exclusive domain, for there were a number of party offices that he had to contend with because some of them offered services and programs to members and their families living abroad.[34] Emil Ehrich, Bohle's assistant, characterized the situation as follows: "There was a strong tendency in the Party to extend to German communities abroad its many branches and organizations. Herr Bohle opposed this energetically right from the beginning, and finally succeeded in persuading the Führer's deputy [Hess] to issue the well-known decree of the 17th February 1934 to forbid any activities by associated organizations of the Party directed towards German communities abroad which were not included in the program of the AO [Auslandsorganisation]."[35]

As the new military stance of the Hitler regime began to receive increasing attention, Bohle found it difficult to defend any support from his office concerning the semi-military groups that had emerged from some of the German communities abroad. According to his assistant, Emil Ehrich, it was a troublesome problem for his boss, but he finally felt that he had to make his position clear, and refute any connection to such groups. Under the circumstance, Ehrich said, this required considerable courage. However, the situation was a bit different with the German intelligence community at home (Abwehr, Sicherheitsdienst, and Gestapo), which was not going to ignore the fact that the AO had party members worldwide.[36]

Thus, try as he might, and in spite of his own feelings on the subject, Bohle was compelled at times to collaborate on certain spy or sabotage schemes undertaken by one or another of the intelligence agencies. When he was interrogated about this after the war, Bohle said that he was aware that his government sent individuals on secret missions abroad, but that this was never initiated by the AO, and that his office never acted as an intermediary for such activity. He insisted that if there had been any real evidence that his organization was involved in such things, its operations abroad would have been banned by foreign nations. Bohle admitted that if one of the German intelligence groups expressed an interest in using one of the people working for him, that he released that person from all of his duties.[37] Since most of Bohle's postwar statements were made while defending himself against war crimes charges, it can be assumed that he made every effort to avoid incrimination in Nazi Germany's misdeeds, including spying and espionage.

An aspect of Bohle's operations that definitely had a confidential side to it was the relationship his office had with German companies that did business overseas, although he made no secret of his support in helping German businesses expand abroad. "We were very closely connected," he said, "sponsoring of German chambers of commerce, and did everything we could to extend German trade and help German business." He also established a liaison office with Walter Funk's Economic Ministry to coordinate closer efforts with German businesses that worked abroad.[38]

In the beginning, Bohle's reception by many German companies was decidedly a cool one. He said he detected a kind of skepticism about the survival of the new Hitler government. No doubt, many of the companies viewed Bohle's organization as an enforcer of Hitler's "coordination" (Gleichschaltung) policy in which everyone was expected to fall in line with the new regime. Just how the companies were to exhibit their sudden zeal for National Socialism was left somewhat vague, but there was no mistaking the meaning. For Bohle, there was a certain urgency in the matter because he had to transfer funds abroad to his people working in the German communities, and it had to done in a confidential manner in order to conceal the action from the foreign news media, where it would receive adverse publicity, if revealed. An I. G. Farben executive named Anton Reithinger said that he helped Bohle in the transfer of funds abroad, and that the company director, Max Ilgner, encouraged cooperation with the AO.[39]

Bohle always denied that he placed any unethical demands upon the German businesses that operated abroad, but the evidence indicates otherwise. If a German who was employed abroad did not cooperate with Bohle's economic advisor, the firm's home office was notified by the Gauleiter directly with the suggestion that the individual in question be replaced. This was usually accompanied by a negative report by the local Landesgruppe concerning the character and behavior of the German employee. Bohle was not above using the same methods when he wished to place one of his own people with a German firm abroad.[40] On the petty side, if a German citizen working abroad expressed some criticism of Bohle and he heard about, then he took steps to have the person dismissed from his position. In one instance, a physician employed by a South African mining company wrote a letter in which he criticized Bohle's opposing stance on the colonial settlements resulting from the Treaty of Versailles. The Gauleiter requested that the company dismiss the physician, but not reveal to him the reason.[41] Bohle also pressured German companies that conducted business abroad to make financial contributions to his organization. He boasted that it was not unusual for a German businessman to voluntarily send his office a thousand marks from time to time, but it was a different story for the diplomatic personnel, Bohle said; they had to be reminded to make "contributions."[42]

One of the departments (Schatzamt) in Bohle's office handled all of the finances, and was responsible to the party treasurer for expenditures. Bohle felt that it was an arrangement that stifled some of his more creative proposals because Nazi Party Treasurer Franz Xaver Schwarz did not have the vision to fully grasp the need to finance them. It was also slightly humiliating, that the accountant who managed these affairs in Bohle's office had to be approved by Schwarz. The Gauleiter said that Schwarz was a "hard taskmaster with the mind of a bookkeeper."[43] But as much as Bohle chafed under Schwarz's restrictions, he knew better than to challenge the party's old treasurer. The Reichsschatzmeister had been a party member since 1922, and controlled its finances since 1925. His party file contained a notarized statement that he had been given full legal control over the finances of the NSDAP by Hitler personally in September 1931, and had the authority to represent it in all maters pertaining to its resources.[44]

Schwarz required that Bohle submit detailed accounts of his expenditures before authorizing reimbursement. This meant that any of the AO staff who traveled or made purchases in the line of duty, had to produce careful receipts and file a written itinerary with Schwarz's office. Bohle kept up a running litany of complaints about the required procedures, and peppered his correspondence to the Reichsschatzmeister with references to the many people who worked for the AO for the honor of it, or accepted only a token salary.[45]

As 1933 ended, however, and despite his annoyances, Bohle's star was rising. He had managed in his brief tenure as Gauleiter of the AO der NSDAP, to gain the notice of influential party leaders, and lay claim to an office that many saw as a potential spokesman for National Socialism abroad. Greater achievements were still ahead.

4 Consolidating Power and Growing Influence

Germany's economic and political problems did not disappear with Adolf Hitler's assumption of power in 1933, but dramatic and fundamental changes in the conduct of government soon occurred. Only weeks after Hitler became chancellor, a mysterious fire destroyed the German Reichstag building. Immediately the Nazis denounced it as a Communist plot, and the aging president, Paul von Hindenburg, was prompted to issue a series of decrees seriously curtailing the freedom of speech and press. Despite a temporary loss of voter support in the March election, the NSDAP succeeded in securing passage of the so-called Enabling Act (Gesetz zur Ehebung der Not von Volk und Reich, or Law to Remove the Distress of People and State), which permitted Hitler to issue laws through the cabinet without consent of the Reichstag. The "coordination" (Gleichschaltung) of all German life with the demands of the new regime had begun.

Action was almost as swift in foreign policy, as Germany announced a withdrawal from the Disarmament Conference in Geneva, and the League of Nations in October. The Führer had already focused his attention on Poland, and in concluding a ten-year non-aggression pact in January 1934 with that nation, succeeded in seriously weakening the French-dominated alliance system in eastern Europe. Thus, in less than a year, Hitler had introduced the beginning of sweeping domestic and foreign policy changes. Just what this would mean for Germany, and the rest of Europe, was not yet clear, but it was not hard to evaluate the effect of gaining power upon the members of the NSDAP. A triumphant euphoria permeated the ranks as members now realized untold opportunities had suddenly become available and preference would go to the faithful. Formerly unimportant party offices could expect to expand into functional arms of the government, wielding new power and authority.

To Ernst Wilhelm Bohle, a young man as eager as any of his fellow party members to seize the fruits of Hitler's triumph, knew that the way had opened for those who were clever enough to steer the right course. He had already shown a talent for maneuvering the world of mistrust, rumor and petty jealously that characterized the Hitler movement, but with the assumption of power over the entire state, these elements would be magnified into personal feuds of deadly proportion. Bohle was aware that during his short party tenure and quick rise to Gauleiter of the Auslandsorganisation(a designation bestowed by Hess in February 1934), that he had made enemies who strongly resented his success and that he faced powerful opposition from the entrenched diplomatic corps and fellow Gauleiters, who regarded the AO as not deserving of Gau status.

It was true that when compared with other Gaue, the AO was not a typical district of the NSDAP for it did not govern a precise geographical land area in Germany, but instead was responsible for German citizens and party members residing and traveling outside the country. The fact that Bohle's Gau carried the title of "Foreign Section" of the party and already exhibited some pretensions toward foreign affairs, was enough to arouse hostile feelings in some quarters. His AO was also proving effective in the distribution of Nazi propaganda abroad, an activity highly important to many party leaders who were anxious to project an impressive image to the world. In keeping with the growing importance of his organization, Bohle was proud to announce that the Führer had personally given permission for all AO staff members to wear a special insignia in the shape of a black diamond with the letters "AO" in the center, on the left sleeve of their uniform.[1]

In keeping with his close association with Rudolf Hess, Bohle employed the Deputy Führer's younger brother, Alfred, in his office. Like Rudolf, Alfred was born in Egypt, and was also a veteran of the First World War. He had joined the Nazi Party in 1920, and for a time worked for the Deutsche Bank in Hamburg and Munich, later returning to Egypt to work for his father in Cairo. He established the first NS Ortsgruppe there in 1932, and later a Landsgruppe.[2]

Being of foreign birth made Bohle's AO the logical place for Alfred to seek employment, and he made a visit to the Gauleiter to explore his opportunities. The fact that Rudolf Hess probably viewed Bohle's office as a spot where his brother could be comfortably employed, may have played a role in the Deputy Führer's decision to throw his weight behind the permanent establishment of the AO as an independent Gau at a time when there was some indecision among party leaders about its future. Later, Alfred expressed his gratitude for his brother's support, but he never occupied a decisive role in Bohle's management of the AO, where he specialized in economic matters; the most important person next to Bohle, was his assistant, Emil Ehrich[3]

As Bohle's office expanded, it became possible to create separate departments for each function, and one of the most significant was that devoted to the development of propaganda in the form of printed matter for distribution abroad, a lecturers' program, and an information service (clippings sent to the foreign press). The responsible department was the AO Presseamt, which had a working liaison with Josef Goebbels' Propaganda Ministry. In fact, Bohle got on well with Goebbels, who seemed to like the young Gauleiter. After a visit to Bohle's office, the Propaganda Minister noted in his diary that the AO "...was large and complicated, and well led by Bohle, one of our most competent people. Everything made a good impression, maybe a bit over organized."[4] This was to prove an important contact for Bohle, but it also had its advantages for Goebbels because the AO was effective in transporting propaganda materials abroad

In addition to coordinating the production of printed matter and other propaganda work with Goebbels' Ministry, the Auslandsorganisation sponsored a large lecture circuit of several dozen persons, various traveling exhibits, musical programs, motion pictures, and newsreels. Bohle tried to select lecturers who had traveled extensively or had lived abroad and understood the life of the Auslandsdeutsche At one point, the AO produced a film described by Bohle as "...a move dealing with the longing of Auslandsdeutsche for the Fatherland." Actually, the film was made by Felix Schmidt Decker, a Goebbels' employee, while traveling in Argentina,[5] and Bohle knew the value of the right kind of propaganda. It was very important to the mission of the AO that the office project a National Socialist image championing the cause of the Auslandsdeutsche.

In its publishing program, the AO produced large quantities of pamphlets and flyers, and occasionally a book The subject matter was mostly of a nature that concentrated on the life of the German who lived abroad, and usually written by an AO member living in one of the overseas communities. The accounts avoided any heavy-handed propaganda message, but tried to weave into the material subtle references to such historical events as the Treaty of Versailles, and its devastating impact upon postwar Germany. The suffering of German minorities was described as one result, but the recent concern shown by the new German government through the creation of the Auslandsorganisation was evidence that Hitler intended to change things. While Bohle himself never authored anything of significance for distribution abroad, he did have a special interest in novels and nonfiction accounts about Germans who lived in foreign lands.[6]

It soon became evident that Bohle's efforts to spread the word about the wonders of National Socialism may have become more successful than he really intended. The basic aim in 1933–34 was to create a world network of German citizens who would assist in the promotion of support and goodwill for the new regime at home, and at the same time embrace the AO and its members who were offering them renewed pride in the fatherland The difficulty was that this message was officially supposed to be for those Germans who held citizenship, but the mix of German citizens with Germans who were not citizens in the communities abroad was impossible to separate, and Bohle quickly discovered that his propaganda was appealing to both groups without distinction. When the Germans residing abroad who were not citizens of Germany became too enthusiastic about National Socialism, the host country usually took restrictive measures against them, such as curtailing their political activity. Even more serious were economic or diplomatic actions initiated against the German nation. Bohle was never able to develop a successful strategy to cope with this problem, although he always insisted that the AO had no involvement in the politics of non-German citizens.

Bohle also found that his organization was increasingly being asked to provide information from Germans abroad — citizens and non citizens alike — about the employment prospects in Germany. The Hitler government had made impressive inroads in the reduction of unemployment in Germany, and this had made news worldwide. The Auslandsorganisation, through its extensive network of contacts and Landesgruppen, became the focus of those overseas Germans who decided that conditions looked better at home, and wanted the AO to assist them in going there. Although all legal arrangements had to be handled through the local German consulate, interested individuals were advised to contact the Landesgruppenleiter or a party member for relevant details. The point was also made that the AO legal office (Rechtsamt) exercised jurisdiction over German citizens abroad as of January 1934. To deal with the hundreds of Germans who now besieged the German consulates and Bohle's representatives in the communities, the AO established a new department to handle only the processing of returnees (Rückwandereramt).[7]

This meant new responsibilities for Bohle, for the work now entailed conducting investigations of the people who applied to return, issuing reports on the results, advising on employment(certain skills received a higher priority), and arranging for travel. In addition, returnees had to be provided overnight facilities at both the ports of departure and arrival, and later, housing arrangements in Germany. All of this AO activity involved interaction with the Foreign Office personnel, the German secret police(Gestapo), and a variety of state and local aid agencies.[8] The burden of this increased work was welcomed by Bohle because it not only meant an expansion of his organization with more people and more money, but it was a significant extension of his diplomatic functions. The AO was now empowered to certify an individual as "politically reliable."

While it appeared that the process for returning Germans home seemed to be in place, the reality was a bit different. To Bohle's credit his organization was the most efficient spoke in the wheel of a limitless bureaucracy that moved at a glacial pace. The AO was at the mercy of numerous offices and agencies that had to provide essential information before people could be processed for return and long delays proved unavoidable. A big source of complaint to his office came from German families who had made it to Germany's border points, but were not being admitted until their status was checked with police, welfare and immigration officials. These were people who had usually exhausted what funds they had and now were stranded. In addition, they were rudely treated by the German border personnel or at the ports of entry, they complained, and references were made to their status as "Volksdeutsche," or not full German citizens. Conditions began to improve somewhat after Bohle personally brought the problem to the attention of Rudolf Hess.[9]

By this point, the structure of Bohle's Auslandsorganisation had expanded into eight sizeable departments (Länderämter I-VIII) representing the geographical divisions of the world based upon the existing party branches (Landesgruppen) led by a group leader(Landesgruppenleiter). Each group leader was responsible for a country-wide network that had units led by party members he appointed. On paper, it was all carefully organized and each group was a piece of the overall apparatus managed from Bohle's Hamburg office, and although it appeared from the outside as a well oiled machine, the reality was a bit different. A basic problem that could not be overcome was the fact that many of the groups that Bohle was presumably managing were simply too far away for any close supervision. In the beginning, he did not know some of the party members who emerged as leaders of the Landesgruppen, many of whom had received their appointments by mail after a recommendation to Bohle's office from a party functionary at home. If the Gauleiter had doubts about a particular individual, it presented a problem if he wanted to remove him because he had to gather information from the local scene, and also take care that he did not offend an influential party member. Over time the situation changed somewhat as the AO began to receive more funding and could hold annual meetings in Germany attended by the Landesgruppenleitern.[10]

The relationship of a particular Landesgruppenleiter to Bohle and his staff depended upon several factors. Obviously, some countries figured more prominently in German foreign affairs than others, and this gave the party branch there a greater importance, and more attention from Bohle's office. It was not uncommon that the man who emerged as a party leader abroad was also a person of prominence in the German community there. Such individuals were accustomed to conducting affairs without too much interference from anyone, and with the added prestige of being appointed a Gruppenleiter, usually made decisions in the name of the party without much consultation with Bohle. The Gauleiter knew that he could not exert absolute control in these situations, and usually ignored the problem unless the complaints became too disturbing. Bohle understood, given the distances involved and the many different local circumstances, that a Landesgruppenleiter had to have the freedom to act on his own when he thought it necessary.

This does not mean that he could not bring pressure to bear when he thought it had to be applied. The AO exerted a strong influence over programs important to a community such as the local school curriculum, the schedule for celebrating German holidays, and certain financial subsidies. Ultimately, of course, there was the threat of party disapproval or censure, but Bohle had to move cautiously on this issue. He knew that a large part of the success of his AO rested with his people overseas, and he had to judge the reliability of each Landegruppenleiter and how that person could be depended upon to work with him and acknowledge his leadership in matters that were important. This required considerable tact, and Bohle usually sensed just how far to go and when to back off: "There were several Landesgruppenleiter to whom I would say, 'If you hear anything, send me a report. You are a sensible chap — you understand this and that'. Others, I would not ask because I didn't think them suitable. The countries were different and the men were different. It was all flexible, and it was not the same iron discipline as here. You can not do that with Germans abroad, I knew that."[11]

Bohle also knew that in the process of building his network that he had created a valuable world-wide listening post that could provide a wide variety of information unobtainable anyplace else. His office received everything from useless local gossip to important state secrets, and Bohle had to decide what had some relevance and what was worthless among the thousands of letters and reports that poured in from abroad. He was not reluctant to let party officials know that he had access to important information that the German embassies did not receive, and that his people were often aware what a foreign government was planning to do before anyone in the German diplomatic corps did.[12] The Gauleiter was justly proud of this accomplishment, but he was unstinting in his praise of the Landesgruppenleitern who provided the most insightful information in their monthly reports. He described these reports as valuable evaluations on "...whether National Socialism was flourishing or nor, if not, why not, reports on the consular diplomatic service, if anything was wrong in their opinion, it would be taken up in Berlin, reports on economic affairs - if there was any chance for German trade to get additional business or if anything was going on detrimental to German trade, then, of course, separate reports to the separate departments."[13]

By 1935 Bohle had his reporting system down to a fine art, although he had still not achieved a uniformity that he desired. The reports were uneven in quality depending upon the capability of each Landesgruppenleiter. In turn, each of these leaders had to depend upon the organization that he had built and the people reporting to him. Structured like a large pyramid, the organization looked efficient on paper, but there were weaknesses that were difficult to correct. Some of the problem rested with the wide variety of items reported upon. For instance, detailed profiles of each German who arrived in a community, description of specific social events, overheard rumors and negative comments about Hitler and National Socialism, evaluations of the local economy and the political scene, and very important to Bohle, the behavior of the German diplomatic personnel serving in the area.[14]

Bohle insisted that he never gave any specific directions for this kind of information-collecting in the field, and that a great deal of useless material was submitted that ended in the waste basket, although he never let this be known outside the office. He said that often times he cold tell that a monthly report by a specific Landesgruppenleiter was not prepared by him, and contained nothing worth reading. But Bohle knew this was the price of managing such a large and unwieldy organization and he accepted its faults without complaint to higher party officials, and rarely did he remove anyone for incompetence. However, for those people whom he found smart and dependable, Bohle gave more support in the way of funding and additional staff sent from the AO. When he found a Landesgruppenleiter who was particularly outstanding, he would dispatch younger members from his office to spend a training period with him.[15]

There was no doubt that the young Gauleiter had made impressive strides during his first two years as leader of the Auslandsorganisation. One problem that seemed to grow and take on more ramifications, however, was that which related to the citizenship question among Germans who resided abroad. There appeared to be considerable confusion in many of the communities about their exact relationship to Nazi Germany and National Socialism. Many thousands of Germans had been deprived of their citizenship as a result of the World War I treaties, and existed as minorities in other nations, while others had chosen to emigrate after the war to German communities abroad. There were also equally thousands of second generation Germans who had never held German citizenship but wanted to be a part of the new Germany, and they refused to be excluded from the Auslandsorganisation. Bohle could issue as many directions as he wanted excluding them from AO membership, but he could not effectively monitor the activities of a Landesgruppe that admitted these people to its functions. He was absolutely dependent upon his network of Landesgruppeneleitern and could not act in an arbitrary manner over this issue, and yet, at the same time it proved to be a serious point of contention in a number of countries where the activities of the National Socialists had become more than a mere annoyance. Bohle tried to ignore it as much as he could, but this was not always possible when conditions sometimes reached crisis proportions and verged upon a diplomatic break between Germany and one of the nations in question. Almost with monotonous regularity, Bohle always responded that he had issued clear directives that non-German citizens were not permitted to participate in AO membership.

Another serious concern for Bohle was dealing with the existing German organizations and clubs, both at home and abroad. Many of them had large memberships and admitted people whether they had German citizenship or not. The composition ranged from small social groups on a local level to very large organizations with a headquarters in Germany. Some of them had a long history of operations that reached back into the previous century, and connections to German communities abroad through several generations of people. The problem for Bohle was the fact that numerous activities of some of these organizations and groups were exactly the kinds of things that the AO wanted to take the lead in and control such as student exchanges, vacation homes, holiday and conference functions, and the distribution of literature about the Hitler government. Bohle was also smart enough to realize that while all of these organizations and groups had rendered services to the Germans living abroad, there was no strong unifying factor until National Socialism appeared on the scene. They had their language and cultural heritage, but no political ideals, only bitterness left over from the post-World War I era. He knew that his AO could provide that political unity by carrying the National Socialist message. It was important, however, that this not be diluted by disorganization and group infighting among the many groups, and therefore, the Auslandsorganisation der NSDAP had to emerge as the recognized leader.

Bohle fully understood that he had to make his appeal for obedience and unity on the basis of the astonishing success the Nazis had achieved at home, and that loyalty to the nation and to Hitler had to take precedence over all else. As welcome as this message may have been to many important party leaders, the Gauleiter was aware that there were others who regarded his grandiose plans as intrusions into their own domains, and there would be resistance. The most formidable, and ultimately the most difficult to deal with, was the German Foreign Office, which viewed Bohle's proposals and planning as unacceptable interference into the realm of official affairs that were conducted by the regular diplomatic personnel.

At first, the animosity between the two offices remained beneath the official surface, but in January 1934, a confidential AO memorandum meant for inner office personnel only, outlined the growing jealously of the Foreign Office. It focused on the success that the AO people were having abroad in spreading the spirit of National Socialism among the German communities, and the intolerance and rivalry encountered from the German consular staffs who seemed intent upon thwarting AO programs at every turn. Mussolini's actions in placing his Fascist followers into the forefront of Italy's diplomacy at the expense of the old time diplomats, was praised as an example for Germany to study.[16] Such sentiments, expressed so early in the Hitler regime indicate that Bohle was already set on a course that intended to place his Auslandsorganisation in competition with the Foreign Office on every feasible issue. It also points to the Gauleiter's conviction that his best course of action in choosing his arguments with the Foreign Office was to base them upon the premise that his organization was a creation that had grown out of the Hitler movement, and therefore, was an expression of the party's will. He felt, and rightly so, that this was a defense that even the most respected of German diplomatic figures could not openly reject.

To implement his vision, Bohle was careful in the selection of people he picked to staff his office. With the exception of Alfred Hess, Bohle was determined to make his own appointments and placed a premium on brains and youth. The degree of commitment to National Socialism appears to have played a secondary role, which seems to be a contradiction when viewing the AO as an instrument which had the primary function of spreading the Nazi gospel. However, Bohle saw the AO as the vehicle that held the potential to bring him the position of authority in Germany's diplomatic world that he craved, and if this meant selling the message of National Socialism abroad, then so be it. The Gauleiter apparently saw little conflict in promoting the mission of the AO, and having staff people who were less than enthusiastic about National Socialism. Doing good and efficient work, having a personal loyalty to Bohle, and keeping any criticisms of the regime strictly to yourself, were the main criteria for employment.

An example of this was Bohle's choice for his most trusted deputy, Emil Ehrich, who had been an exchange student in England. He became an invaluable assistant to Bohle, and had come to work for the Gauleiter in July 1933. In describing these early years, Ehrich's account brimmed with youthful exuberance about his future. He said that the office atmosphere was eager and interested, often working well beyond ordinary office hours. Everyone knew that the future looked promising, and that Bohle would someday head a new "Ministry for Foreign Germans." Ehrich was certain that "by a proper exploitation of the Auslandsdeutsche, an extraordinarily important political factor can be created."[17] Ehrich estimated that there were some forty million Germans spread around the world waiting to be influenced by Bohle's work, and without reference to citizenship status, indicated that there was no limit to what could be accomplished. This early optimism of Bohle's future was even shared by some of the important party leaders. Martin Bormann, Hitler's private secretary, on a visit to Bohle's AO offices in March 1933, wrote the following in the guest books: "The AO is a greater undertaking than any other Gau. It has already achieved a great deal, and has even more to accomplish."[18]

However, the fact that Bohle could not really resolve the problem of the Germans who were attracted to the National Socialist state, and were not German citizens, did not only represent a continuing diplomatic tension with foreign countries where many Germans resided, but was the root of much of his trouble with certain organizations at home. These organizations only existed because of the Germans who lived abroad, most of whom were not citizens, and they viewed the AO as a distinct threat to their survival with its infiltration into the communities. Bohle attempted to mollify these organizations by announcing in April 1934, the creation of an AO office (Verband der Reichsdeutschen Vereine im Ausland) that focused only upon German citizens living abroad. However, the Gauleiter continued to maintain that it was a party aim to bring unity to the Germans who lived beyond Germany's borders.[19]

In an attempt to circumvent the criticism directed at the AO over the non-citizenship question, Bohle endorsed the strategy of creating front organizations that enlisted Germans who were not citizens of the Reich. This usually entailed establishing a group with a title or name that reflected its support of the Nazis, but was not officially connected with Germany. In this manner, they hoped to avoid being prohibited by the host countries, and for a period of time, depending upon the local circumstances, the subterfuge was tolerated. However, the situation was always a source of friction between the growing anti-Hitler feelings abroad and the various front organizations. This generally resulted in the lodging of diplomatic complaints with the German Foreign Office, and the possibility of strained relations. Bohle had to also constantly contend with the problem of how to answer the charge that he was actually directing the front organizations when it was revealed that AO party people were really members of many of them. Of course, he always denied any involvement, but the fact of a party connection remained an open secret. The situation relating to the German population that lived in North America was a prime example of the policies of duplicity employed by both the German Foreign Office and the Auslandsorganisation der NSDAP.

In one instance, in January 1934, the Landesgruppenleiter for Canada, Karl Gerhard, together with a Nazi Party member from Montreal named Lothar Pfau, discussed the prospect of creating a major front organization with German consular officials there. What they had in mind was an organization that would include all people of German descent in Canada, and call it the "Deutschen Bund." They also suggested that it was probably possible to establish openly at the same time a branch of the Nazi Party, but were dissuaded by the German consul, who advised that the Deutschen Bund was probably the best way to go. It was undecided, however, if it was necessary to receive permission from the Canadian government before proceeding. The name finally selected was "German League of Canada, Inc."(Deutscher Bund, Kanada, Inc.). In preparing to apply for a charter from the government, an English text was composed that read: "The League desires the formation of an unpolitical body comprising members of the German race in Canada, with the object of fostering German culture and interests in the cultivation of the ideals of the new Germany." A confidential note to Berlin explained that the core of the proposed league would be made up of party members.[20]

To check the legality of their position, the German consulate consulted a Canadian law firm for an opinion. Their concern focused on two questions: In organizing the German communities in Montreal, Toronto, Winnipeg, and Vancouver, into the proposed League, would a charter be required? Secondly, since there are also German nationals living in those same cities who wish to form a branch of the National Socialist Party of Germany, do they need a charter, too? The law answered that an incorporation document was sufficient for proceeding with their plans, but cautioned that any possible conflict with Canadian law must be avoided, and suggested that all references to any association with an existing organization in Germany be eliminated.[21]

The entire charade was typical of what the AO played over and over again in various parts of the globe as it attempted to establish a foothold for the propagation of National Socialism among the German communities. Sometimes an extremely contentious situation developed when these incursions were not only resisted by local governments, but by German diplomatic personnel working in the areas involved. While they did not openly object to the National Socialist theme, they strongly resented the challenge to their traditional authority to manage the details of German foreign affairs. The diplomatic corps saw themselves as more experienced, better educated, well traveled and generally, more knowledgeable, than Bohle's party members, and there was enough truth in this assessment to provide them some protection against simply being replaced. Thus, a kind of stand-off existed, with neither side capable of making the other disappear. As Hitler's hold over the nation increased, however, it was inevitable that the Foreign Office people had to make the best of the inroads into their duties by the AO, although there were innumerable ways in which Bohle's aims and progress could be thwarted without displaying any criticism of the regime.

Both the AO and the Foreign Office became adept at employing subtle forms of harassment against each other, always careful to choose who could be offended without serious retaliation in the internecine war that continually raged among Nazi Party officials. For example, the Foreign Office made a point that it would only add to the hostility felt toward Germany abroad if the consular officials permitted people from the AO to have the use of space in their offices. In fact, there was already an instance whereby an AO member, using an office in a consulate, gave the impression that he was a fully accredited diplomat of the German government.[22] At this time, the problem for the Foreign Office was how to pursue an internal policy that protected their ranks from being infiltrated — and ultimately controlled — by untrained and inexperienced Nazis, and yet at the same time, not appear hostile toward a party-created organization bent upon assuming some of its duties.

After all, Bohle had the blessing of most of the party leadership to organize the world of the German abroad in the image of National Socialism, and could not be faulted for carrying out the wishes of the Führer. In a bold move to reinforce his position, Bohle devised a plan that would completely disarm his Foreign Office opponents by enlisting them as party members into his Auslandsorganisation. Actually, the idea was not new for there had been the intent earlier to bring all diplomats of higher rank into the party as a unit ("Auswärtiges Amt der NSDAP"), but this had been delayed due the initial ban on party membership when Hitler first assumed power. In February 1934, it was finally agreed that those permanent employees of the Foreign Office who served abroad, and wished to become members of the NSDAP, would have to make their declaration through the Auslandsorganisation in Hamburg.[23] This was an important piece of authority that was now placed in Bohle's hands, for it meant that every new recruit to the Foreign Office going abroad who took party membership, passed through the Auslandsorganisation. While party membership was not stated as a requirement to join the Foreign Office, the implication was clear that an individual's future depended upon party approval. While no figures indicated the percentage of new Foreign Office personnel after 1933 who belonged to the Nazi Party, it can be assumed that the majority were members, especially among the younger people.

By the terms of the new arrangement between Bohle and the Foreign Office personnel, those persons who accepted party membership were now expected to participate in the activities of the AO Landegruppen, and give full cooperation to the Landesgruppenleiter in affairs scheduled by the Hamburg office. In the event of any disagreement over the performance of duties or crowded schedules, the issue was to be referred to a resolution committee of personnel from both the AO and the Foreign Office. For the diplomats already serving abroad who did not have party membership, it was now permitted to make application to the AO office in Hamburg. Bohle's announcement of this new relationship with the Foreign Office, ended with the encouraging statement that party applications would be dispatched to each overseas consul with the next courier.[24] With this step, the AO Gauleiter had not only succeeded in channeling virtually all of Germany's diplomatic corps that desired to have a future in the Third Reich into an affiliation with his Auslandsorganisation, but he had also secured permission to open party membership to German citizens living abroad when it was still not allowed at home.

It is important to recognize that while Bohle placed this great emphasis upon party membership, he obviously saw it as a tool that reinforced his position in competition with the Foreign Office. To always champion the party line placed him in an unassailable stance in any disagreement with the diplomatic corps, However, many of his actions indicate that he was not a fanatic National Socialist, but used the implied force of party support to gain his ends when he deemed it necessary. Some evidence of this came from descriptions of former German diplomats who spoke of Bohle after the war. One such was Vicco von Bülow-Schwante, who had served as chief of protocol in the Foreign Office at one time, and had become acquainted with Bohle in the course of his duties. He said that he worked closely with the AO leader for a period, and knew him quite well, but never did the young Gauleiter attempt to use his position and influence to pressure anyone into joining the party. Another account, from the wife (Ingeborg Alix) of a German diplomat serving abroad, encountered Bohle when he made a visit to the consulate, and described him as a man who was certainly not a narrow-minded fanatic. Brigitta Reich, a longtime secretary in Bohle's office also stated that the Gauleiter never tried to persuade her or any other office member to join the party, and that they felt perfectly comfortable in not doing so.[25]

Despite this seeming tolerance in the matter of party affiliation when it suited his purpose, Bohle never missed the opportunity to press the point of loyalty to the National Socialist state when he dealt with issues involving the Foreign Office. Although the animosity between the diplomatic corps and Bohle's AO remained largely below the surface most of the time, it was clearly a situation that grew more aggravated as the Gauleiter's influence increased. Both sides engaged in a kind of infighting that often focused upon petty issues that were made bones of contention, like the use of consular space by Bohle's people, for example. In this instance, however, the Foreign Office had a legitimate concern that the presence of AO personnel in the consulates left the impression that the diplomats were collaborating in spy operations conducted by Bohle's office. Such was the reputation of the Auslandsorganisation that any suspected association with German diplomatic personnel abroad was sufficient to raise the ire of a host country, and possibly cause a diplomatic rife.

Bohle seemed to accept these criticisms as part of the job, and carried on a never ceaseless effort to discredit the Foreign Office at every opportunity. Through these first years of Nazi power, he moved steadily forward in extending his influence into the diplomatic ranks with a series of intrusions into Foreign Office protocol. A significant step was the ability of the AO to bring pressure to bear upon the diplomatic personnel assigned abroad to become party members, and at one point, Bohle informed the Foreign Office that they were to employ only party members in those situations that were of a confidential nature.[26]

As time passed, and new people entered Germany's foreign service as party members, it meant that they were far more sympathetic to the aims of the Hitler regime than their older colleagues, and tended to view the AO as an ally rather than an enemy. It also resulted in introducing a strong element of the rivalry and jealously characteristic of the history of the Nazi Party. Now, diplomats had to be cautious that they always followed the correct procedures to the letter, or be possibly reported by their colleagues. Failure to end a correspondence with "Heil Hitler!," not hanging the swastika flag in each and every room, and the absence of the latest Hitler portrait, could bring sharp reprimands from Berlin. However, by the end of 1934, the first full year of Nazi control, Bohle could survey his progress with some satisfaction. His AO had been endorsed by such powerful Nazi leaders as Martin Bormann, Josef Goebbels, and Rudolf Hess as the single responsible office for all NSDAP members residing abroad (except for Austria, Memel and Danzig), and the young Gauleiter had begun to edge into the rarified atmosphere of German diplomacy.

5   Foreign Policy Concerns

The National Socialist Party of Germany had succeeded in its first two years in power in taking total control of the nation's institutions, and eliminating all visible opposition. The process of implanting National Socialism into every conceivable fiber of German life had already made considerable progress. Although the world had been momentarily shocked by Adolf Hitler's ruthless methods of dealing with his political opponents, much of the outrage was overshadowed by the signs of some economic recovery. For many Germans, numbed by the years of political strife, inflation, and depression, the stringencies introduced by the new government were a willing price to pay for a revitalized economy, and the restoration of political and social order. Even the transfer of presidential responsibilities to Chancellor Hitler after the death of President von Hindenburg, was accepted as an act in accordance with the spirit of the new Germany.

This was accompanied by the emergence of a new pride in Germany's international standing as the January 1935 plebiscite in the Saar reflected the overwhelming desire of its inhabitants to return to German rule. Hitler was suddenly a new and powerful player in European affairs, and when he denounced the disarmament clauses of the Versailles Treaty as unfair, and indicated his intentions to do something about it, other nations began to show serious concern. Great Britain already appeared ready to make significant concessions regarding German naval expansion.

By 1935, even Germany's critics were being forced to admit that Hitler and his National Socialists were pulling the country out of an economic depression that still burdened the rest of the industrial world. The more oppressive aspects of the Hitler movement were largely ignored as the new regime was compared to the successes of Mussolini in Italy. There was an outpouring of praise for a leader who brought hope to a people who had suffered military defeat, ruinous inflation, and economic depression. Not surprisingly, there were voices raised in some of the democracies, still deeply mired in the depression and suffering mass unemployment, that suggested Hitler's ideas had merit and should be seriously considered as possible solutions to their own problems.

Understandably, the new Germany became a magnet for millions of Germans who lived abroad. While many of them may have had some reservations about the messages being sent by the new National Socialist government, there was a renewed pride in the respect now being shown Germany. If properly harnessed, these Auslandsdeutsche represented a world-wide network that could be extremely helpful to Germany's foreign policy in many ways, and no one was more aware of this than Ernst Wilhelm Bohle, the Gauleiter of the Auslandsorganisation der NSDAP. He knew, from his own background, that the job of bringing a meaningful unity under the banner of National Socialism was fraught with complexities. Each and every German community had its own history, and while all of them had a language and a culture in common, they varied considerably in political outlook. Those with an older German population tended to regard the advent of the Hitler government with a more conservative attitude, while the communities that had witnessed the influx of younger Germans, especially after World War I, were more ready to welcome contact with the Auslandsorganisation der NSDAP.

Of course, geography and recent history played a large role in the prevailing politics of the German communities. Those Germans who lived along Germany's borders obviously had a different attitude toward the Hitler government and its nationalistic appeals, than a long established German community in Argentina. More important for the immediate future was the degree of relevance a particular German group had to German foreign policy. A disputed border minority involving Germans separated from the fatherland by the war settlements, was of far more concern in Hitler's scheme of things than an Auslandsdeutsche community overseas.

Bohle was aware that the resolution to some of these problems lay beyond the limits of his organization, but his ambition was to bring some semblance of political unity to the German world beyond Germany's borders. He hoped to be able to say one day that his AO, with its Landesgruppen and party apparatus, had created a solid network of those Germans who lived abroad, into National Socialist supporters, but first there was work to do. He knew that old feuds and arguments were just as rife among the German communities abroad as they were among the party members at home, and that many times these conflicts were carried on in the name of serving the community. Sometimes, the root of the trouble rested with individual party members at home who had connections to a community abroad, and insisted on involving themselves in a local controversy. Bohle had to walk carefully in such instances, especially when elements in a local German community rejected the AO representatives. If the situation was not handled diplomatically and quietly resolved, it could reach the news media, and negative publicity for the Auslandsorganisation; perhaps even banning its activities from the country concerned.

In one such instance, that got out of control, a German club in Melbourne, Australia, decided to expel several members who held party membership, and the affair was reported in lurid detail in the local press: "The beginnings of this upheaval became noticeable about two years ago when a number of young Germans arrived, Nazis to the bone. As a result, something approaching a state of civil war exists in the German colony in Melbourne."[1] When such events occurred, it was not unusual for the German Foreign Office personnel to find themselves in the middle of it. In 1935, the German consul in Manila decided to hold the May First celebration in the local German club, and invite the crew of a German ship that happened to be in the harbor. Since German seamen belonged to the Auslandsorganisation, it was logical that the members of the Ortsgruppe in Manila be included, however, the club had already banned members of the Nazi Party from their activities, and refused them admission. The consul complained to Berlin, that he had a very busy day having to schedule two separate celebrations.[2]

The AO Gauleiter was sensitive to such matters, but could not always anticipate what might happen. Anything that brought unwanted publicity was a concern which he tried to avoid, and sometimes he was successful. When the German Foreign Institute (Deutsches Auslands-Institut) was in the process of preparing a reference work on the German communities abroad, it included a description of the role of the Auslandsorganisation, but when Bohle read the proposed account, he quickly informed the editors that any mention of the AO should be eliminated because in "...many countries where our groups are quietly tolerated, we run the risk of having them prohibited if it's brought to the attention of governments openly in a handbook."[3]

Bohle was not premature in his concern, for some countries were already mounting investigations of Nazi groups on their soil in late1933. In fact, the United States government began a probe of Nazi activity that same year, which is ironic since Bohle, who had a good grasp of the American situation, had concluded that his organization had little future there. He said that he did not try to exert any influence in the United States, nor put pressure on German diplomatic personnel working there. The problem was that there were a number of party members residing there who were determined to establish a National Socialist presence in spite of Bohle's reservations.[4]

Actually, there had been some Nazi activity in the United States ever since the Hitler-Ludendorff Putsch in Munich in 1923, but it was spasmodic, disorganized, and went largely unnoticed. Only later, when the Hitler movement began to attract more notice, the Nazis in the United States started to get some attention, but even then, it was not very much. The United States had a long history of radical immigrant groups in its history, and they were usually regarded with a certain tolerance as simply part of the fabric of a democratic society.

Bohle denied that the AO ever had an official branch in the United States, although he admitted that an informal group did exist, and AO records for the year of 1929, make reference to a "Landesgruppe USA." The first person to have any direct connection to the AO was a party member named Heinz Spanknöbel, who was living in America in 1931. Bohle said that when he took over the office from Hans Nieland, some contact existed with individual party members there, however, Rudolf Hess "...told us that he wanted no trouble ...and the first thing he did was to dissolve the AO in the United States by telegram in April 1933. He said he wanted no organization there. It would only lead to trouble." [5] However, in the meantime, a group of Nazi Party members in the United States had created a front organization called the "Friends of New Germany" (Bund der Freunde des Neuen Deutschlands) led by Heinz Spanknöbel, who was now informed by Bohle that he should surrender his position to a German who held American citizenship, but the Gauleiter did not expressly forbid participation by German citizens in the new association.[6]

In addition to the flow of information that the AO received from the Friends group and the German consul in New York City, Bohle requested the North German Lloyd representative there, Captain F. C. Mensing, to maintain regular contact. In a show of caution, Mensing decided to ask the German Ambassador to the United States, Hans Luther, if he knew of any objection by the U.S. State Department to these arrangements by the AO. The captain was especially concerned that Bohle had asked him to collect dues from party members. Luther replied that he had heard nothing specific from the U.S. State Department, but he felt that anything resembling Nazi activity on American soil would certainly be seen as unwelcome.[7]

An investigation into Nazi activity by a United States House of Representatives committee started in late 1933, and while it signaled trouble to German Ambassador Luther, it appeared to have little impact on the party members living in America. At first, the committee was headed by a congressman named Samuel Dickstein a Democrat from New York, and was authorized to investigate not only the Nazis, but the Communists, too. However, the House of Representatives decided that Dickstein, being Jewish, would be too much of a target for Nazi propaganda, and therefore appointed Congressman John McCormack the chairman. The German news media ignored this though, and always referred to the committee as the "Dickstein Committee."

Hearings were held in various cities around the country, and some Nazi Party members were called before the Committee to testify, including Captain F. C. Mensing, who appeared in July 1934. He said that Gauleiter Bohle and the Auslandsorganisation did not direct any National Socialist group on American soil, but there was communication with individual party members from time to time. In fact, Mensing said, when he visited Germany recently and met with Bohle, and conveyed greetings from Heinz Spanknöbel, the Gauleiter threw up his hands and said: "I do not want to be in any connection with Mr. Spanknöbel. Every officer in this land [Germany] has tried to hook Mr. Spanknöbel onto me, but I refuse the responsibility."[8]

Kurt Lüdecke, who was also called before the hearings as a witness, supported Bohle's denial that he had not had any direct dealings with Spanknöbel, and had certainly not appointed him to anything. Actually, according to Lüdecke, the AO leader did not really know very much about the situation in the United States. Several other Bund members who were called as witnesses stated that Spanknöbel was active in the movement in America before Bohle was appointed as head of the AO, and at the time, answered to Bohle's predecessor, Hans Nieland.[9]

The October hearings proved disturbing to several groups in the United States that sponsored relations between Americans and Germans, and one of the most notable was the Steuben Society of America. A leading figure in the Society, T. A. Hoffman, thought the congressional investigation serious enough to discuss it personally with Hitler, and in a visit to the Führer, Hoffman expressed his growing concern that the continuance of contact between officials in Germany and the Bund was creating very serious harm to German-American relations. Although Hitler repeated the official position always given when Germany received such criticisms, that party members were forbidden to engage in any politics when abroad, he stated that there were no restrictions on meetings among themselves to share their National Socialist ideology.[10]

Bohle's reaction to Hoffman's visit to Hitler was defensive. He immediately contacted Hess, and explained that he had never agreed to support any sort of official status for the American group, and when he first heard that some party members had joined the Friends group, he ordered them to resign. There was a rumor, he said, that the Steuben Society had become jealous that the Friends organization was gaining support from some of the German Americans, but insisted that the problem was one that had to be taken care of there because the AO had no connection to the situation. He suggested that steps had to be taken by the group that would clearly indicate that they had no official link to the Third Reich, and the German Ambassador to the United States fully agreed.[11] However, Bohle conveniently omitted some relevant details in his communication to Hess. For example, he neglected to tell the Deputy Führer that he had arranged to have a number of party members in the United States temporarily "retired" from active membership in order that they could continue to participate in the Friends. The Gauleiter had, in fact, forwarded twenty-five names of party members currently in the United States to the party treasurer in Munich for placement on a special status that suspended membership until a future "reinstatement."[12] It was apparent that Kurt Lüdecke's remark that Bohle knew little about what was going on in America, was not very accurate. He had an informant in the German consul in New York named Dr. Draeger, who regularly supplied him with lengthy reports on what the Friends were doing. Actually, Draeger's major assignment was to supply Bohle with confidential communiqués on the German diplomatic personnel there, as well.[13]

Despite his efforts at evasion and secrecy, and the official denials of any involvement in the American situation, animosity toward Germans and Germany mounted. The Friends of New Germany was finally dissolved, but quickly reemerged as the German-American Bund, and appeared to most American observers as the same organization as before, just a new name. By this time, a far more strident tone was being heard from voices in America, as accusations were surfacing that charged Bohle and his organization with carrying out spying and sabotage missions for Germany. This was nothing new for Bohle, because the same charges had been made before in other countries, and provided the foreign press with a series of sensationalist stories that painted the AO as a direct arm of Germany's espionage apparatus.

There were those in Germany who did not take the rising criticism of Germany as calmly as Bohle did. They not only resented his growing influence, but regarded the AO as a threat to their own activities. Such was the case with the League for Germandom Abroad (Verein für das Deutschtum im Ausland or VDA), led by Hans Steinacher. The relationship between the two men had taken on a very personal note marked by mutual animosity. Their open dislike for each other began to assume larger consequences as both men sought support from various factions within the party. While Bohle had a more solid position as the appointed spokesman for National Socialism, Steinacher and his organization had a much longer history of service to German communities abroad, and some influential friends both in the party and beyond.

Their rivalry began almost as soon as Bohle had assumed the leadership of the AO. One of the first disagreements arose from Bohle's decision, together with Hitler Youth leader Baldur von Schirach, to introduce programs for young people into a number of German communities, both in Europe and abroad. Although this primarily involved activities of camping, hiking, singing, and celebrating national holidays, Steinacher was concerned that it was an effort to bolster the image of the AO at the expense of the VDA Rudolf Hess tried to smooth over the differences between the two, but to no avail. In fact, Steinacher was certain that Bohle was plotting against him and that Hess supported the AO leader.[14]

By early 1935, according to Steinacher, Bohle's efforts at undermining his position had become very threatening. Not only was Bohle demanding a share of the funding that the VDA received, but was building a case that Steinacher's actions were contrary to party welfare. Following the Winter-Help relief campaign in February, Steinacher wrote: "On the 12th, Bohle demanded from me half of the collections...I said no! A few days later, I received a written request from Hess that I give 50% of the collections to Bohle. I did not immediately comply... from Hess, a limit of three days, the VDA shall transfer 350,000 Reichsmarks to the Party!"[15]

Bohle continued to press the theme that Steinacher and the VDA were not supportive of the goals of National Socialism, and as proof he charged that Steinacher was using funds from his organization to assist newspapers that were unfriendly to Germany.[16] Bohle brought this charge publicly at the 1935 Party Day (Parteitag), and as Steinacher described it, the

AO Gauleiter "...declared me Germany's enemy number one."[17] It is not clear just what kind of reaction this caused from those assembled for the party celebration in Nuremberg, but evidently Bohle's harsh words were not taken literally by Hess, for Steinacher remained at his post for a couple of more years before the Deputy Führer "retired" him. However, it was becoming increasingly evident that in the short two years that Bohle had been in office, he was determined to make the Auslandsorganisation the most important voice in any dealings that Germany had with the German communities abroad. Groups or organizations like the VDA were the easy targets; his real challenge remained the German Foreign Office.

In these first years of the Third Reich, as National Socialist Party members permeated the commanding positions in government, that element of the German professional diplomatic corps that tried to remain somewhat aloof from enthusiastic pledges of loyalty to Führer, must have wondered many times what the future held for them. There were clear signs that a fundamental change was underway, and no segment of German society would escape total integration into the Nazi fold. It would only be a matter of time. Already, a number of German consuls were complaining to Berlin that they were encountering interference in their daily functions from local AO representatives. For example, Bohle's office often dispatched instructions on what kind of celebrations were proper for German holidays, and this sometimes conflicted with what a German consul had prepared. The right of the AO to use consular space for holiday functions was also a contested issue. When the AO insisted that either the format or the content of a particular program planned by a German consul be changed, the Foreign Office defended itself by explaining that the local German community had grown accustomed to it, and any change would be disturbing to them.[18]

It was customary for the Foreign Office to sponsor an annual speakers' program, and certain distinguished people, or experts in some area, were invited to participate. Before Hitler's government, these events had usually been devoted to topics on travel, science and literature, but this changed after 1933, and Bohle's AO began sending out speakers whose major theme was extolling National Socialism. By 1935, when the Foreign Office prepared its list of speakers for the May Day celebration, twelve of the fifty-two people were Bohle's pick, and he presented two of the speeches himself, in London and Birmingham, England.[19]

Ever alert to any real or imagined snub by the Foreign Office, Bohle never neglected to make it an issue, and almost always on the basis of the party versus its detractors. The Gauleiter took the matter of respect for his AO members very seriously, and was not reluctant to inform Hess or Bormann, when he detected any sign of discourtesy or disrespect from Foreign Office personnel. Social functions by German consuls were often a target of Bohle's complaints because his local Ortsgruppe people were not always invited. Hess, obviously on Bohle's behalf, did not hesitate to contact German Foreign Minister Constantin von Neurath, and point out specific instances where his AO people were snubbed on social occasions by German consuls. On one occasion, the Deputy Führer sent Neurath a newspaper clipping describing a piano recital in Belgrad at the German embassy that made reference to the fact that the AO Landesleiter had not been invited.[20]

As Bohle continued to press for greater authority over what had been traditional consular duties, resentment and confusion arose in Foreign Office ranks. With no clearly defined lines of authority, the German diplomats serving abroad had to make decisions on what they regarded, from time to time, as unacceptable AO intrusions. The Foreign Office was particularly sensitive to the AO practice of assigning one of their people to a consulate office even though the individual in question did not have any official diplomatic status or function. However, considerable care had to be exercised in complaining about the AO presence because Bohle's propaganda activities were strongly supported by the party.

While these differences between the AO and the Foreign Office were often over petty issues, it was not unusual for Hess and Neurath to become involved before some resolution was reached, but it seemed to never end, and as soon as one argument had been settled, another arose. No doubt weary of the continuous hassle, the Foreign Office notified all missions and consulates in May 1935, that there was far too much time and correspondence wasted upon the current procedures involving differences of opinion with the AO representatives, and henceforth every effort should be made to settles things orally and on the spot. Only when such an effort failed should it be pursued officially through channels. It was noted that these same instructions had been issued by Bohle to the Auslandsorganisation.[21]

Soon thereafter, Neurath informed his people that he wanted to maintain good relations with the AO, and reminded them that all party functionaries were officials of the Reich, but he was obviously also concerned about the extent of Bohle's infiltration into Foreign Office territory as evidenced by a communiqué to all Foreign Office personnel abroad, wherein answers were requested to the following questions: How many party members working in the missions and consuls belong to a local Ortsgruppe? How many of the same personnel belong to a local German club? Exactly how large is the local German community? How many are German citizens? How many of the Foreign Office employees are fulfilling a party function in addition to consular duties?[22]

Of course, there were instances when the cooperation between the Foreign Office and the AO went smoothly, but this usually occurred when a mission or consul staff had a significant number of party members employed. In 1934, in Cuba, for example, a German consul had informed Berlin that relations with the local Ortsgruppe had been difficult in the past in trying to arrange any mutual functions, but by 1935, and presumably with more party members on the staff, matters were going well and there were no problems.[23]

In the same year, Bohle's main office moved from Hamburg to Berlin (Tiergartenstrasse 4-4a), instead of to Munich with the other party offices; he was now in close proximity to the German Foreign Office. In announcing the move, Hess noted that the AO was no longer administered as a department of his office, but was a fully independent Gau, and would continue to enroll all party members living abroad as well as German seamen (about 25,000). The Gau retained its original designation of Auslandsorganisation der NSDAP, and was now responsible for the entire activity of the party membership outside of Germany.[24]

The Hess announcement reinforced Bohle's position enormously for it clearly strengthened his desire to play a larger role in the affairs of the border Germans. He knew the immediate concerns of the Führer were far more focused on the situation involving the German minorities in the border areas than the communities overseas, and his new status now opened the way for him to be more aggressive in establishing Landesgruppen there. This meant that the AO could now engage in activities that the regular German diplomatic corps could not, and could carry Hitler's message of 'protecting' the German minorities. It was a theme that was the centerpiece of Hitler's foreign policy, and Bohle was eager to present the AO as the instrument of the party directing the pro-Nazi agitation through a series of Landesgruppen.

In neighboring Austria, a strong pro-Nazi element had emerged early, but not long after Hitler's victory in Germany, Engelbert Dollfuss, the premier, had dissolved all political parties except his own, the Fatherland Front, and allied himself with Mussolini as an insurance against the Nazis. However, in July 1934, Dollfuss was killed in a failed coup by the Austrian Nazis, and German-Italian relations began to improve. Under the new leader of Austria, Kurt Schuschnigg, an agreement with Germany created an atmosphere that permitted the AO to openly represent the German Party members living there. National Socialism found fertile ground in the Führer's homeland.

Actually, the border state with the largest number of German citizens was Holland, although some 15,000 of the 55,000 who resided there were housemaids who had been recruited through various religious organizations, but the size and location made it important to the AO.[25] Bohle was also encouraged by the fact that National Socialism had taken early root there with a significant number of paying party members already active in 1932. Perhaps, they had actually been a bit too active, because the year after Hitler assumed power in Germany, the Dutch government restricted their actions so severely that Bohle dissolved the Landesgruppe. Without missing a beat, however, the AO leader quickly gave support to a newly formed organization which called itself the Association of German Citizens (Reichsdeutsche Gemeinschaft), and the propaganda machine continued as before.

This did not end the matter for the Dutch, however, and the government complained to Germany that the Association was nothing more than a disguised arm of the AO der NSDAP. The responsibility fell to the German Foreign Office to deny that there were any connections between the Association and the NSDAP. The Foreign Office's explanation was that the AO did have the duty to keep its members informed on affairs in Germany, and to maintain other contacts related to their citizenship, but that was all. The information bulletins that the AO distributed to party members abroad only focused upon the affairs at home, and carried no political references to situations in other lands. However, politely but firmly, Holland requested that no further information originating with the AO be sent, and while the German Foreign Office continued to defend Bohle's organization as only distributing innocent news items, a high ranking German diplomat involved in the controversy complained that his office had never even been given a copy of the AO bulletin, but had to be confronted with a copy presented him by a representative of the Dutch government.[26]

At this point, Hess stepped in and defended Bohle's administration, and informed the Foreign Office that all during 1934–35, the Dutch had been fully aware of the political sentiments of the German community in their country, and its support of the NSDAP. In any event, the Deputy Führer concluded, Germany was not ready to abandon the basic right of their citizens abroad to have contact with their own nation, and while there was no direct organizational connections between the German citizens living in Holland and the Nazi Party, they were subjects of the German state and obliged to obey its institutions, which included the offices of the NSDAP.[27] But this position was not good enough for the Dutch, who declared the AO Landesgruppe illegal in their country, and informed the German government that they still regarded the community of German citizens (Reichsdeutschen Gemeinschaft) living there as a disguised branch of the Nazi Party, and would not tolerate any further propaganda activities.[28]

The AO experience in Switzerland was similar to that in Holland, except it reached an earlier and more dramatic climax. Bohle saw Switzerland as fertile ground for his organization because of the large number of German citizens living there. By the mid-thirties his Landesgruppe there had some 1,360 party members, and was very active. The Landesgruppenleiter was an ardent National Socialist named Wilhelm Gustloff, who was well connected in party circles, having been recommended to Hess for his position by Alfred Rosenberg. He was a fervent admirer of Hitler and a NSDAP member since 1923. Bohle considered him a valuable leader in Switzerland, but the Foreign Office was not pleased by the unfavorable publicity he attracted.[29]

In April 1935, the German minister to Switzerland, Ernst Freiherr von Weizsäcker, informed Berlin that there was growing animosity toward Germans there, who were complaining that they were being subjected to public insults and threats from the people, and Weizsäcker said even prominent Swiss politicians were showing anger at the activities of the Landesgruppe and Gustloff.[30] In reporting to Berlin in September about a session of the

Swiss National Assembly, Weizsäcker wrote that specific questions had been raised about Wilhelm Gusloff's role as head of the AO Landesgruppe. He was described as a provocateur who had created an organization of a military character, whose members wore uniforms with Nazi insignia, and saluted a German flag. A Swiss politician posed the question to the assembly members: "Aren't the activities of Gustloff a misuse of Switzerland's guest laws, and isn't it high time that this man and his accomplices be removed from our community.?"[31]

Weizsäcker assured Foreign Minister Neurath, however, that while the language in the Swiss assembly sounded threatening, he did not expect the government to take any action against Gustloff. After all, he continued, there was no law in Switzerland against displaying the Swastika flag, and the restrictions about wearing uniforms were confusing and uncertain. He concluded, that as far as he was concerned, "...it does not appear that the continued presence of Mr. Gustloff in Davos as the Landesgruppenleiter der N.S.D.A.P. in Switzerland is threatened."[32]

Although Gustloff's behavior was making Weizsäcker's job as Germany's chief diplomatic representative in Switzerland difficult, there is no indication of this in the communications to the Foreign Office in Berlin. This probably meant that as a senior diplomat with a career to protect, Weizsäcker was exercising the usual precautions when dealing with matters that concerned the party. He was, no doubt, well aware of the tensions between the AO and the Foreign Office, and any negative opinion expressed about a well known party member like Gustloff could have unpleasant consequences. The wisdom of silence on his part was amply demonstrated when, only four months after his report on the Gustloff affair, the Landesgruppenleiter was murdered in his home in Davos by a Jewish student. The assassination immediately elevated Gustloff to martyr status in Germany, where he was hailed as one who had given his life for National Socialism.[33]

The Swiss reaction to the murder was to immediately place a ban on all AO activity, but not before Bohle personally led an entourage of people from his Berlin office to Gustloff's funeral in Bern. Bohle also used the trip to personally visit the German embassy for a discussion of the continuing role of the Auslandsorganisation among the Reichsdeutsche community in Switzerland, which he regarded as a very important group. In stressing the need for discretion in light of the Swiss ban, the Gauleiter said he would personally oversee a reorganization plan. While there is no indication that Weizsäcker participated in the discussion, Bohle was assured of complete cooperation from the embassy staff.[34]

A further indication that the German Foreign Office was eager to avoid any sign of conflict with the party, was the response of von Neurath. In an indignant note to the Swiss government, the German foreign minister complained that their decision to forbid all AO activity in their country was a complete reversal of earlier policy, that there had been no violation of the law by the German citizens living there, and he requested an explanation for the ban that had been invoked. German citizens everywhere, he wrote, are part of the national movement that constitutes the foundation of the German state, and during the past three years, the NSDAP had created a new internal political life for the German people. It was only natural, he continued, that German citizens living beyond Germany's borders desired to participate in this life, and under these circumstances the German government anticipates that the Swiss government will revoke the ban upon the NSDAP Landesgruppe there.[35]

Considering the potentially powerful threat that the Nazis posed, the Swiss showed considerable courage by responding with a polite but firm rejection: "No other colonial organization in Switzerland has a local or national structure directed by a political party functionary. The German citizens can participate in the events in their homeland without a central organization such as the Landesgruppe."[36] By no means did this signal the end of Bohle's activity in Switzerland, for he continued to stay in close communication with the Nazi Party members who lived there.

What both the Dutch and Swiss situations illustrated was Bohle's determination to exploit every conceivable avenue to enlarge his authority and influence to the point that the Auslandsorganisation actually became the voice of the party abroad. While there were still influential Germans in government and party positions who continued to regard the Foreign Office as the instrument for Hitler's foreign policies, Bohle's success in gaining worldwide name recognition for the AO, had convinced many foreign statesmen that the demarcation between the Foreign Office and the AO was virtually nonexistent. If the Foreign Office continued to be overshadowed in its little skirmishes with the AO, Bohle knew that he had a chance to establish himself as a force in shaping Germany's image abroad.

6 The AO and the Foreign Office (AA)

Even the strongest critic of the new Germany had to acknowledge that by the end of 1936, Adolf Hitler's National Socialist government had lifted the state from economic distress and near collapse to one of full employment and financial growth. The introduction of the first Four Year Plan, combined with a variety of social and political measures, had proven so successful that the German recovery was being hailed abroad as a model of planned economy. A favorable public image of Adolf Hitler, both at home and abroad, had grown with each government program, and the earlier negative views of National Socialism were fading into the background. If there were some doubters, their criticisms were drowned out by the masses of the German public who reveled in the spectacular rise of power and prestige now enjoyed by Germany in the international arena. Hitler's policies had weakened the League of Nations, his troops had reoccupied the Rhineland, a Rome-Berlin axis had been formed with the powerful fascist leader Benito Mussolini, German forces were assisting Francisco Franco in his war against the Spanish Republic, and Berlin was chosen as the site for the Olympic Games of 1936!

Not all of the credit for Hitler's success was due entirely to the changes introduced by the National Socialist government. A major factor in influencing both German and world opinion in favor of the dictator was the perceived menace of communism. The emergence of a cooperative attitude from Great Britain was based upon the deep rooted fear of many British leaders, both public and private, that communism was the alternative. Germany, even under a dictator, provided a bulwark against the Soviet Union. For those people who still had some reservations, the answer was that every dictator acted harsh in the beginning, but after assuming power, things changed. Mussolini was often cited as an example. After all, he had created a benevolent regime highly praised by western statesmen, and Hitler would, no doubt, take the same route.

By 1937, life for the rank and file of the Nazi Party could not be better. The successes of the past four years had been nothing short of phenomenal. No one was more conscious of this than Gauleiter Ernst Wilhelm Bohle, the leader of the Auslandsorganisation der NSDAP, whose official title, as of the 30th of January 1937, became the Leader of the Auslandorganisation in the Foreign Office(Chef der Auslandsorganisation der NSDAP im Auswärtiges Amt). It was a recognition that the Gauleiter had been after for some time, but the Gustloff affair, with much adverse publicity abroad, had delayed the announcement.[1]

His appointment not only reinforced Bohle's authority over all German citizens abroad, including the Foreign Office personnel, but the AO now monitored the loyalty of all German officials working abroad. This was an awesome control to command because the slightest hint of disloyalty to the regime, real or imagined, could result in the direst of consequences. In addition, Bohle's office decided on any financial assistance that went to German citizens abroad, and negotiated directly with foreign governments on matters of compensation due the German government. Military and work obligations that German citizens living abroad were responsible for were processed through the AO, as well as questions regarding citizenship or any plans to return to Germany.[2]

When informing the diplomatic corps of Bohle's newly announced position, Foreign Minister von Neurath outlined the impact upon the ministry. He stated that the AO Gauleiter's responsibilities now extended into any department or special office of the Foreign Office that involved the welfare of German citizens living abroad. Any decisions that concerned these German citizens were not to be finalized until referring them to the Auslandsorganisation. In a closing note that may have been meant to assure his own people that Bohle's new authority would not compromise the integrity of the Foreign Office, Neurath wrote that the AO leader "...is directly and personally under me."[3]

Bohle decided that all Foreign Office personnel should be afforded the benefit of his version of the new arrangement, and within days of von Neurath's message, dispatched a communiqué to all diplomatic and consular personnel emphasizing that his appointment to the Foreign Office simply represented a logical extension of party involvement. It was also a recognition of the loyalty shown by the German citizens abroad, who deserved a strong endorsement for their support of National Socialism. To meet these new challenges, Bohle wrote, it was vital that a close and confident working relationship be maintained between his office and the Foreign Office, and any differences resolved in the spirit of party unity.[4]

In introducing himself as a new voice in the Foreign Office, Bohle's message, although polite, carried a clear signal that he had the authority of the party behind him, and this took precedence in any situation of conflicting views. Following this up, he wrote: "My personal adviser, and office manager, Dr. Emil Ehrich, as a result of my appointment, will shortly be installed as a legation secretary in the Foreign Office. He has extensive knowledge of the Auslandsorganisation and my leadership, and will be responsible for establishing my office in the desired manner in the Foreign Office." [5] In assuming his position within the Foreign Office, Ehrich was actually embarking on a diplomatic career, but for the moment he was representative of the growing influence of Bohle, and was operating as his closest associate. Not yet thirty years old, Ehrich would later act as AO Landesgruppenleiter in Italy and France, where he also fulfilled important diplomatic duties.[6]

Bohle could not resist bragging to a friend that his communiqué to all diplomatic personnel in the Foreign Office had been agreed to by von Neurath without discussion, and that it signaled to all concerned that the AO der NSDAP was a voice to be heard. The Gauleiter now requested that von Neurath support his request that all AO people working abroad receive diplomatic immunity, but the foreign minister refused, and the issue remained in dispute. Perhaps, as a small concession, von Neurath directed that Bohle be provided a diplomatic passport and a ministerial pass for his wife.[7]

When Bohle's appointment to the Foreign Office was announced, it probably appeared to many of the party's leaders who were not connected to any aspect of foreign policy, as a logical step in implementing the original intent of a National Socialist state, and there was virtually no overt protest from within the ranks. This was not exactly the private reaction from some of the diplomatic personnel, however. In speaking of the event some years later, two of the diplomat's active at the time agreed that the new influence of the Auslandsorganisation in Foreign Office affairs was definitely unwelcome.[8]

When Bohle referred to his 1937 move into the German Foreign Office after the war, he left the details vague, and indicated that it had no real significance to his career as head of the AO. He implied that the whole thing had been engineered by influential party members who wanted a more direct influence in the Foreign Office, but insisted that the diplomats welcomed him, too. Actually, Bohle said, the position was not very important anyway: "It was definitely a side-line. I went to the Foreign Office for a couple of hours every morning and then to the Foreign Organization[AO] for the rest of the day."[9] However, when Bohle spoke these words, he was a prisoner of war awaiting his fate at the hands of an Allied military tribunal, and was, no doubt, trying to minimize his role in the Nazi regime. He said that the final decision for the appointment had been made by Rudolf Hess, but the record indicates that he went with Hess to see von Neurath and discussed the matter with him. To avoid the impression that the Foreign Office was a mere bystander in the process, it was agreed that the foreign minister would secure Hitler's approval.[10]

Up to this point, much of Bohle's success in edging into the areas that had been hitherto the domain of the Foreign Office, was due in large part to the reluctance of von Neurath to openly take a stand against him. Such a move could have been construed by some in the party as not showing the proper National Socialist spirit, and ultimately, a risk to his future career. Von Neurath was also well aware of Hitler's game of permitting competitive voices in foreign affairs, and never giving the foreign minister too much control. As one who understood the nuances of party behavior better than the foreign minister, Bohle was more astute at reading the situation and, no doubt, did not see von Neurath as an insurmountable object to his future ambitions. He felt that the foreign minister, like many of Germany's older diplomats, viewed the Auslandsorganisation as a band of opportunists totally unsuited for the foreign service, and he was right. Von Neurath later admitted that Bohle's entry into the Foreign Office was a "...terrible thing for me as Foreign Minister. That was an organization entirely of the Party... it was very, very annoying to our representatives and ambassadors because they mixed in everything and every[one]...thought he would be a better ambassador than the official ambassador."[11] He characterized the AO representatives who served abroad as "...men who had either gone bankrupt or who had not any kind of work, or had no success in their business and so on. Mostly men who were morally not clean."[12]

Although Bohle gave no indication officially that he was aware of von Neurath's contempt for the AO at the time of his appointment to the Foreign Office, but the Gauleiter was, above all, a pragmatist by nature and could afford to be generous under the circumstances. He once described the foreign minister as "...a wonderful man, an excellent diplomat, absolutely a gentleman."[13] Being somewhat of a diplomat himself, it is hard to tell if this was a true opinion that Bohle held or not, however, he seemed to have no problem getting along with von Neurath. He said that there had been a "...slight friction at first. No personal friction, but, of course, the AO was something new to the foreign service and they had to become accustomed to it." Bohle was honest enough to admit that his people were not as well trained as the professional diplomatic personnel, but felt that this difference would change over time.[14]

The AO leader said that von Neurath was always available to him on a moment's notice, and their discussions were friendly and never contentious. The working relationship was a good one from Bohle's standpoint, but he noted that the subject of their discussions always related to situations or problems relating to the German citizens living abroad, and never touched upon any aspects of German foreign policy. According to Bohle, while the foreign minister was always interested in any matter dealing with a possible encroachment upon diplomatic privileges by the AO, he showed little curiosity about its work with Germans abroad.[15]

Actually, according to the head of protocol for the Foreign Office at the time of Bohle's appointment, Vicco von Bülow-Schwante, von Neurath was very disturbed about the whole thing: "The battle between the Foreign Office and the NSDAP was without doubt one of the most serious problems for Frh. V. Neurath. The NSDAP began immediately after the 30 of January, 1933, to make unreasonable demands and intrude into the concerns of the Foreign Office."[16] By the time of Bohle's 1937 appointment, there already existed a long list of petty complaints between the two departments, and most of them had their origins in challenges to the authority by one or the other. Bohle was often the first to seize upon an issue of little consequence and in a show of authority, insist that it was the wish of the party. In one such instance, a disagreement arose over the question of who should open functions held in honor of visiting seamen in consuls abroad, an AO or Foreign Office member. Bohle insisted that the ship's highest ranking officer, a party member, do the honors by opening and closing the visitation with a rousing "Sieg Heil!"[17]

Ernst Bohle always maintained that it was never his intent to intimidate those diplomats who did not belong to the party, and, when mounting his defense after the war, the former Gauleiter said: "All civil servants who held office in 1933, when National Socialism came into power, well over 90 percent were still in office at the end of the war. There was never anything like a purge in the Foreign Office, and I believe that the German Foreign Office was the only Ministry which held such a high percentage of old officials of who everybody, especially myself, knew that they were not National Socialists." In fact, Bohle continued, there were people from the Foreign Office who sought his recommendation when applying for party membership. He added, that in his opinion, some of the diplomats accepted were not the most desirable of candidates.[18]

Bohle failed to explain that his recommendation was virtually essential for any applicant, since his office provided the political clearance necessary. The procedure was based upon the law that all German civil servants appointed or promoted were to have the approval of Deputy Führer Rudolf Hess, and after 1941, the Party Chancellery. The information on a particular individual went to the responsible party office, which, in the case of the Foreign Office was the Auslandsorganisation der NSDAP. Bohle said that he undertook these duties in his capacity as the Gauleiter of the AO, and that his recommendations were not always followed. The law, was, he said, a loyalty test administered in the name of the party, and: "I did my best to be fair. I by no means made my approval upon whether a civil servant was a Party member or not."[19]

Bohle's could have added that his office often investigated Foreign Office people on a regular basis. The investigation was usually conducted by one of the AO people working in a consul or embassy, or by a trusted party member in the diplomatic service. Bohle boasted at one time that he had been instrumental in the recall of a number of higher echelon diplomats who did not show the right National Socialist spirit. The basis for recall was often the lodging of complaints against a particular diplomat who had failed to show the proper respect toward visiting party members. It was Bohle's contention that the complaints had a basis in fact because of the elitist attitude that prevailed among many of the diplomats: "For the ordinary everyday German, it was very hard to speak to speak to a consul at all. There was a general dissatisfaction on the side of the German abroad with the whole consular corps." He cited instances where German abroad in need of assistance even went to foreign consulates for aid.[20]

Despite all of Bohle's later claims that he acted fairly toward Foreign Office personnel, it is important to note that, in the cases where he was instrumental in recalls, he was ready with recommendations for replacements, and, of course, they were men from the AO. Hans Schroeder, Otto Bene, Hans Bernard, Otto Langmann, and Rudolf Schleier, all AO people, reached ministerial rank in the Foreign Office.[21] Protocol chief Bülow-Schwante said, however, that if a diplomat was doing a good job in Bohle's view, the Gauleiter never complained if the person was not a party member. After the war a former German diplomat named Günther Altenburg testified that at one time he was in danger of losing his post in the Foreign Office because he did not belong to the party, and that Bohle saved his job by going directly to Hess on the matter.[22]

A large part of Bohle's success in advancing himself was due to von Neurath's inability to conduct the kind of infighting so ingrained in Nazi politics. Although he had a relationship with Hitler before the Nazi takeover in 1933, his career was really in the mode of a traditional diplomat. He had entered the German foreign service in 1901, and had served in several high positions abroad long before the Nazis became a political force in Germany. His elevation to foreign minister had occurred the year before Hitler became chancellor. There is no denying, however, that despite all of his reservations about serving the Nazi dictatorship, he held onto his job for over five years.[23] It was a period of dramatic achievements by the National Socialist government, and the general perception was that Hitler did not appear unhappy with von Neurath's leadership of the German Foreign Office. In fact, in the same year that Bohle assumed his role in the Foreign Office, a leading Berlin newspaper noted that von Neurath had been given an honorary rank in the SS, and the golden party pin "...as evidence of the Führer's confidence in the caretaker of his foreign policy."[24] Less than six months later von Neurath announced that he was resigning as foreign minister at his own request, but would remain available in a confidential capacity to advise Hitler on foreign policy matters.

In judging von Neurath's problems as foreign minister, von Bülow-Schwante, the ministry protocol chief at the time, said that it was a very difficult position to fill. There were a half-dozen Nazi Party leaders (Goebbels, Hess, Himmler, Rosenberg, Ribbentrop, and Bohle) who all meddled in foreign policy, and through all of this, von Neurath had to try and guess Hitler's intentions: "If you did not actually experience it, you can't really picture the many disparate difficulties that Frh. V. Neurath confronted."[25] Although he had never exhibited openly any animosity toward von Neurath, Bohle must have felt a sense of triumph at the foreign minister's departure from the Foreign Office. The way was now open to advance his ambitions for the Auslandsorganisation to become the true representative of National Socialism in foreign affairs. He would not have felt nearly so confident if he knew what was to come.[26]

In emphasizing his expanding responsibilities, Bohle notified all overseas missions and consuls in October 1937, of the exact authority of the AO over activities pertaining to German citizens abroad. It was an impressive list that included the right to arrange the celebrations for holidays, resolve all citizenship questions, voting, immigration and return, military and work service, legal rights, financial assistance, and awards.[27] Some of these activities obviously spilled over into the communities where many of the Germans did not hold citizenship, but were admirers of National Socialism. It also highlighted the important but unanswered question of just how deeply was the AO involved with the thousands of Germans in these communities who were not citizens.

Meanwhile, Bohle had acquired one of the second highest rankings within the Foreign Office, when he was named a State Secretary. Additionally, he was named a member of the Reichstag, where he served on a committee that advised on foreign affairs. In 1936, he had received the rank of Brigadier General (Brigadeführer) in the SS, although later he disputed the importance of it by describing it as a very casual happening at the party rally that year when an adjutant of Himmler simply told him of the appointment. A year later, however, he received messages from Himmler and Hitler personally, stating that he was being advanced to the rank of major general (Gruppenführer) in the SS.[28]

During an Allied interrogation after the war, and still very much uncertain about his fate, Bohle said that he took no pride in the fact that his SS appointment had placed him on Himmler's personal staff. He insisted that on the occasions when he wore the striking black SS uniform, which was very rare, he did so either because it was required or his regular brown uniform was being cleaned.[29] Considering his situation at the time of this statement, it can be assumed that Bohle was attempting to minimize his involvement in the Hitler regime, but the record of his ambitious agenda to broaden his role in foreign affairs leading up to 1937, belied his defense.

During that same year, in the exercise of his increased responsibilities, Bohle took up the question of dual citizenship, a matter that had begun to prove vexing for both the Foreign Office and the AO, as more and more Germans who held dual citizenship indicated that they wished to return home. Especially eager to resolve their status was a group of German citizens living in Mexico. They numbered about 6,500 people, and approximately 1,600 of them had accepted Mexican citizenship, largely for employment reasons. Some 1,000 of the German children in the community held Mexican citizenship by virtue of birth It was an issue that had attracted the attention of the Mexican government, and Bohle decided that his office had to take some action. Hopefully, to prevent further concern by the Mexicans, he ordered that no one holding dual citizenship be permitted to participate in party affairs. Since Bohle himself held dual citizenship, it was obvious that he would have to surrender his British citizenship in compliance with his own order.[30]

Clearly, this was not something that Bohle wanted to do for it represented a basic denial of the AO propaganda that had always regarded dual citizenship as an acknowledgment that the German who lived, or had lived, abroad was more worldly than the German who stayed at home, and had a fuller understanding of life outside of Germany. Of course, a leading example was Alfred Hess himself, and Bohle had rarely missed the opportunity to point this out when extolling the virtues of belonging to the AO. The legality of dual citizenship had remained somewhat murky because a nineteenth-century law specified that German citizens who remained abroad more than ten years without consular approval lost their citizenship. However, the situation changed with the Imperial and State Citizenship Law of 1913, which not only lifted the earlier restriction, but encouraged Germans to hold dual citizenship after approval by the proper authorities.

It was probably a painful decision for Bohle to give up his British citizenship for he had been raised bilingual and had absorbed much of English culture and life style. When the Bohle family moved to Capetown, South Africa, he was enrolled in an English school, which he finished before going to Germany to study. This background served him well for he found employment with both English and American import firms later. Later, when Bohle discussed giving up his British citizenship with the British ambassador to Germany, Sir Eric Phipps, he was assured that retaining the citizenship presented no problem for the British government. The Gauleiter decided, however, that considering the AO position, it was only proper for him to do so.[31] He obviously felt it necessary to immediately tell Himmler that he had given up his British citizenship: "I am pleased to inform you", he wrote, "that this morning I relinquished my English citizenship before the British consulate in Berlin, and I am now exclusively a German citizen." Evidently feeling that a further explanation was in order, Bohle continued: "I had the English citizenship as a result of my birth in England, although both of my parents are German citizens. I did not do this before because England does not normally recognize the relinquishment of citizenship, but by special arrangement with the British ambassador, I was able to do so."[32] The following day Bohle also contacted Hans Heinrich Lammers, who headed the Reich Chancellery with the same information, and asked him to make sure the Führer saw it. Later, Lammers informed Bohle that he had mentioned the Gauleiter's explanation to Hitler.[33]

Evidently Bohle's action had not created any tension with the British government for shortly after the formalities at the consulate in Berlin, Bohle decided to make a visit to Britain. He had always viewed the AO Landesgruppe there with a special regard. It had been created before he came to the head of the AO, and when he assumed that post, he reaffirmed the Landesgruppenleiter there, Otto Bene, who had held the position since 1932. Bene had lived in England since 1927, and dated his party membership from 1931. He and Bohle both shared a common interest in England, and had been close friends for some time. Under Bene's leadership the AO Landesgruppe had kept its distance from the British fascist elements, although he told Bohle that his group was under constant police surveillance and found it necessary to move their meeting place from time to time despite the inconvenience for the membership. At one point, this became so annoying that Bene proposed to Bohle that they purchase a hotel in London for their group to use, and rent the rest of the rooms to German tourists who were visiting the city. After the German Foreign Office warned Bohle that this was going too far, the Gauleiter rejected Bene's proposal. Not long thereafter, Bohle recommended Bene for the position of German general consul in London, but withdrew it after the British government made it known that he was unacceptable.[34]

Ernst Bohle's name was not unknown in England, and his actions in surrendering his British citizenship was reported widely in the press. This was followed by more negative coverage when, shortly before his departure for England, he delivered a speech in Stuttgart at the "Congress of Germans Living Abroad" that was critical of what he termed "old liberal ideas", a clear reference to English liberalism.[35] In a sharp response to Bohle's speech and coming visit, Winston Churchill publically expressed the view that the AO had no business in England, and should be carefully watched by the authorities There should also be no fear of any retaliation, the future prime minister said, because there are far more Germans living in England, than English in Germany.[36]

Although Churchill was out of favor with the Baldwin government at the time and considered a political exile, he was still an important public figure, and according to Bohle, "...the German Embassy in London informed the Foreign Office at that time that a question by Churchill in the House of Commons regarding the activity of the Auslands-Organisation would be extremely undesirable. As a result a meeting between Churchill and myself was advocated as urgent."[37] Anxious that there be no problems during his visit, Bohle ordered that all AO Landesgruppe activity in England be suspended until further notice.

In what must have been seen as a rather bizarre episode by some observers of the British political scene, Churchill and Gauleiter Bohle met in a private residence in London, where they discussed the situation of the German citizens living in England, and the interests of the Auslands-Organisation. Bohle said that he assured Churchill that his organization was only interested in the cultural relationship with its citizens who lived abroad, and that this explanation seemed to dispel any misgivings that the future prime minister may have had. The parting was very friendly, according to Bohle, and Churchill accompanied him to his car, where they posed for a photograph together. "There was no inquiry in the House of Commons", Bohle boasted, "and Churchill never uttered a word of objection about the activity of the Auslands-Organisation." After his return to Germany, the

AO leader received a cordial letter from Churchill, who characterized their London meeting as very satisfactory.[38]

Before the rise of National Socialism, the presence of German communities had rarely been a problem for foreign nations. They had always represented a productive and peaceful addition to the economy, and their tendency to preserve their language and customs had not been socially disruptive. Although the communities often placed a high value on their Germandom(Deutschtum), with an emphasis upon German culture, they did not promote a political agenda, and therefore, foreign governments usually adopted a policy of tolerance. All of this began to change, however, with the advent of AO activities and the spread of Nazi propaganda. The previous attitude of tolerance by many foreign governments began to be replaced by suspicion and distrust when it became apparent that Bohle's AO representatives in the German communities were attempting to organize them into support groups for Hitler's National Socialist regime. It had also become obvious in a number of the German communities that Bohle's order that only German citizens were allowed to participate in Landesgruppe activities, was being ignored.

One of the most persistent complaints from abroad about the AO was that it was a spy organization, and its people were infiltrating the German communities, and sponsoring subversive activities. Given the aggressive nature of some of the Landesgruppen leaders, and the steady drumbeat of National Socialist propaganda, this seemed to be a logical assumption. The result was an unfavorable reaction by many foreign governments toward those German colonies residing in their midst that had the most active AO branches. It was also a ready made situation for the local news media to take a few facts mixed with much rumor and conclude that the communities were spy nests. It usually found a fascinated reading public who devoured stories about German agents dispatched from either the Abwehr (German intelligence service) or the Gestapo, to carry out secret missions for the Führer.

A major difficulty for Bohle in trying to deal with the spy-espionage charges was the fact that many of the AO members had the best qualifications for such undertakings. They had lived abroad, spoke the language, knew the culture, and were dedicated National Socialists. This made them attractive candidates for Germany intelligence services. Also, Bohle was really in no position to refuse to cooperate when a request came for the loan of one of his people for some espionage or spy mission. An aide to Heinrich Himmler reported that the SS Reichsführer always read the reports that came from Bohle's office, although some of them were very extensive. He said that Himmler often added notes to the margins that read "very good observation" or "very interesting."[39]

Bohle was fully aware of the serious damage to his work that was caused by the general perception abroad that the AO was actually a front organization for Hitler's spy apparatus. He tried to contain some of it by increasing his own flow of propaganda that portrayed the AO as an organization only interested in promoting German culture, but privately he admitted that he had no control over one of his people who was selected by one of Germany's intelligence for spy work. Bohle claimed that he was always notified in advance when this was going to happen, and given time to transfer the individual in question out of the AO.[40]

During his postwar interrogations, Bohle tried to appear naive and somewhat uninformed about Germany's spy and espionage networks, but the invaluable resource his organization provided at times was obvious. He was unable to deny the fact that the AO had a liaison man, Erich Schnauss, assigned to work full time with the Abwehr and Security Service (Sicherheitsdienst, SD). Schnauss had been active in Spain, where he had headed an AO branch. He returned to Germany in 1934 to accept the liaison position.[41] However, Bohle denied that the liaison job represented any active involvement of the AO with the intelligence groups, and described the relationship as one of constant friction. This stemmed from the constant demands of the Abwehr and the SD for the compilation of voluminous amounts of information on a wide variety subjects. This meant, Bohle said, that he had to secure this data from one or the other of his Landesgruppenleiter; it was a time consuming undertaking with little reward: "...they hardly ever gave us any information. The Abwehr never did, and the SD, I don't think, ever did either. That was a big fight. We always had that fight with them. It was an absolutely one-sided affair." All requests for information that came from the Abwehr and the SD went to Schnauss, first, who then made the decision which Landesgruppenleiter to contact. The Landesgruppenleiter's report went directly to the requesting agency with a copy to Bohle's office.[42]

The reports were not coded and were transmitted via a diplomatic pouch of the Foreign Office. Bohle said that he did not always read the copies that he received, although he did meet occasionally with Himmler or Admiral Wilhelm Carnaris, head of the Abwehr, because some of the information received required clarification or discussion. At one point, he said he asked Carnaris to limit the use of borrowed AO personnel to Germany only, and the admiral agreed, but he found out later that his request had been ignored. It was ironic, Bohle added, because often the individuals picked by either the Abwehr or the SD were not the most suited for the missions undertaken, and while he could have been helpful in the selections with his far greater knowledge of the AO men in the foreign communities, he never recommended anyone.[43]

Although Bohle may have had some reservations about cooperating fully with the Abwehr or the SD, according to his own account, this was certainly not true about the Gestapo. From almost the beginning of his AO career he had proven zealous in providing the Secret State Police with detailed reports on those Germans who applied to return to Germany. This meant a thorough examination of a person's attitude toward and degree of participation in Landesgruppe activities. The Landesgruppenleiter's evaluation was a decisive factor in the approval or disapproval of an applicant, especially in his judgment of the individual's 'political reliability'. Himmler took a personal interest in the procedure, and discussed it with Bohle several times. He told the Gauleiter that those individuals with acceptable records had nothing to fear upon returning home, but there were some who would require "compulsory training."[44]

It's clear that Bohle and his organization were more involved in the spy game than he was willing to admit to his interrogators, but the reality of the situation was quite different than that portrayed in the popular press. The media hysteria that sometimes surrounded the exposure of a failed spy attempt by German agents obscured the degree of AO involvement, which may have been minimal or even non-existent. The Auslands Organisation was not the conduit for a world wide German spy network. Bohle knew that he had a mandatory obligation to cooperate with German intelligence, but his eye was focused upon developing a party organization that would have a major voice in the conduct of Germany's foreign affairs.

7   Bohle and Ribbentrop

On Sunday, August 30, 1937, the Auslands Organisation der NSDAP celebrated its fifth Reichstagung in Stuttgart, the City of the Auslandsdeutschen. It was an impressive affair as some 80,000 people, including 10,000 Auslandsdeutschen, filled the Adolf-Hitler-Kampfbahn: "At 4 o'clock, Rudolf Hess and Gauleiter Bohle appeared and delivered lively welcomes. Then, accompanied by martial music, a company of new Wehrmacht troops marched through the Marathon Gate."[1] A number of other important Nazi Party leaders were present, including Joachim von Ribbentrop, who was the German ambassador to England.

Whole both Bohle and Hess spoke in the usual platitudes, praising the virtues of the Germans who resided abroad, von Neurath offered a bit of insight into the tensions that marked the relationship between the AO and the Foreign Office. With a comment that was both defensive and conciliatory, he said that Hitler's order placing Bohle into the Foreign Office as the head of the Auslandsorganizsation der NSDAP, and his elevation to State Secretary, were not only a positive examples of the unity of party and state, but clarified the relationship of both his office and the AO to the Germans living abroad. In this way, he continued, both he and Bohle knew their exact positions, and it was his hope that this meant the difficulties that marked the past between the two offices would now disappear for good.[2]

Perhaps, while von Neurath's comment might be interpreted as a firm statement of his position toward the activities of the AO, it was also a reluctant confirmation of Bohle's importance. The AO leader could now boast of Landesgruppen in dozens of countries and a combined party enrollment of over 25,600 persons. This did not include the people in AO Amt VI (United States and Canada), since it had been officially dissolved, nor the approximately 24,000 German seamen. The total number of German citizens living abroad in the summer of 1937 totaled about 515,680 people.[3]

In late 1937, Bohle contacted Goebbel's Propaganda Ministry, requesting that proper distribution be given a statement agreed upon with the Foreign Office on the terminology to be used when referring to the Germans who resided abroad. The Gauleiter explained that during the last few years there had arisen considerable confusion about the right terminology to use in referring to the status of Germans living abroad, and that this had caused some problems. It is time, he wrote, to bring some clarity to the situation, and therefore it was proposed that more exact definitions be employed when referring to an individual's status. First, Germans citizens (Reichsdeutschen) abroad are to be referred to as Auslandsdeutschen; second, the Germans abroad who possess foreign citizenship, and this included the German minorities in other countries in Europe, are Volksdeutschen; and, finally, when referring to Auslandsdeutschtum and Volksdeutschtum the correct designation is "Das Deutschtum im Ausland."[4]

Just how much clarity was provided for an already confusing situation is difficult to measure since many of the groups and organizations associated with the Auslandsdeutschtum scene were not eager to abandon the terminology that predated the Hitler government. There was also some resentment toward the AO for not engaging them in some consultation before simply announcing a change. Of course, Bohle knew that if he tried to consult with every group that was concerned in some way with the German communities abroad, it would be an unending process. In 1936 there were some seventy-four official and unofficial groups that were involved, some of which were important to Bohle's work, and others that were, at times, a serious nuisance. One such was the Association for Germandom Abroad (Verein für das Deutschtum im Ausland, or VDA), led by Hans Steinacher. It had voluminous records and valuable contacts that interested the AO, but Bohle found that there was competition from some other party officials, most notably, Heinrich Himmler, who commanded a Racial Assistance Office (Volksdeutsche Mittelstelle, VoMI), that also found the resources of the VDA interesting. The idea behind it was that all Germans had a racial or biological connection, and therefore, concern should be shown for all of them. VoMi was under the direction of an SS general (Oberruppenführer) named Werner Lorenz, who took it over in 1937, and continued until war's end in 1945. It had a tenuous connection with the Foreign Office, and was supposed to coordinate its efforts, but rarely did, which remained one of the sore points between Ribbentrop and Himmler.[5]

Although Bohle found Himmler a competitor, he also knew that the SS leader represented a powerful vote for retiring Steinacher, and thus, it was not exactly unwelcome news for him when it was announced in October 1937 that the VDA director had gone on indefinite leave. Steinacher later claimed that only the support of important personages like Admiral Erich Raeder and Dr. Karl Haushofer had allowed him to remain in office so long. He said that Rudolf Hess threatened to imprison him if he tried to win public support to retain his position.[6] With Steinacher's removal, Hess intended to place the VDA under his own control, but Himmler prevailed, and Lorenz was put in charge. Bohle said: "They [VDA] had nothing to say. They were absorbed absolutely. There is no doubt about that at all." Obviously Bohle had to cooperate with Lorenz, but he did not like him, and described him as a "colorless person" who insisted on addressing the

AO leader in the familiar "du," which Bohle said he did not do even "... with my best friends."[7]

Bohle's most serious challenge, however, came from Joachim von Ribbentrop and his so-called Bureau or Dienststelle Ribbentrop. The office had been created by Hitler in the spring of 1933, and was located opposite the Foreign Office in the Wilhelmstrasse. While it did not duplicate the Foreign Office, the intent was to advise Hitler on foreign affairs, and by the time von Ribbentrop was appointed Germany's ambassador to England in 1936, the office numbered some three hundred employees.[8]

In the beginning, the relationship between Bohle and von Ribbentrop was certainly not one of mutual hostility, as it later became. While competitors in certain areas, they had some things in common. Both of them viewed von Neurath with a certain disregard, and did not take his management of the Foreign Office seriously, and both were convinced they could do a far better job, if given the opportunity. They also strongly embraced the idea that German life should reflect the principles of National Socialism, and that definitely included the Foreign Office. This meant that Bohle could not easily undermine von Ribbentrop's position by implying, as he did with some of his opponents, that perhaps his loyalty to the party was questionable. The atmosphere still appeared to be cordial in 1937, when Gauleiter Bohle made his visit to England, and met with Winston Churchill. Von Ribbentrop invited him to an embassy dinner, and Bohle said later, that at his suggestion, the ambassador was kind enough to include his uncle and aunt, who were living there at the time.[9]

Von Ribbentrop was not an old party member, having only joined in May 1932, but he had succeeded early in impressing Hitler, who named him in April 1934 as a special minister to advise on disarmament questions. One seasoned German diplomat said that the Foreign Office did not regard the Ribbentrop Diesntstelle as a challenge, but rather something that was meant to satisfy von Ribbentrop's ambitions.[10] Another said: "The competitive business of the Dienststelle Ribbentrop was for us in the Foreign Office , for professional reasons, highly unwelcome. Ribbentrop was arrogant, ignorant, with no mind of his own, and completely subservient to Hitler."[11]

The relationship between Bohle and von Ribbentrop dramatically altered when the ambassador was named Germany's foreign minister in February 1938. The Foreign Office liaison officer, Vicco von Bülow-Schwante, recalled: "The picture changed totally when Foreign Minister von Ribbentrop took over the Foreign Office and introduced his new way of doing things, but there was much tension between Herr Bohle, who did not disguise his critical feelings, and Ribbentrop."[12] There was no doubt that the AO leader regarded von Ribbentrop's appointment as a serious mistake by Hitler, a view he continued to hold the rest of his life. [13]

Bohle said that soon after von Ribbentrop took over, he summoned the young Gauleiter to his office, and it was soon evident that the new foreign minister wanted to make it clear who was in charge of Germany's foreign policy. "He told me that himself," Bohle recounted, "showing me at the same time, several foreign newspapers in which I was mentioned as a promising young man who might one day be German Foreign Minister. At any rate, he certainly very strongly disliked me and kept me away from everything in the Foreign Office unless in someway connected with the affairs of Germans abroad."[14]

Von Ribbentrop very much enjoyed the power that went with his new position, and used it to feed an enormous ego, according to Bohle. For example, Bohle said, von Ribbentrop always wanted everyone from his Berlin staff, including spouses, to meet him in formal dress whenever he returned from a conference: "That is his whole way, driving around Berlin in a big car with at least six or seven SS men in it, to safeguard him. Nobody dreamt of attacking him. Everybody laughed...when he went to Munich or anywhere in Germany, when he came back all the top shots had to wait and greet him, sometimes we had to wait three hours, and he would get out of the plane and in two minutes it was all over."[15]

Despite their mutual dislike, Bohle continued to maintain a small staff in the Foreign Office, but instead of going in for a couple of hours daily, as he had done before, he only went in for the 10 am daily briefings that were held, and which von Ribbentrop never attended. As he later explained: "I could not get on with Ribbentrop. We were at loggerheads right from the beginning. He had a haughty and often insolent manner of treating subordinates. I refused to put up with that and spoke back. He always made everything as difficult and as unpleasant as possible for me."[16]

Obviously, the situation was bound to lead to serious disagreements, and Bohle admitted that they had a number of very heated arguments. He claimed that the foreign minister engaged in all kinds of petty maneuvers aimed at curtailing his authority, and absorbing the functions of the AO. It started when von Ribbentrop directed Bohle to send him any reports that came through the Foreign Office, even though they were addressed to the Auslandsorganisation. Bohle refused on the grounds that his primary rank as a Gauleiter was a party position, and Hitler had decreed that no state position took precedence over it, and he knew that von Ribbentrop would not disobey a Führer order. Of course, he knew that Hitler would do what suited his convenience, but he also knew that von Ribbentrop was afraid to challenge the ruling. As Bohle explained it: "It was a matter of personal courage. He [Hitler] was this way. If he was very passionate about something and somebody was against the idea, he might lose his job, but if you are a politician, you must risk that, if you want to stick to your convictions." He insisted that, unlike von Ribbentrop, he was prepared to go to Hitler personally, if an issue warranted it.[17]

While Bohle may have felt confident that the foreign minister would not take their arguments to Hitler, that did not translate into a victory for the AO leader, because Ribbentrop found other ways to reduce his influence.

One of the most effective was to exclude Bohle from the flow of information from the Foreign Office. This was done by simply excluding his name from the distribution list of daily communiqués, and when he protested, he was reminded that the AO was not in the diplomatic business. It reached the point that there was literally no direct communication between the two men, and when it was necessary for Bohle to go to the Foreign Office to conduct discussions on something, he always dealt with other personnel. His major contacts were State Secretary Ernst von Weizsäcker, Protocol Chief Baron Gustav Steengracht von Moyland, and Personnel Chief Hans Schröder.[18]

Weizsäcker usually presided over the Foreign Office sessions that Bohle attended, but he also met with von Moyland when there were specifics that pertained to the AO, and he became the principal liaison person. Bohle said that he got along with von Moyland all right, but he had been deliberately picked by Ribbentrop because he was completely loyal and did no thinking for himself.[19] Von Moyland described the relationship between Bohle and Ribbentrop as being "...on exceedingly bad terms, and conflicts were frequent," but personally he found Bohle "...a rather agreeable fellow and an honest fanatic who was definitely pro-Western in orientation."[20]

Shortly before von Ribbentrop's appointment as foreign minister, Bohle had received party approval to establish an AO unit (Ortsgruppe) for all National Socialist members in the Foreign Office, and this was announced in December of 1937. The following month, all the affected members, who were formerly enrolled in the Gau Berlin, were now informed that they were transferred to the Auslandsorganisation. According to Bohle's decree, the new order included not only the party members in the Foreign Office in Berlin, but also those who were employed outside of Germany's borders. The intent, he wrote, was to bring all members under a central administration, and to provide support in assisting them to spread National Socialism.[21]

Although this happened only days before von Ribbentrop's appointment was announced, Bohle must have regarded it an assurance of the solidarity of his position within the Foreign Office. His language left little room for ambiguity about what he regarded as his new authority: "I expect you to fulfill your duties as Party members in an exemplary manner. As long as Party members of the Ortsgruppe Foreign Office ...are active in a group abroad, they are members of and responsible to this group and under the direction and discipline of the current group leader."[22] To be able to extend his authority over members of the Foreign Office in such a fashion must have given the Gauleiter a great deal of satisfaction, but it would be short- lived.

Von Ribbentrop was not about to accept such a bold move into his newly acquired territory by the young upstart from the AO. Unlike Neurath, he thought of himself as a party man, and stood ready to defend his domain against all comers. If this meant a contest with Bohle over what was the proper party protocol involving the membership of his Foreign Office personnel, than so be it. Von Ribbentrop voiced his strong objections to Hitler, who supported his new foreign minister with a short but decisive order: "To clarify the supreme Party rights for the personnel of the Foreign Office, I declare: The Ortsguppe Foreign Office of the Auslandsorganisation der NSDAP to be dissolved."[23] Von Ribbentrop and the State Secretaries were transferred to the Reichsleitung of the party, and the leading personnel who were serving abroad were placed into the Ortsgruppe Braun Haus.

Whether Bohle was surprised by von Ribbentrop's quick reaction is difficult to surmise, but he certainly knew that he was in for a fight. His opponent was skilled in all the tricks of party infighting, and had shown that he was not going to let any real or imagined encroachment by Bohle slip by. While von Ribbentrop appeared receptive to suggestions from other party leaders about potential appointees to positions in the Foreign Office, he made it clear that Bohle was not included in the group. In an attempt to circumvent the isolation that von Ribbentrop was trying to impose upon him, Bohle began forwarding his more important reports to Himmler, because he knew that the foreign minister never sent anything from the AO to Hitler's attention.[24]

Himmler, who found von Ribbentrop opposed to the stationing of Gestapo agents in certain embassies abroad, shared Bohle's feelings about the foreign minister, but he was not the only important party figure who sympathized with Bohle's dislike for von Ribbentrop; Bohle had allies in Hermann Goering and Martin Bormann, as well. Perhaps his strongest ally, aside from Hess, was Josef Goebbels, who made no secret of his contempt for von Ribbentrop. After a meeting with the foreign minister, Goebbels confided to his diary: "He is insignificant and repulsive. A loathsome fellow that no one wants as a friend He has also struck out by Himmler."[25]

Bohle said that when he had something significant to report that required an explanation, he contacted Himmler personally on his own initiative: "The object of these visits," he said, " was to utilize Himmler as a medium to get reports from leading German citizens abroad which were directed against Ribbentrop's foreign policy to Hitler." The AO leader denied that this represented any intrusion into the making of German foreign policy, and insisted that his organization was in a unique position to gather information from abroad in a way not available to the traditional avenues pursued by the Foreign Office.[26]

Obviously, Bohle had to deal differently with von Ribbentrop than he had with Neurath, but he still had some support from people within the Foreign Office, especially the party members who viewed the AO as a friendly extension of the party. Bohle already had been involved in several cooperative ventures with the Foreign Office before von Ribbentrop's arrival, and it had worked smoothly. An important part of the cooperation had involved the transmission of funds abroad through the auspices of the various consuls. It was a large operation, amounting to hundreds of thousands of marks, that went to Landesgruppen to pay for different services. Another program of importance was cooperating in returning Germans home. Bohle had taken the initiative in the process, and the AO provided the background checks for all of the individuals who applied.[27]

Nineteen-thirty-eight was a big year for repatriating Germans home, as the labor shortage intensified. Goering's plan to create a labor pool to support the second Four Year Plan, and hire skilled applicants by offering a guaranteed wage, housing and some travel expenses. The program was widely publicized by both the Auslandsorganisation and the Foreign Office. The screening process conducted by the AO was an expensive undertaking, as the goal was to return some ten thousand skilled craftsmen plus dependents, estimated at thirty thousand additional persons. This was to take place over a period of five months at a cost of about eight and one-half million marks.[28]

The AO repatriation office (Rückwandereramt), described by Bohle as one of his most important, processed all of the German citizens who were accepted for return and provided them with proper identification (Rückerwandererausweis). The office became the major contact for the returning Germans, providing them with necessary funds, clothing, and assistance in finding housing. Elderly dependents were admitted to homes for the aged administered by the National Socialist welfare office (Wohlfahrtsamt). Bohle's director for the repatriation office was an old party member named Hans Hellermann, who had had experience evacuating Germans from Spain during that country's civil war. He worked out of the AO main office in Berlin, but had branch offices at receiving points in Hamburg, Munich and Stuttgart. Temporary shelter for new arrivals was also established in Berlin-Tegel. Bohle dubbed the office the "kindly aunt" for homecoming Germans.[29]

He may well have added that all of this activity quickly overtaxed his financial resources, and new funds were urgently needed. In his request to the Party Treasurer (Reichsschatzmeister) Franz Xaver Schwarz, Bohle carefully pointed out that the Führer had personally promised that the Germans living abroad would never be neglected as they had been in the past. He also noted that their needs were unique, and that they had received no government financial aid before Hitler came to power. The Gauleiter could not resist a reference to the poor record of the Foreign Office regarding the plight of Germans who found themselves in financial distress while living abroad.[30]

Bohle requested that the sum of 750,000 Reichsmarks be transferred into the AO account, but that the entire transaction be kept confidential because some of the expenditures might arouse unnecessary concern from other quarters. The request for confidentiality was granted, but the sum was reduced to 200,000 Reichsmarks, although it was noted that more would be forthcoming the next year.[31] A major irritation for Bohle had always been the fact that he did not have total control over the funding for the Auslandsorganisation. Although the AO had its own treasury (AO Schatzamt), the funds were managed by a party member named Theodor Leonhardt, who answered more to Schwarz than to Bohle. It was a frustrating arrangement for the AO leader because he felt that neither Leonhardt nor Schwarz had the professional background to understand the importance of the projects he proposed for funding. Schwarz was an old time party member, however, having joined in 1922, and he had been the watchdog over the money for many years. He was not particularly impressed by the young Gauleiter's arguments, and occupied an unassailable position within the party hierarchy. Bohle was not unaware of this and knew better than to challenge him on anything unless he had the full support of Rudolf Hess.[32] The largest items in Bohle's budget were the salaries and expense accounts of his Landesgruppenleitern in over twenty countries. A 1938 budget showed the monthly costs submitted by the AO group leaders abroad ranging from a low of 250 marks to a high of 15,600 marks. This amounted to about half of the allotted funds that Bohle received to maintain his network abroad, however, he did succeed in concealing an exact accounting from curious party leaders, and especially von Ribbentrop.[33]

Although the tensions between Bohle and von Ribbentrop continued to mount, the Gauleiter still held a distinctly unique position within the larger framework of German foreign policy. Unlike the Foreign Office, which continued to conduct its business in much the traditional manner of international diplomacy, the Auslandsorganisation was strictly the creature of a political party, and actually directed branches of the National Socialist movement beyond Germany's borders. This was, of course, a result of the curious blending of party and state, but without a clear concept of just how some institutions could be absorbed to fully reflect the National Socialist spirit and still fill the functions necessary for the conduct of state affairs. Bohle obviously felt confident that just as long as the party reigned supreme, the AO was on solid ground, and so was his future.

The young Gauleiter was already a skilled veteran in understanding how National Socialist doctrine applied to his organization, and moved accordingly. He had learned early in his career that his success depended not only on running an efficient bureau, but to offer the proper support to major policies of the NSDAP, even though some of them had little application to the problems of German living abroad. When the possibility arose that Bohle could extend his authority into a policy area traditionally a diplomatic one, he could not resist the opportunity. One such policy was the racial discrimination that existed in Germany, and after the 1935 Nuremberg Laws on Citizenship and Race, when Neutrath discouraged any marriage of his diplomats to individuals with foreign backgrounds, Bohle quickly followed suit, and forbade his political leaders to marry foreigners.[34]

As the pressure grew to isolate Jews from German life, the AO faced the problem that many of the key representatives of German firms abroad were Jews who worked closely with the Landesgruppen. At the same time, however, the Nazis were determined to eliminate Jewish influence in German foreign trade, and in early 1937, Bohle drafted a confidential memorandum to all of his employees that outlined a policy: He directed that in the current situation those Jewish representatives who were long time employees of German firms should remain, but no hiring of new ones. However, if there was any evidence that any of the present Jewish employees were unfriendly toward the Third Reich, they were to be dismissed. New business with any Jewish company was permissible only if it offered substantial advantage to Germany. Finally, all future employees were to be German citizens, people of German descent, or non-Jews of other nationalities who were friendly to Germany.[35] When reflecting upon such policies after the war, Bohle acknowledged they were serious mistakes, but the record was clear that his organization had played an active role in encouraging Jews to emigrate from Germany, and before the concentration camps became their fate, he personally had signed documents that agreed to pay Jewish families to depart.[36]

Germany's Jews were encouraged to leave the country for any place that would accept them, but a special effort was made to direct them to Palestine. Bohle denied that he played any significant role in negotiating a trade agreement with Palestine in order to facilitate Jewish emigration there. He admitted, however, that he had discussed the question with the German consul general there in 1937. By Bohle's account, he was informed by the consul that an informal arrangement had been arrived at with Palestine, which involved promoting German trade there. The arrangement, called the *Haavara* (Transfer) Agreement, allowed a company of the same name to have a monopoly on goods shipped from Germany to Palestine in exchange for permitting Jews to emigrate there. The German consul reported, however, that the Arabs resented the fact that they were excluded from any of the trade handled by the *Haarvara* Company, and the trade was only enriching Palestine.[37] But a German government report on the problem noted that most of the Jews who expressed the desire to emigrate, wanted to go to Palestine. It stated that already many of them had extensive investments there, much of which had been made starting in 1932, and it was estimated that approximately 410,000 German Jews already resided in Palestine.[38]

By the terms of the *Haavara* Agreement, the Jews who decided to emigrate were allowed to recover some of their assets by buying German goods destined for Palestine and draw from their frozen accounts in Germany. The Foreign Office and the Economic Ministry supported the idea at first, but when it became evident that Jews were receiving credit against their assets while Germany received no foreign exchange, opinions changed. Although German exports to Palestine had increased substantially, without hard currency in return there was no advantage. Bohle also now became a negative voice, urging that the *Haavara* Agreement be ignored because it was creating a hardship upon the some 2,500 German citizens who lived in the Templerkolonien there since trade fell exclusively into Jewish hands.[39] Strong support for Bohle's argument came from Foreign Minister Neurath, who said that the whole affair was increasing the possibility that Palestine could become an independent state and mount a world wide protest against

Germany's racial policies. It was important, he stated, that other countries understand that an independent Jewish state was definitely against Germany's interests.[40]

To insure that there would be an official termination of the *Haavara* Agreement, Bohle informed Hermann Goering that it was not only causing harm to the German consumer, but was detrimental to the economics of the Four Year Plan that he was directing. The Generalfeldmarschall agreed, and the so-called informal arrangement was cancelled in early 1938. It is significant to note that all of these maneuvers by the AO leader might well be regarded as actions that should have rightly fallen into the province of Germany's foreign minister. However, it also illustrates the drive toward influence in diplomatic decisions that Bohle was achieving , and the fact that a number of German citizens resided in the Palestine area had given him the opportunity to intercede. A very important factor in Bohle's little success was Neurath's inability to command policy from the Foreign Office. Nineteen-thirty-seven was a good year for Ernst Wilhelm Bohle.

While the Gauleiter was not a rabid anti-Semite, he was generally unconcerned about the prejudice and cruelty directed toward the Jews, and reluctant to know any of the details concerning their fate. "Naturally, the National Socialist Party was anti-Semitic", he admitted, "but from all of the utterances that I heard before 1933, when I joined the Party, it was the object only to deprive them of German citizenship, and place them on the same level as foreigners....To be quite frank, I did not give that very much thought at all at the time."[41] He maintained throughout all of his postwar interrogations that in his position as head of the Auslandsorganisation his only concern regarding Jews was to exclude them from influence in Germany's economic affairs, and to insure that none of those who lived abroad held German citizenship.

This is obviously not the whole story, however, for just as other Nazis in important positions, the Gauleiter had some discretionary authority to enforce anti-Jewish measures strictly and harshly, or depending upon the circumstances, ignore the letter of the law and show leniency. He said that when the excesses against Germany's Jews began, he had some misgivings about it, but that all revolutions engaged in such things when taking power.[42] Bohle ignored the obvious fact that the worst excesses against the Jews came well after Hitler's regime assumed control of government, and not in the beginning, as he implied.

The difficulty in attempting to make a truthful assessment of Bohle's attitude toward Germany's Jews is that any favorable testimony in this regard was by former colleagues after the war. With this in mind, the more charitable statements of support must be weighed accordingly. One such statement that did substantiate Bohle's defense, however, came from a diplomat named Graf von Dürkheim, who served in England during the thirties, and was apparently threatened with dismissal because of his racial background. "My impression of Bohle's attitude was strengthened by my personal experience", he said. " I was considered a non-Aryan according to the Nuremberg Laws...I shall never forget how at that time Bohle not only expressed his regrets, but even told me clearly that he wanted to disassociate himself from the narrowness of the Aryan paragraph. He sent word to my mother that she could rely absolutely on his personal protection if she was in any danger."[43] The former Foreign Office personnel chief, Emile Yung, also offered a positive testimony for Bohle. He claimed that he had never heard Bohle utter an anti-Semitic remark, and that he often defended persons in the diplomatic service who faced dismissal because of accusations that they were not racially acceptable.[44]

When questioned about having any knowledge of Germany's concentration camp system in the years before the war, Bohle said that he had seen occasional references to camps in material that passed through his office, and, of course, rumors that circulated among people. He insisted, however, that it was not his habit to do much socializing with other senior Nazi officials, and therefore did not exchange much gossip about such things. He agreed though, that he could not avoid what was expected of him when his office had to supply data relating to a situation that aroused the attention of Nazi leadership. Such an episode was the murder of Ernst vom Rath, a young German diplomat, who was killed in Paris in November 1938.

Rath had been attached to the German embassy in the French capitol, and became the unintended victim of a planned assassination by a young Polish Jew named Herschel Grynszpan, who really meant to shot the German ambassador. Grynszpan had lived in Germany before moving to Paris in 1936, and still had family there. It was apparently the forced move of his family to Poland from Germany that ignited his determination for revenge. On November 7, he went to the German embassy, and was admitted to Rath's office, where he shot the youthful third secretary. Mortally wounded, Rath was rushed to the hospital, and the German ambassador was immediately notified. And so was Bohle, who telegraphed Rath a get well message, and expressed his outrage over the cowardly attack. Rath died, however, and Bohle was instructed by order of the Führer to represent the party at the funeral in Düsseldorf.[45]

The assassination of Rath triggered an outburst of public fury against the Jews in Germany, and there were brutal personal attacks against them and their property during the week of November 9. Bohle's office was flooded with telegrams from Germans abroad, who were concerned that the pogrom would bring retaliatory measures against them. Some of the messages indicated that business was already being affected. According to the head of Bohle's legal office (AO Rechtsamt), Dr. Lubbe, the AO leader had informed his staff that he was definitely opposed to such extremes as the pogrom. He said that it was bad publicity, and had economic consequences too, because all of the damage inflicted upon the Jews had to be paid for. Goering was in full support, he stated, and told him that he would order punishment for those responsible if such a thing occurred again.[46]

When interrogated about the matter after the war, Bohle denied any extensive involvement: "The only explanation I can give about knowing anything about the whole affair is that the murdered man was a German abroad and a Party member and that he was murdered in a foreign country," Bohle said: "So that somebody in the ministry of Propaganda who was evidently planning a trial, thought of me as a witness."[47]

Of course, any account regarding Bohle's actions before the war based upon documentation of that period, obviously provide a far more accurate version of events than postwar testimony by participants on trial as war criminals. Bohle was, after all, a high official in the Nazi regime, and could not have been as ignorant as he later indicated of the plight of the German Jewish population. It was possible, that he attempted to avoid what he found as distasteful, and maintained the illusion that he was really unaware of what was happening.

Bohle exhibited a somewhat similar attitude toward the Nazi persecution of Germany's churches, but while he was not hostile toward organized religion, his record indicates an indifference. He did deny that he was an atheist, however, and gave the following explanation: "My mother is a devout Catholic, my father was just as ardent a Protestant. In spite of their otherwise exceptionally happy wedlock, religion was the one question on which they could not agree. They could, therefore, not agree whether their five children were to be Catholics or Protestants. The result was that three of the children were baptized Catholic and two of them Protestant, including myself. None of us, however, ever received any religious education outside of our home at all. We never attended Sunday school or church, we knew practically next to nothing in all our youth about Christianity." He said that he felt no attachment to any kind of church, although he did believe in God.[48]

The Gauleiter knew that the party did not encourage church membership or religious affiliation, but he said that he never questioned any of his employees about their religious beliefs, and it was not a subject in his communications to the Germans living abroad: "Our Germans abroad were for the most part deeply religious, and I was fully aware that our German churches in foreign countries had for years been the center of German life, of the German language, and of German customs. My functionaries or collaborators in Berlin could leave the church or remain in the church, just as they pleased. The whole question just wasn't any issue with me at all."[49]

He said that he had instructed all of his AO subordinates abroad not to engage in religious discussions at party meetings, but admitted that from time to time a German clergyman ignored his order. Bohle indicated, however, that most of the time, his instructions were obeyed because it was within his power to approve or disapprove the state subsidies the Reich Catholic and Protestant churches abroad received. He had the authority over the German schools abroad that received funds from the Reich, as well.[50]

In evaluating Bohle's performance in this period before the beginning of the war, he can be seen as a man who did not exhibit extreme tendencies in either race or religion, and generally avoided those problems that could reflect negatively on his climb toward a share in conducting Germany's foreign affairs. Without question, he placed great faith in the future success of National Socialism, and nothing in his written record up to this point in his career indicates doubts about having committed himself to following Hitler. But 1938 represented a turning point in his career. He now had to confront a German foreign minister who was just as ambitious as he was, and who regarded the AO leader as a potential challenger to be relegated as soon as possible to the level of a minor functionary tending the non-policy needs of Germans abroad. This would not be so easy to accomplish, however, for Bohle still headed an impressive National Socialist organization that had wide support among many party leaders. As long as there was no war to interrupt communications, the Auslandsorganisation, with innumerable contacts abroad, also served as a listening post that could provide information as no other agency or source could.

8 A Worldwide Network

It is unlikely that even the new challenge that he faced from Ribbentrop dampened the pride that Ernst Wilhelm Bohle must have felt when, on his birthday in 1938, he opened a personal message from the Führer, which read: "It gives me great pleasure to extend my heartfelt good wishes to you on your birthday on the 28th of July."[1] At thirty-five years of age, Bohle had every reason to believe that his meteoric rise in the new Germany was due to the impressive strides he had made in establishing the Auslandsorganisation der NSDAP as an important influence in the German communities around the world.

The young Gauleiter could no more predict Hitler's actions in Germany's foreign policy than could any other party member, however, he had no reason to doubt that the future would be as successful as the past five years had been. Despite his relatively recent commitment to National Socialism, he had quickly learned to evaluate the party's political nuances. Bohle knew that ability alone did not guarantee his position; for that, one needed powerful friends. In his case, that meant first and foremost, Rudolf Hess. So long as he had the support of Hitler's old and trusted friend, he felt that his position was secure. However, Ribbentrop represented a new challenge. Unlike Neurath, the new foreign minister displayed such an enthusiasm for National Socialism that it made it difficult for Bohle to fault him on grounds that he was not acting in a manner compatible with the party's philosophy.

In addition to the support he received from Hess, and several other important party leaders, Bohle felt that his greatest strength in competing with Ribbentrop lay in the fact that his Auslandsorganisation could be far more aggressive in promoting National Socialism among the German communities abroad than the Foreign Office could. Essentially, von Ribbentrop's actions in this regard were limited by what was acceptable in the world of diplomacy. Through his Landesgruppen, and support from sympathetic German residents abroad, Bohle had virtually an army that he could direct in furthering the aims of the AO among the communities. This fostered a degree of interaction with the Germans abroad that was not possible for the Foreign Office. It was an activity that older party members, still reluctant to forget their prejudices against some of the Foreign Office personnel that predated Hitler, strongly approved.

Although Bohle had these elements of strong support at home, he knew that his organization rested upon a structure that largely functioned outside of Germany's borders, and therefore was subject to forces that were often beyond his control, but he had been successful in bringing some unity to an amorphous mass that heretofore had been loosely tied by language and a relatively strong feeling of a common homeland. The AO reinforced these attributes, and brought a political meaning that had been lacking for a true cohesiveness to exist. Important to note is the fact that it was not welcomed by all of the Germans abroad, and was actively resisted by some who saw National Socialism and the Hitler movement as an oppressive dictatorship.

A vital area of Bohle's operation was his relationship with the men who led his Landesgruppen. Earlier on, he recognized that these were men with widely varying backgrounds and ambitions that were not always bound by his own visions. He knew that he had to deal with each one on an individual basis, and could set no hard and fast rules that would apply to all. This was especially true as it related to the assignments that each Landesgruppenleiter was entrusted to carry out. Bohle's approach was to allow a maximum of freedom of action, and only intervened if a particular Landesgruppenleiter began to attract too much negative attention from the government of the host country.

Obviously, not all of the Landesgruppen had the same importance in German foreign policy. Prior to 1939, the deciding factor was geopolitical. The relevant question was how a particular area related to Hitler's current plans for expansion. In the beginning, in pursuing his political aims, Hitler directed his energies toward the so-called border Germans in Holland, Belgium, Czechoslovakia, and Poland, whose recent past was tied to the Versailles Peace settlements. The border German question presented some complications for Bohle that did not exist with the communities outside of Europe, however. He was eager to be involved with their fate because it offered the greater opportunity to actually exercise some policy decisions in foreign affairs, but his AO was never able to play a really significant roll in what transpired for several reasons.

The primary one was historical. The problems surrounding the border German question had emerged as a result of the peace settlements following the First World War, and had long established themselves before Hitler's assumption of power in 1933. The nucleus of political groups with their own leaders existed before the emergence of the Third Reich, but they had a commonality with National Socialism and its appeal for a return to Germany. With the exception of the Germans in Holland, who welcomed Bohle's attention, most of the border German areas already had organization and leadership, and for them the Auslandsorganisation was largely superfluous. They wanted Hitler to reclaim them through annexation

During his years at the helm of the AO, Bohle had familiarized himself with most of the community histories, and knew that with some he could exert a direct influence, while with others, he had to step carefully. Aware of these complexities, Bohle did not adopt any single standard that had to be applied to each community. There was some common ground in language and fatherland, but just how a community related to the AO was an individual matter. Bohle recognized that important local German leaders who had attained some status in a community had to be respected, even if they were not party members, and in some instances, were not citizens of Germany. Bohle was also conscious of the fact that there were party member with extensive experience abroad who would gladly take over his position if they could.

Unlike von Ribbentrop, who enjoyed a personal relationship with Hitler, and had already been entrusted with certain foreign policy assignments, Bohle had had virtually no direct contact with the Führer. His youth precluded any significant party history before 1933, and this weighed heavily against him when Hitler made his selections of individuals for important positions. By all logic, as Nazi Party offices absorbed the functions of the state, an office with the title of Auslandsorganisation der NSDAP should have begun to play an increasingly important role in the conduct of Nazi foreign policy. However, logic never dictated Hitler's behavior, and there was never any clarification specifying the exact limitations of function and authority of either the Foreign Office or the Auslandsorganisation in regard to certain points of contention on policy. Bohle knew that he was on firm ground if he pursued the goal of joining language and fatherland with National Socialism in the German communities abroad, and he geared his actions accordingly. To be effective, he had to establish priorities on the basis of what constituted Hitler's policy at the time. This required a good deal of flexibility, and some ability to try and determine Hitler's intentions, even though Bohle was not always privy to formal briefings at the Foreign Office.

Unlike some of his colleagues, Bohle was a good administrator, and the AO was an efficient operation. He had reorganized the Berlin headquarters in 1934 into a number of administrative units reflecting the areas of the world where the AO was active. These consisted of eight land offices (Landerämter): I-Northern Europe, II-Western Europe, III-Southeastern Europe, IV-Southern Europe, V-Africa, VI-North America, VII-Latin America, and, VIII-Far East. In 1937 the office for returning Germans (Rückwandereramt) was added, as well as offices consisting of a speakers' bureau and community school concerns. At times, depending upon the shifting world situation, specific countries were excluded, or moved from one office to another.[2]

One of Bohle's significant accomplishments was to direct an exhaustive research project that provided a massive body of information on the German citizens and Nazi Party members who lived outside of Germany as of

1937. It was broken down country by country, with the focus upon those Germans who held party membership, both before and after Hitler became chancellor. The total figure came to 29,099 persons. As might be expected, before 1933, the number of party members was relatively small, with the big increase coming after that date (membership was permitted for German citizens living beyond Germany's borders, but was not immediately available for those within Germany). [3]

The statistics for 1937, presented interesting contrasts. Some of the countries with a large number of German citizens did not always have the largest number of party members. For example, Holland had 75,000 German citizens, but only 1,925 party members; Czechoslovakia had 32,000 German citizens and only 1,006 party members; Austria had 44,000 German citizens and only 1,678 party members; and, Switzerland had 120,000 German citizens and only 1,364 party members. In certain instances, some of the disparity was due to the large number of German girls working as domestics abroad, and who were in temporary residence only, but this did not account for all of it. In countries like Argentina and Brazil, where this factor did not apply, the ratio between German citizens and party members was equally low. In addition to classifying the people into seventeen occupations and professions, the lengthy project report listed the ages. The majority of the party members outside of Germany, but who lived in Europe were under fifty years of age, while those who lived abroad were mostly over fifty years of age.[4]

While the project data provided a detailed profile of the German citizens and party members who lived abroad, there is no indication that it resulted in any policy changes by the AO, or that the information received wide distribution among party leaders at home. For Bohle and his co-workers the report must have raised a number of interesting questions, however. Why were the party members in the most distant areas from Germany so much older than those in Germany? Why was party membership relatively weak in certain areas where many German citizens resided? Did the data have any discernable relationship to the number of German citizens who indicated a desire to return to the Reich? Was there a method to measure how effective AO propaganda was among the German citizens abroad?

Nineteen-thirty-seven was a very good year for Nazi Germany, and on the basis of the survey, Bohle may well have considered developing more aggressive outreach programs. After all, depending upon what element of the world's population was consulted, public opinion of the new Germany and its leader Adolf Hitler was a relatively positive one. He had succeeded in bringing Germany out of an economic morass during the first years of his regime, and had raised its prestige and influence to a dominant place in European affairs. No doubt, Bohle was elated to be part of this, and more determined than ever to do his part in promoting National Socialism.

A major responsibility for Bohle was to decide where and when to allocate his resources. He had to determine just which of the AO's activities should be increased and exactly where. The expenditures for propaganda were extensive, but the Landesgruppen could not be neglected either. Some of them required more money than others, but at times the situation changed quickly and he had to be ready to shift funds from one to another. The Landesgruppen in Europe needed not only more funding, but more attention, however, to maintain the image of a worldwide organization, it meant that the flow of propaganda and services had to be kept at a certain level in areas that had little relevance to current political problems in Germany, such as China, India, and South Africa, and maintaining that image was vital to Bohle's plans. In addition, the growing number of Germans, citizens and non-citizens, who were clamoring to return to Germany, was requiring more time and money than Bohle had anticipated. To deal with the influx of people, it was necessary to open eight receiving centers throughout Germany and Austria (annexed in 1938).

The economic success of the Third Reich, plus the gathering of war clouds, decided many Germans living abroad that it was time to return home. In the beginning, returning Germans had not been a significant activity for the AO, but by 1938 the world situation had changed dramatically, and Bohle found that his Auslandsorganisation had become the primary agency in the operation. Actually, the assistance that the AO extended was a diverse undertaking because it had to distinguish between Germans returning from overseas, and Germans who were being added to the Third Reich, either through international negotiations(annexation), or military conquest. The largest numbers were coming from the border Germans who were being added to Germany, but their needs were different, since most of them remained in the area where they were.

A persistent problem that Bohle had to deal with was the tangled relationship between the German citizens (Reichsdeutsche), and those Germans (Volksdeutsche) who were not German citizens. It was an subject that the Foreign Office deliberately ignored, but which Bohle obviously saw as an additional opportunity for extending AO influence. The problem applied almost exclusively to the overseas Germans, and especially in areas of large concentrations, like Latin America. The protests that the AO was really an undercover agency for Germany's intelligence services, and was using German citizens and non-citizens alike in its operations, mounted as international tensions increased. At one point, the AO was forced to look at the question of punishing German citizens who were found to be involved in illegal activities while living abroad. In October 1937, a German citizen named Max Reichle was charged with supplying weapons to a rebel leader bent upon overthrowing the government of Honduras. The AO legal office (Rechtsamt) was given the task of researching German law for an answer. The result was a report that examined in detail existing law that applied to such situations.[5]

Current German law called for a prison sentence of five to fifteen years for a German citizen convicted of attempting to alter or change the government of a foreign nation. However, it was pointed out, that the exact nature of what constituted an attempt or an alteration had to be clarified. For example, what was the penalty if a German citizen abroad contributed financial support to a political party or candidate in a foreign country, or participated in a protest against a certain political movement (communism), or displayed the German flag in a community of German settlers? Since none of these activities were covered by German law, it was suggested that a special court would have to be convened, and because this involved German citizens living abroad, it was more appropriate to place the court under the jurisdiction of the Gauleiter of the AO, rather than the Ministry of Justice (Reichsjustizminister).[6] It was found that the involvement of Germans in the internal politics of foreign nations usually fell into three categories: 1) the political connection to the Reich by different German groups abroad; 2) an attempt at connecting to the NSDAP by fascist parties or movements abroad ; and, 3) the existence of political or economic ambitions of private individuals (especially in South and Central America, i.e., the Reichle case). However, it was not necessary to draft any new legislation dealing with German citizens abroad, the report continued, because the authority to return an individual to Germany made any new law in this regard superfluous.[7]

As he had in the past, Bohle made a renewed attempt in 1938 to bring some clarification to the morass of names applied to various German groupings that had grown over the years. Such designations as border Germans (Grenzlanddeutsch), folkgroups (Volksgruppen), folk islands (Volksinseln), and language islands (Sprachinseln), only created confusion, Bohle said, because there were only Reichsdeutsche (German citizens) and Volksdeutsche (people who did not hold citizenship, but were of German descent). In January, Bohle delivered a speech on the subject before the Hungarian parliament, which was widely reported in German newspapers. According to the account carried in the *Völkischer Beobachter*, and speaking to a capacity crowd, the Gauleiter said: "When we generally speak about Germandom abroad, we usually mean both German citizens and those of German extraction. We know very well, however, the distinction between German citizens abroad (Reichsdeutsche) and the Germans without German citizenship (Volksdeutche), but who share a common language and culture even though they are not citizens."[8]

Although it might be questioned if Bohle's speech brought clarity to the situation, it received praise from several leading Nazis. Hans Heinrich Lammers, Reich Minister and head of the Reich Chancellory, and one of Hitler's closest legal advisors, thought Bohle's speech was important enough to be brought to the attention of the leading state officials, while Goebbels was impressed enough to note in his diary: "Bohle delivered a good and impressive speech in Budepest about the A.O."[9]

While Bohle was obviously impressing a number of the important Nazi hierarchy with his energetic leadership of the AO, he was, no doubt, wondering if he was impressing Adolf Hitler. Did the Führer see the young Gauleiter as a potential foreign minister of the Third Reich? Did he view the AO as a significant element in German foreign policy? Was there anything more Bohle could do to bring his competence and ambitions to the attention of Hitler? Such questions must have occurred to the Gauleiter many times as he tried to calculate his relationship to the Führer in the years before the outbreak of war.

Bohle was well aware that a major policy area for Hitler in those years focused upon the border states, and he knew that he would gain Hitler's attention if he could play a larger role in what was happening there, but the situation was extremely complex. While these regions were at the center of much of Hitler's unfolding foreign policy at the time, most of them, as already noted, had existing political movements and local leaders who had embraced National Socialism, and did not always look to the Auslandsorganisation for leadership. Many of the local leaders looked more directly to the NSDAP in Germany, and some of them had close contacts with important Nazi leaders, who often involved themselves without regard to Bohle's AO.

The Gauleiter deserves the dubious credit, however, for devising ways to avoid serious consequences from a number of hostile states that were intent upon outlawing Nazi activity within their borders before the war. After the Dutch government protested the aggressive behavior of Nazi Party members in Holland in 1937, Bohle initiated the creation of a cover organization called the "Reichsdeutsche Gemeinschaft", and installed an AO man from the Dutch East Indies as the leader. However, since the Nazi Party was already outlawed in Holland, Bohle was forced to further subterfuge by using a member of the German Foreign Office to direct the Gemeinschaft. Presumably, with diplomatic rank, and engaged in legitimate consular activities, the individual selected, a Dr. Windecker, would not be found persona non grata by the Dutch government. Bohle said, however, that the Gemeinschaft was, "...for all practical purposes the Party. This group in Holland has been a problem child for some time, and I hope the work of my new representative will consolidate the situation and unite all factions of Deutschtum{Germandom} there."[10]

The very fact that Bohle could avoid any direct censure by using the Foreign Office as a shield for AO activities that had already been outlawed by a foreign nation, indicated the strength of his position with party stalwarts. He did not escape censure entirely, however. Dr. Graf von Zech-Burkersroda, a German diplomat from the pre-Hitler era, and the Foreign Office legation head in The Hague, dutifully informed the Dutch government of the Windecker appointment, but informed Bohle that he was not pleased by the Gauleiter's choice. While Bohle offered a slight compromise by appointing another individual, Dr. Otto Butting, he did not back away from his original intent that the person appointed would carry out his instructions to lead the Gemeinschaft. "In this area," Bohle wrote the

Graf, "he is clearly responsible to me and occupies a position in relation to the Gemeinschaft that a Landesgruppenleiter does in other countries."[11]

In naming Butting, Bohle had selected a person with a strong party background. He was a medical doctor who had joined the NSDAP the year before Hitler became chancellor, and soon headed an SS clinic with the rank of an SS captain (Hauptsturmführer). Concerning his appointment by Bohle to the German legation in The Hague, a note in his file read: "Dr. Butting was relieved of his duties to serve abroad in Holland from 1.7.1937 to 30.6.38. The wearing of the SS duty uniform is not permitted."[12]

With the Butting appointment, Bohle had again demonstrated his increasing ability to influence the direction of the Foreign Office before von Ribbentrop took control. The story did not end there, however. First, the Foreign Office did register a mild complaint with Bohle that Butting's appointment did not fool the Dutch government, and they knew that he was not a diplomat, but a party faithful and might not accept his accreditation. Second, Bohle received a complaint from Goebbels that Butting had been careless about distributing propaganda materials in Holland when Dutch citizens were present. The Propaganda Minister warned that such actions could result in restrictive measures by the Dutch government against sending in materials to that country.[13] Despite the protests, Bohle did not withdraw Butting. He may have seen any retreat on his part as a loss of the hard-won prestige he had gained in the diplomatic field, and a weakening of his authority to appoint his own people to the Foreign Office.

In the meantime, the entire episode was receiving full treatment in the Dutch press. As a dutiful employee, Butting forwarded daily accounts and clippings, accompanied by his own analysis that the hostility toward the Germans in Holland was the work of the Jews and the communists, but there was nothing to worry about. Public anger in Holland did not subside, however, and Bohle was growing concerned about the situation. The Dutch police had already issued warnings to the German residents that they could not guarantee their safety if they continued to display the German (swasitka) flag. Butting was already involved in a heated debate with Graf von Zech-Burkersroda and the Foreign Office over the matter, with Butting insisting that the Germans had every right to display the flag, and that they should not let the warning intimidate them, but reports of beatings and smashed windows were pouring into the Foreign Office.[14]

Although Bohle did not have a reputation for being fanatic about displays of the flag or the Führer's photograph, he was obviously not willing to allow the Foreign Office to undermine his appointment, and refused to recall Butting, although the ban on the AO in Holland continued. However, Bohle apparently decided to make an issue out of the fact that Graf von Zech-Burkersroda did not require the diplomatic missions to have pictures of Hitler prominently displayed. In a petty gesture of retaliation for the earlier complaint, Bohle notified the Foreign Office about the lack of attention given the Führer's photo, and the Graf was persuaded to place new orders for display.[15]

Holland was not Bohle's only worry, but every situation was different, and he did not have the same level of interest in every country that presented the AO problems. Spain was an example that did not excite Bohle very much, but it had an active branch of the Nazi Party that had formed in 1931. In the 1937 survey that the AO conducted, Spain was listed as having some six thousand German citizens living there, most of whom were engaged in import-export businesses. Five-hundred-forty-two of the German citizens in Spain held party membership.[16]

As much as Bohle may have preferred to ignore Spain, it was a country that held the world's attention with a civil war that involved a battle between military insurgents and the republican government. Although developments in Spain had been largely ignored by the European powers prior to World War I, the postwar period brought many of the problems that beset the rest of Europe. A military dictatorship under General Primo de Rivera emerged, but ended in 1930 when a republic was proclaimed. The new government was threatened by extremists from both the left and right, however, and by 1936, the country was in the throes of disintegration. Liberal republican forces struggled to direct government in a leftist coalition named the Popular Front, which claimed broad support, but in July, the Spanish army under the command of General Francisco Franco, mounted a revolt from Morocco against the central government in Madrid.

These events would not have normally been regarded with alarm by the major European powers, except Italy had been involved in assisting Franco prepare for the revolt, and both Mussolini and Hitler were offering military forces to him. This was signal to a number of Europe's leading statesmen that Spain had become the battleground between fascism and democracy, and a victory for Franco would be a victory for the dictatorships. Meanwhile, the floundering republic was receiving assistance from the Soviet Union, and volunteer forces from a number of the western democracies, including Great Britain and the United States.

As noted, prior to this time, Bohle had exhibited little interest in Spain, and he later admitted that when he had attended affairs at the Ibero-Amerika Institut in Berlin, everyone only spoke Spanish, and since he did not, he felt out of place. In addition to the six thousand German citizens in Spain, Bohle estimated the number of Germans without citizenship who lived there at about ten thousand people. According to all of his reports on the country, Bohle thought that the Germans residing there lived quite well, and that the Auslandsorganisation gave support to the "Union Alemana Nacional, NSDAP."[17]

In spite of Bohle's earlier indifference, the Landesgruppe in Spain continued to thrive. The leader was a man named Walter Zuchristan, whom Bohle had appointed in 1933. He was an industrious organizer and had developed a party structure with branches in a dozen Spanish cities. However, in 1935, one of his people was accused of meddling in local Spanish affairs, which gave the German Foreign Office the opportunity to criticize AO behavior, and cite the incident as the kind of action that brought discredit to Germany abroad. When the civil war began, the Spanish government seized the records of the AO Landsgruppe. A German diplomat named Hans Völckers, who was serving in the Madrid embassy at the time, wrote that Zuchristan had fled in such a hurry that he had left all kinds of incriminating materials behind, including personal data on members of the embassy staff. The material found its way into the hands of American journalists, and was soon made public.[18]

The outbreak of the Spanish civil war starkly emphasized the inability of the western democracies to take any collective action against the growing power of the dictatorships. This was further driven home with Mussolini's attack upon Ethiopia, and the emergence of the Berlin-Rome axis, affirming the mutual interests of the Italian dictator and Hitler in the Mediterranean region. When the civil war began, Hitler appointed a retired general named Wilhelm Faupel as German ambassador to Franco's government in Salamanca. The general had previously headed the Ibero-Amerika Institut, and had the strong recommendation of Rudolf Hess. Faupel's appointment was considered by some as a success for Bohle, since the general had worked closely with the Auslandsorganisation, although he was not a party member, but neither did he have a background in the Foreign Office. Bohle said he had not been consulted about the appointment, and only heard about it after it was publicly announced, nor did he think the general was the best man for the job, but he was pleased to get an ambassador who was not part of the Foreign Office clique, and was friendly to the AO.[19]

While Bohle's negative comment about Faupel came after the war, his correspondence with the general during his Spanish appointment in 1937, presents a somewhat different story. Faupel kept up a steady stream of reports to Bohle's office about his activities in Spain, including accounts of visits to the combat zones. He also often complimented the Gauleiter about AO work, writing at one point: "What you and your staff have accomplished is an absolutely marvelous instrument of foreign policy." In responding, Bohle wrote: "Let me say in closing , I am proud that I am permitted to work with you in the service of the Führer."[20]

By this time, Bohle was exhibiting a far greater interest in Spain, and felt that the Landesgruppe there needed some regeneration. He had already received some encouragement from one of his AO people there, Willi Köhn, who had become the German counsel general in Salamanca. In a note to Köhn, Bohle informed him that he had appointed a new Landesgruppenleiter to Spain named Arthur Dietrich, and suggested that Köhn could be helpful with a problem that had arisen. It seems that some of the AO party members had appeared in Falangist (Franco) uniforms, and Bohle was concerned that this made for bad publicity, and implied that a word of caution to these party members was in order.[21]

Considering the event many years later, Völckers, who was assigned to the Madrid embassy at the time, wrote that Foreign Office relations with the AO were at a low ebb. There was really no close cooperation with Bohle, and the continued negative and false reports of Dietrich, and other AO personnel, about the diplomats, was an attempt to undermine the position of the Foreign Office. He also noted that these AO people obviously expected to become Germany's official representatives to Spain.[22] Although these observations were made by Völckers long after the event, they were not wrong. Everything in 1937 supported the view that Bohle's ability to place his own people into what had been traditional diplomatic posts had increased significantly. The fact that he had been named a state secretary in the Foreign Office, only strengthened the possibility that he would soon play an even larger role in the conduct of German foreign affairs.

This was evident in the vital part that the AO played in the evacuation of Germans from Spain during 1937. Bohle led the initiative to create a working arrangement with Franco's Falange, and the German Interior Ministry to transport Germans home as quickly as possible, and to locate them near their former homes. Since some of these people arrived without funds, they needed immediate assistance, and Bohle had secured a fund of some 600,000 marks through public subscription to help them. He also was able to provide some reimbursement for those German citizens who simply had to abandon their assets in Spain with money that came from the funds allotted for the German volunteer military force (Kondor Legion) assisting Franco.[23]

Although most German men who were citizens were called home for military service, a number of Bohle's people remained in Spain throughout the entire conflict, and the AO received regular reports about the situation there. A key figure for Bohle in Spain was his Landesgruppenleiter from Portugal , a man named Friedhelm Burbach, who had transferred there to assist in the evacuation of the Germans. He informed the AO leader that the Catholic Church was not playing the positive role that it should in the war, and partly blamed the Jesuit Order for not understanding what the conflict was all about. However, Burbach was optimistic that Franco was going to win, but was doubtful if Spain would ever develop a political system comparable to Italy and Germany.[24]

As 1938 unfolded, Bohle was still confident that his power was spreading in the diplomatic field, and rewarded Burbach's good work by assisting him in securing a permanent Foreign Office appointment as the German consul at Bilboa, Spain, but there was growing evidence that von Ribbentrop was working diligently to halt any further inroads into his domain by the AO. Bohle's faithful assistant, Emil Ehrich, who had been sent to Paris to head the AO Landesgruppe there in July, complained that he was receiving very poor treatment from the German Foreign Office people. They bickered about providing him office space in the embassy, and would not provide any furnishings: "Even now, I do not have writing supplies. I do not say this to grumble, but only to give you an idea that the Landesgruppenleiter here has to fight for his place. My arrival here has reminded me in many ways of your reception at the Foreign Office."[25]

It is difficult to say just how aware Ernst Wilhelm Bohle was of the challenges he now faced from Ribbentrop. He knew, of course, that every move was going to be scrutinized, and the foreign minister would try and block anything that even remotely appeared to be an encroachment on the functions of the Foreign Office. Bohle knew, however, that he had compiled an impressive record during the past five years, and that in addition to having a powerful ally in Rudolf Hess, there were other party leaders who regarded Ribbentrop unfavorably. Most importantly, perhaps, the Auslandsorganisation had demonstrated its value in ways that were significant to many dedicated National Socialists.

9 Administrative Problems

To many Germans who advanced to positions of prominence and authority with the advent of the Hitler regime, the experience must have had an occasional sense of unreality at times. The speed with which Germany was transformed from a nation trying to recover from war, inflation, and depression into a country with a thriving economy and renewed international prestige, was very impressive. Many outside observers, however, pointed to the oppressive measures that were being introduced into German life by the dictatorial regime. Others choose to overlook the persecution of political foes of National Socialism, and the brutal treatment of racial and religious minorities, as the price to be paid for economic recovery. For Ernst Wilhelm Bohle, whose earlier prospects for a successful career in business or government had looked bleak in 1930, Adolf Hitler and the National Socialist movement proved a blessing.

Some of the credit was due his own ability to recognize an opportunity, and be in the right place at the right time, but his success was also a reflection of Germany's rapid economic recovery and the expansionist policies of the Hitler dictatorship. It was a time of opportunity for many in the Nazi Party, and while Bohle had the advantage of a powerful mentor in Rudolf Hess, it was no guarantee that he could avoid the invidious politics that permeated not only the leadership, but also the rank and file of the party. Bohle was a quick learner, however, and quickly proved adept at skirting the pitfalls that had relegated some of his colleagues to minor posts and career oblivion.

Although the young Gauleiter had no background in government administration or managing a large organization, he was able to recognize almost from the beginning, what the pursuits were that would enhance his position as the leader of the Auslandsorganisation He was fully aware that a major concern of Hitler's in developing foreign policy, focused upon Austria, Czechoslovakia, and the Polish Corridor, and he also knew that these areas had a history and leaders that did not require much direction from the Auslandsorganisation, however, he was not inclined to pass up an opportunity to involve himself in diplomatic affairs. He was able to take advantage of his position as Gauleiter of the AO, and his appointment as a state secretary in the Foreign Office, to inject himself at certain times into on-going diplomatic negotiations in both Austria and Czechoslovakia. Leading up to the annexation of Austria in March 1938, and the dismemberment of Czechoslovakia in 1938–1939, Bohle conferred with the foreign ministers of both of those nations on certain aspects of Nazi Party activity in their countries. This did not mean, however, that he was privy to what Hitler's intentions were toward these countries, and claimed he knew nothing in advance of the plan for annexing Austria, insisting that it was Ribbentrop's doing "... that I had to be kept out of foreign policy altogether."[1] Actually, the Auslandsorganisation der NSDAP had been openly involved with the Austrian Nazis until their failed attempt to take control of the government in 1934. After that date, Bohle operated more circumspect, but continued contact with German citizens residing there. Of the 44,000 thousand German citizens in Austria, 1,678 of them held German Nazi Party membership.

When speaking of the situation in Czechoslovakia, Bohle said that he had only been in Czechoslovakia once before 1939, and it was just an overnight visit. There had been an organization of German citizens in the country since 1926, and an AO Landesgruppe since 1933. However, Bohle said, the AO never provided any funds, but he knew that Konrad Henlein, the leader of the Sudeten National Socialist Party there, received money from the Volksbund für das Deutschtum im Ausland (VDA) in Germany. The AO leader insisted that his organization had no contact with the political movement led by Henlein, although he had met him once in Stuttgart in 1938, and they had discussed the Czech situation.[2]

These comments, made by Bohle while awaiting his sentence on war crimes charges, do not reflect accurately the activity of the AO in Czechoslovakia at that time. He may have had little contact with Henlein and the Sudetendeutsch movement that desired annexation to Germany, but the AO did maintain a steady relationship with the German citizens there through the Landesgruppe, and funds were expended for various programs, such as German holiday celebrations, and educational exchanges. Sometimes, these activities proved to be irritants to the Czech government, especially such public displays as the flying of the German flag. Tensions continued to mount through the 1930s, as the attitude of the Germans grew bolder. As one of Bohle's people in Czechoslovakia informed him in a note in 1937: "There is no reason for us to creep back behind German borders to celebrate. This creates a cowardly impression and more suspicion."[3]

At a meeting with the Czech foreign minister Vojtech Mastny in Berlin, the AO leader told him that the only concern his office had was to safeguard the welfare of the German citizens living there. In a devious attempt to persuade the foreign minister that the NSDAP in Germany was not working closely with Henlein's party in Czechoslovakia, he said: "I explained to him, I personally had never seen Henlein nor spoken to him nor exchanged any correspondence, which astounded him."[4]

Even though Bohle's conversations with the Czech foreign minister centered upon the subject of German citizens in that country, the AO leader was engaging in high level diplomacy that directly concerned Germany's foreign policy. He said that Mastny told him that his government had every confidence in Germany's good will, but there were certain negative forces at work, and he named several of the Sudetendeutsch who continued their agitation against Czechoslovakia, including a deputy of Henlein's. He said that although these men had now taken refuge in Germany, they continued their agitation work just as before, and he suggested that perhaps they could be silenced. According to Bohle, the implication was that if he could use his influence to silence these agitators, the AO could continue to function in Czechoslovakia undisturbed.[5]

Whether Bohle knew it or not, his conversations and any understandings with Mastny were meaningless because the Munich Agreement was already taking shape. The crisis between Germany and Czechoslovakia had been building steadily during the summer of 1938, and all of Europe was on edge. The British had been trying to play the mediator, and secure some acceptable compromise, and finally Prime Minister Neville Chamberlain made two trips to Germany to confer with Adolf Hitler. Ultimately, and agreement was signed in Munich in September, which permitted the British prime minister to return home with the claim that he had secured a peace settlement. It was, however, far from a peace settlement, for it literally destroyed Czechoslovakia. Germany now proceeded to annex the Sudetenland, and some three million Germans. The result was the ruin of the system of alliances that France had maintained in central Europe (Little Entente), and the elevation of Germany to the position of the most dominant power on the European Continent. The Munich Agreement was a great victory for Hitler, and revealed the tragic weakness of the western nations and their inability to prevent German expansion.

In the process of the German annexation of the Sudetenland, Bohle was given the task of establishing the necessary machinery that would permit the new Germans to vote. This involved an information campaign that informed them of their rights, and where polling places were located for the coming election. Since this included all of the Germans who had formerly resided in the Sudetenland, the message was broadcast to all AO branches abroad, informing them that these people could now vote at all German consulates and ships in ports. As the processing for citizenship for the Sudetendeutsch from Slovakia began, Bohle could not resist the pleasure of informing a number of party leaders that the Foreign Office had not been very helpful in the process.[6]

The so-called frontier questions illustrated amply to Bohle that he had to be constantly alert to the shifting winds in Hitler' policies, and that unexpected dead ends could occur. It was clear that the AO involvement in countries like Austria and Czechoslovakia had been of limited usefulness, and secondary to the role played by the Foreign Office. This meant that Bohle had to focus his energies where he could be more directly involved, which was outside of the European continent, but this permitted less opportunity for any diplomatic involvement in those areas that were uppermost on Hitler's schedule. It left Bohle with little option, except to do the best he could in working with the overseas German communities, spreading propaganda, and biding his time

The AO leader did, on occasion, follow a personal interests in a German community abroad, even though it did not have a great deal of relevance to his diplomatic ambitions at home. One such example was South Africa, where Bohle had spent part of his youth, and his father had been active in local politics. The AO 1937 survey listed almost 19,000 German citizens resident in the various African states, with 2,100 of them living in the Union of South Africa; 336 of them were members of the Nazi Party.[7] Hermann Bohle, Ernst's father, had resided in South Africa a number of years, and was an ardent National Socialist, who had joined the party before his son did. He had long been a critic of the German Foreign Office for its neglect of the German community in Cape Town, and had made his complaints known to Ernst's predecessor, Hans Nieland.[8] Actually, the German community in Cape Town had begun to divide on the issue of National Socialism and the Hitler movement as early as 1929, and Bohle's father had organized the first National Socialist branch in May 1932. With fewer than two dozen listeners on hand, the elder Bohle told them that no one could remain neutral in the coming struggle for Germany, and strongly urged them to join the NSDAP. The news of Hitler's appointment as chancellor caused an immediate surge in applications for membership among the German citizens in South Africa, and soon an AO Landesgruppe emerged in Cape Town. This did not resolve the bickering that had started in 1929, however, and a number of Germans, both citizens of the Reich, and non-citizens, voiced their opposition to National Socialism and the Hitler triumph in Germany. Bohle's father was still trying to gain control over the community, when his son became the leader of the Auslandsorganisation.[9]

All of this activity did not go unnoticed by officials in the Union of South Africa, who had always been concerned about any revival of the colonial question by Germany. The return of Germany's lost colonies had always been a part of the rhetoric that most German politicians had included in their post-World War I campaign activity, and when Bohle sent an emissary from the AO to visit the Germans living in South West Africa, the Union of South Africa viewed it as an unfriendly gesture. The result was a police raid on the AO Landesgruppe headquarters in Cape Town in July 1934, and the seizure of materials that the Union authorities found unsettling. Rather than face the possibility of a legal ban, Bohle decided to dissolve the Landesgruppe and reorganize with a cover group called the "Deutsche

Bund," which contained the same leaders and membership as the old Landesgruppe had.[10]

The maneuver did not really fool anyone, and the German-language press reflected the raging debates that were destroying the German community in the Cape. On the opposing side, Bohle was accused of stirring up the old argument of the 1919 mandated decisions, and attempting to force the acceptance of National Socialism on the German community. Even the German Foreign Office was growing concerned that Bohle's actions were endangering diplomatic relations with South Africa, and felt that all citizens of Germany residing there should not be involved with local politics. Therefore, the suggestion was made that they separate their activities from the Germans who were not citizens, and confine their pursuits to cultural endeavors only. Under no circumstances, should the memberships of the two groups mix. If this suggestion was not followed, Bohle was warned, there would soon be a government ban on all forms of party activity.[11]

As usual, when it came to Foreign Office proposals about his organization, Bohle ignored the advice, and tensions continued to simmer in the German community. Meanwhile, more and more of the Germans who opposed National Socialism were taking Union citizenship. Those German citizens who still strongly supported National Socialism were mostly persons who had come to South Africa in the years after the First World War, and now found that they were under pressure to curtail any political activity related to their National Socialistic beliefs. The options for those German citizens who were fervent in their adherence to National Socialism were not many. They could engage in some quiet espionage by taking Union citizenship, and continue to promote National Socialism; accept the curtailment of their work and wait for another time; or, join a front organization that was legal (i.e., Deutscher Südwest Bund), and try and take over the leadership.[12]

Before any of these directions could be decided, a law was issued by the German government in February 1938, that required all German citizens living abroad to register with their local consulates every three months. This prompted the Union of South Africa to declare invalid a regulation that had permitted German citizens to reside there without a visa. Henceforth, all German citizens residing in or traveling in the Union or South West Africa would require a visa. This meant that the Union could now remove any German citizen from their territory on the slightest pretext by simply revoking his or her visa.[13]

While much of Bohle's motivation in involving the AO so extensively in the German community affairs in South Africa had stemmed largely from his own background, and his father's activities there, he had no such motivation in Latin America, despite the fact that there were many more Germans there with an extensive history. There was a strong German presence in countries like Argentina, Brazil and Chile, and even before Hitler became chancellor, these states had a combined Nazi Party membership of 1,033 persons.[14]

Historically, trade and investment were the reasons for Germany's interest in Latin America, and this had been the influencing factor in designing policy. German import-export trade with Latin America had lagged in the 1920s, but then dramatically increased after 1933. By the late 1930s, Germany was second only to the United States as a trade partner in Latin America. Although German political influence remained limited, there was a military relationship with certain countries. Both Argentina and Chile had received military supplies of various kinds from Germany, and German military advisors had played significant roles from time to time in assisting in the development of the armed forces in those nations. Following World War I, German migration to Latin America increased noticeably, and in 1937, Bohle's office listed 143,610 German citizens residing in Latin American countries. The largest numbers were in Brazil (75,000), Argentina (42,600), and Chile (5,300). The total number of German Party members in 1937 was 7,602 persons.[15]

Bohle readily admitted his ignorance of the languages and culture in Latin America, and had never made a visit to any of the countries, although he noted that his wife had traveled with the wife of one of his employee to Brazil. When later interrogated about Latin America, Bohle exhibited an attitude of both amusement and condescension toward his relationship with the Latin American diplomats he encountered in Berlin before the war. He said that he was required to attend many functions in Latin American embassies in Berlin as part of his job, but paid scant attention to what was going on, and sometimes did not even know which country was hosting. Bohle confessed that he did not know the names of many of the individuals he encountered, but found that things went smoothly when he addressed everyone as "Excellency." He did recall receiving a decoration from the Bolivian government(a large star called the "El Condor de los Andes"), which completely surprised him, but could not remember what the honor was for, however, he did remember the name of the Bolivian ambassador, General Sanjines, because he spoke such good German, and praised Germany's National Socialism.[16]

Bohle's lack of enthusiasm for the Latin American states extended somewhat to those Germans who had chosen to emigrate there. He said that they tended to adopt a relaxed attitude toward life, and forget their good, solid German virtues. It also annoyed him when he encountered them at home in Germany on a visit "...because they always hung together at the South American Club, and often spoke Spanish among themselves."[17] On the positive side, the AO Gauleiter admitted that the Germans living in Latin America were among the most prosperous of all Germans living abroad, and his office rarely had to send anyone from the Berlin staff, because it was so easy to recruit there for party work.[18]

Bohle claimed that there were party members all over Latin America, including Mexico and Central America, but outside of Argentina, Brazil, and Chile, the figures were not impressive. For example, in Puerto Rico there were only three party members, and in Panama, fifty-one. All combined, Uruguay, Bolivia, Peru, Venezuela, Paraguay, Guatemala, Columbia, and Mexico, had fewer than one thousand party members.[19] As in the other nations with large German communities where the citizens of the Reich mixed with the non-German citizens, Latin America presented the same situation of local Nazis antagonizing the authorities with National Socialist organizing and spreading propaganda. An early problem developed in Argentina, which had a party branch dating from 1931. Later, some party members were expelled from the country for political agitation. By then, Bohle was head of the AO, and hoped to improve relations by appointing a new Landesgruppenleieter named Alfred Müller, whom he described as "...a sober, hard-working Nazi, rather sloppily dressed and unpretentious."[20]

The problem did not end there, however, and soon the AO was embroiled in a struggle that Bohle could never have anticipated. He found that he may have momentarily pacified the Argentine authorities by the Müller appointment, but had aroused the ire of the German ambassador to Argentina, Dr. Edmund Freiheer von Thermann. He was exactly the kind of career diplomat that proved the most difficult for Bohle to handle. He was an honored veteran of the First World War, having been wounded in action on the eastern front, taken prisoner by the Russians, managed to escape, and was a recipient of the Iron Cross first class. There was also no way that the AO leader could fault him along party lines, because not only was Thermann a member, but he had applied to and been accepted into a special SS unit despite his age. ("The experience in the World War has shown that a man in his mature years can better endure the hardships of war easier than the young volunteers.") The fact that his daughter was married to a member of Hitler's personal staff was another reason for Bohle to step carefully in opening any disagreement with Thermann.[21] Bohle was dealing with an ambassador that had all of the cards in his favor, and Thermann was set upon extending his duties to include not only control of the party members in Argentina, but to take the leadership of the entire German community. This was an obvious affront to the AO, and an encroachment upon Bohle's authority. However, he knew that any challenge to Thermann was a risk, because not only did the ambassador's record protect him from attack, but he had strong ties with a number of party leaders. Bohle's position was made more difficult because his new Landesgruppenleiter, Alfred Müller, was drawing the same kind of criticism from the Argentine government as his previous man had At the same time, Thermann had gained ground with Argentine officials by letting it be known that he favored a greater emphasis upon cultural activities, and less propaganda.[22]

Thermann was aggressive in pursuing his aim, and mounted a publicity campaign promoting his interest among both the German citizens and the Volksdeutsche communities. His office regularly provided material for the German-language press in Argentina, and although he had promised more attention to cultural affairs and less propaganda, his photo in a full dress SS uniform was not unusual when a German day of celebration was scheduled. The ambassador was quoted as saying that he brought personal greetings from the Führer and SS Reichsführer Heinrich Himmler. At one celebration in 1934, Thermann was pictured on a stage with some Argentine dignitaries against a backdrop of an audience of Germans saluting the flag of the new Germany. [23] In none of the press releases from Thermann's office was Bohle or the AO mentioned.

Themann was also successful in enlisting the support of a German organization in Buenos Aires called the "Deutsche Volksbund für Argentinen," which had a membership containing a number of influential Germans from the community. Significantly, its leader was a German physician named Wilhelm Röhmer, who just happened to be employed at the German embassy. The organization was politically conservative and strongly representative of German business interests, and found the noisy propaganda of the AO's Müller disturbing.[24] Now on the defensive, Bohle could have backed off and removed Müller, but this would have meant a victory for the diplomats in the Foreign Office, and a loss of his own hard won authority over the Germans who lived abroad, including party members.

At this point, the whole situation became further inflamed by the so-called "Patagonia Affair." There appeared a bizarre report that Germany intended to annex Patagonia, and Müller's name was at the center of it. The story was that Müller had gathered some military data for the proposed annexation and dispatched it through diplomatic channels to Franz Xavier Ritter von Epp, director of the Nazi Party's Colonial Political Office (Kolonialpolitischen Amt der NSDAP) in Germany. Presumably, the entire idea had originated with some members of the AO Landesgruppe, who envisioned a German state in Latin America, and had contacted von Epp. When the story broke in the press in Buenos Aires, the German Foreign Office immediately branded it as false, and the work of Germany's enemies.[25]

The Foreign Office was now put in the position of having to defend Müller and the Auslandsorganisation, or admit that a high official of the party was involved in an espionage plot. Von Epp was one of Hitler's earliest supporters, and had been instrumental in assisting the party acquire its first newspaper, the *Völkischer Beobachter*, and held a number of high level positions after Hitler became chancellor. Obviously, he was not a figure to be dismissed lightly, and the possibility that he was acting at the behest of higher forces in the Hitler government was not lost upon the Foreign Office. In the beginning, Bohle thought the whole affair to be largely a fabrication, but he also knew that von Epp had requested some military and economic data on Patagonia, and that Müller had supplied it in a confidential dispatch through diplomatic channels.[26]

Forcing the Foreign Office and Thermann to reverse course was a victory that Bohle must have relished, but there was a price to pay. On orders of Argentine authorities, Müller was arrested for a brief time, and Bohle's entire operation was threatened. His people did not have diplomatic immunity, and were subject to deportation at any time. Fearing that the authorities were about to seize all of the Landesgruppe records, Bohle had them moved into the German consular offices in Buenos Aires. In an attempt to strengthen his position with the Argentine government, Thermann told Bohle that he was going to inform them that the AO was in the process of restricting its activities, which meant no uniform wearing, no non-German citizens permitted at meetings, and no German citizens in any leadership role in organizations or clubs in the German community.[27]

This action earned Thermann a promise from the Argentine Foreign Minister Cantillo that there would be no further measures taken without prior notice, but the situation already appeared beyond repair. In the meantime, Thermann, while attending an ambassadors conference in Montevideo, was told by several representatives from Brazil, Chile, and Uruguay, that anti-German sentiment was building all over Latin America. He was informed that feelings were running especially high against the Auslandsorganisation der NSDAP, and that the recent action taken by Bohle to separate the German citizens from the Volksdeutsche groups, had not been effective in quelling any of the growing hostility toward Germans. The Argentine government, now under increasing pressures from the United States to take action against the Nazi agitators, announced on May 15, 1939, that all private associations, clubs, organizations and clubs were to disengage from any aspect of local politics, discontinue the use of any Nazi signs or symbols, and conduct all affairs in the Spanish language.[28]

Despite these serious setbacks, Bohle was still not ready to admit defeat, and continued to try and persuade the Foreign Office that his work could continue behind the façade of a front organization that met all the restrictive requirements imposed by the Argentina government. By this time, of course, the Gauleiter was not dealing with Neurath, and Ribbentrop was having none of it. He refused outright to even consider the proposal and Bohle was informed that Foreign Office consular and embassy quarters could no longer provide space for AO personnel, supplies and records because the political situation had become far too fragile to offer such privileges.[29]

Bohle argued that the warnings being transmitted by Thermann, that unfriendly feelings were mounting against the Germans all over Latin America, were not true. He cited the example of Bolivia, where party members, although forbidden to wear uniforms or display Nazi insignia, were treated in the most friendly of terms. A successful cover organization had already been created, and there was no danger of any party members being expelled, and Bohle noted, there was a harmonious mingling of both German and non-German citizens. There was virtually no discernable turmoil in the German community in La Paz, he said, and the AO was in the process of initiating an exchange police training program with the country.[30]

Bolivia was not the only country that displayed a friendly face to the German residents. AO files recorded the oldest National Socialist cell founded outside Germany was in Brazil in 1928, and although it quickly dissolved, by 1931 it was back in business. A German consular employee named Hans-Henning von Cossel became the first Landesgruppenleiter for the AO there, and later worked closely with Bohle, who described him as a man with wide connections in Latin America.[31]

About the same time that Thermann was cautioning the Foreign Office concerning what he regarded as the too aggressive attitude of Bohle and the AO in Argentina, Cossel was working diligently to develop a closer relationship with Brazil. He told Bohle in 1937, that he had been approached by the Brazilian Interior Minister Campos, who expressed concern about the growing strength of communism. According to Cossel, this led to some discussion about the possibility of joining with Germany in an anti-Comintern[32] pact. The idea obviously excited Cossel, who described Campos as the most important man in Brazil next to President Vargas. Urging the AO leader to treat the information with the greatest of secrecy, Cossel said that Campos was ready to dispatch some of his most trusted people to Germany for specialized training in combating the communist menace.[33]

As talks progressed, the German ambassador to Brazil, Dr. Karl Ritter advised against pursuing the project, and later notified Bohle that the Brazilian government had just banned all groups and organizations that owed allegiance to other governments. The ambassador said that the ban was aimed especially at the German organizations, and that he had filed a protest with the Brazilian government. His recommendation was that the whole affair be aired on a short wave broadcast from Germany. Ritter told Bohle that he was convinced that the United States was behind the anti-German move.[34]

The situation had become extremely intense, and Bohle immediately ordered all German citizens in Brazil, and elsewhere in Latin America, to withdraw from all groups and organizations that contained Germans who were not citizens of the Reich, and to discontinue any association with them. His order came too late for some of the Germans in Brazil, however. A number of them were arrested in violation of the recent ban, and charged with belonging to Nazi Party cells, and desecrating the Brazilian flag. This last charge stemmed from the accusation by Brazilian authorities that several party members had pasted membership stamps all over a Brazilian flag. One of the involved members informed Bohle that he had taken a Brazilian flag to Germany on a visit, and at several party functions members had pasted stamps on it from their party books. When he returned to Brazil, he had presented the flag as a gift to the local AO Ortsgruppe.[35]

In what can only be described as another of Bohle's encroachments upon Foreign Office protocol, he asked Ritter to carefully explain to the Brazilian government the role of the Auslandsorganisation der NSDAP in the German state. As he phrased it in his communiqué: "The Party is an autonomous body in Germany and abroad, which rules its affairs by virtue of its own authority." Bohle admitted that relations with Brazil should be preserved, but that government, and others, should understand that National Socialism in Germany was not a traditional political party. It was an all-encompassing peoples' movement, and applied to all German citizens at home and abroad.[36]

Whether these fine points in the governing philosophy of National Socialism were successfully conveyed to the Brazilian authorities by Ritter remains a moot question, but for many of the German citizens living in Brazil, the meaning was clear. Like hundreds of their countrymen in Latin America, they were packing their bags and returning home. Bohle did not try to hide his disappointment or his bitterness. The Germans who had gone to Brazil in the first place, he said, had left Germany with very little, so they should not have much to pack, upon returning. He described them as people with great illusions but little knowledge of what life was like outside the Reich. Shortly thereafter, when Brazil presented Germany with a gift of two thousand pounds of coffee, Bohle said: "We should not lose sight of the fact that the Brazilian government is carrying on stiff opposition against Deutschtum [Germandom], that Party organization is forbidden there, and that a series of specific decrees have been issued in these suppression attempts....The 2,000 sacks of coffee have little significance for a country that sinks 100,000 such sacks in the ocean every year just to raise the price."[37]

Curt Prüfer, former head of personnel in the Foreign Office, who served as the German ambassador to Brazil in the very critical period from the start of the Second World War in 1939, until diplomatic relations between the two nations ended in January 1942, said in a statement after the war, that the party functionaries who remained in Brazil ceased all illegal activities upon Bohle's direction in 1939, and the complaints of the Brazilian authorities stopped. He praised Bohle for this, and said that it made his tenure in Rio de Janeiro during that period much easier.[38]

The story of the AO in Chile is similar to that of Brazil. It had its origin with five party members in 1930, and increased to 155 members by the time Hitler became chancellor in 1933. Some early friction developed between Bohle and Neurath regarding Chile, when the Foreign Office reported that there was virtually no party activity in the country. Angered by this, Bohle replied that the work of the AO there was being ignored by the German diplomats, and said that there were almost a thousand party members among the 5,300 German citizens living in that country. However, just as in Argentina and Brazil, there was mounting criticism of the Germans living there, and much of it was directed at a National Socialist party (Nacistas) that boasted a large membership of both German citizens and non-citizens. The close relationship between the Nacistas and the AO Landegruppe was often cited. When the 1938 elections in Chile brought a popular front (coalition of liberal parties) to power, there was a campaign to curb the political right that permitted such fascist groups to function. Interestingly, however, the AO Landesgruppe was able to continue its existence until Chile broke relations with Germany in 1943.[39]

When Bohle prepared a lengthy report on Latin America for the German Foreign Office in April 1939, he defended the record of the Auslandsorganisation, on the basis that it had not become illegal in most of the states there. He said that his Landesgruppen had established solid relations with the German communities, and cited as evidence that all of the German national holidays were celebrated, and the German flag was prominently displayed. In fact, there was even wide use of the Hitler salute. Bohle credited some of these achievements to the steady supply of reading materials and guest lecturers that the AO had supplied over the years that had acquainted the Germans there with the National Socialist viewpoint. He warned, however, that all of this progress was now endangered because of the pressures from the United States to have the AO der NSDAP declared illegal. It was extremely important, he continued, that the AO structure be protected so that the good work could continue, but to do so, meant that all of the personnel presently active in Latin America should be integrated into the Foreign Office, in order to avoid the threat of expulsion in the event of a general ban.[40]

Ribbentrop was not about to follow Bohle's suggestion, and let it be know that he thought the AO had done a poor job in Latin America. In June 1939, the Foreign Office held a conference on Latin America affairs, and while Bohle and many of his people attended, Ribbentrop completely ignored it. The conference was opened by Baron von Weizsäcker, who stated that the purpose of the gathering was to examine the reasons for the recent deterioration of relations between German and Latin America. There was general agreement that historically, Germans had always been welcome there, and that the current trouble seemed to stem from the hostility fostered by the United States.[41]

Von Thermann was alone among the German ambassadors, who pointed to the activities of the AO as part of the problem. He said that Gauleiter Bohle had presented himself abroad as the spokesman for the NSDAP, and had intruded upon matters that were the province of the Foreign Office. This burdened the diplomat in the field, who then had the problem of trying to explain activities that were not compatible with his diplomatic duties. This most often occurred, Thermann said, when the AO insisted upon mixing German citizens with the non-German citizens in various affairs. This always awakened the mistrust of the host governments.[42]

To make his point, Thermann related an instance in his own experience. At one time, the Argentine government opened the door to second-generation Germans, offering them citizenship in that country, but the AO was absolutely opposed to the idea. Since there were Germans who wanted to accept Argentine citizenship, the opposition from the AO created some sharp conflict in the community, Thermann stated. He also said that he warned Bohle that his scheme of a cover organization to conceal AO activities would not fool Argentine authorities.[43]

As a veteran of disagreements with the Foreign Office, Bohle was not one to let such attacks go unanswered, and he was prepared for this one. The primary mission of the Auslandsorganisation, he said, was to instill among Germans living abroad, a passion for National Socialism, and a desire to support its foreign policies. This, he claimed, he had accomplished, for the German communities around the world were far more supportive of Germany now than they had been in 1914. The primary purpose of this conference, Bohle continued, should be to determine how this spirit of unity can be sustained wherever it is threatened. Returning to his earlier proposal of incorporating AO people into the Foreign Office, which had already been rejected by Ribbentrop, Bohle insisted that this was the only way that the spirit could be kept alive, and his people could easily blend into the diplomatic corps as "official advisers."[44] Fully cognizant of the fact that the international situation was changing rapidly as Germany moved closer and closer to war, Bohle admitted that his organization may well face a total ban in all of Latin America, but he was persistent in his belief that the party apparatus could be kept alive by his plan for incorporation into the Foreign Office consuls abroad.

Several factors must be considered when analyzing the relationship of the Auslandsorganisation der NSDAP to the nations in Latin America. Bohle never appreciated the deep concern the United States felt whenever the stability of the hemisphere was threatened. He ignored the history of U.S. reaction whenever the possibility of a European penetration appeared on the horizon.[45] Despite the risks involved, Bohle pursued his plan to build National Socialist branches into every German community in Latin America, and while this was inspired in part by both his own ambition and belief in the Hitler movement, it was also the avenue to securing a greater share of Germany's diplomatic activity.

Ernst Bohle's lack of interest in the culture and history of the states of Latin America ultimately weakened his ability to draft the kind of working relationship that would have been more effective with the German communities there. He failed to recognize the fact that the German population, both citizens and ethnic Germans, while full of pride about the new Germany, did not want to be forced to make a choice when the authorities in many of the Latin American states began take restrictive measures against the Auslandsorganisation. This was obviously a much stronger feeling among the non-Germans who had deeper roots, many of them being second and even third generation settlers. As the hostility toward Germans mounted, most of them probably felt that they had to choose to either support the Hitler regime or declare a kind of neutrality by retreating to what Bohle cynically labeled their "bürgerliche Veriensleben," an obvious reference to the non-political pursuits of beer drinking and bowling. No matter which choice the Germans made, the Auslandsorganisation der NSDAP was finished in Latin America.[46]

10 A Case Study
Germans in the United States

The Auslandsorganisation was operational in many areas of the world, but its reception by the local German communities, some dating their origins back to the nineteenth century, varied considerably, and depended on a number of factors. The history of a community's relationship to Germany was very important, and this rested, to a large degree, upon its immigration pattern. Older communities were oriented toward language and culture, and, until the First World War, usually compatible with the politics of the host country. Their ties to the fatherland often depended upon a variety of organizations in Germany that maintained connections through the promotion of language studies, visiting lecturers, student exchanges, and the celebration of traditional holidays.

The situation began to change when Germany was defeated in the war, and the punitive Versailles settlement of 1919 stripped the country of all colonies and territories. This aroused new feelings of nationalism among the millions of Germans who now found themselves to be a minority in the European nations that surrounded Germany. While the impact on the Germans who lived abroad was not as dramatic, the peace settlement did add a stronger political dimension to their feelings of nationalism, and this would be intensified by the influx of postwar German immigrants. Thus, whether in Europe or abroad, Hitler's messages found fertile ground among certain elements in the German communities, especially the newer immigrants, and, when the AO came courting, there was a positive response. There were regions of the world that had a significant German population that did not react so positively to the new Germany, however, and a major one was the United States.

German migration to the United States had played major role in the country's history since colonial times, and while some communities retained much of their ethnic identity, the vast majority assimilated into the American main stream. However, the anti-German sentiment that emerged during the First World War, and the large number of immigrants who arrived in the 1920s, created an element that viewed the rise of the Hitler movement favorably. For Bohle, a key point was the number of Germans living in America or Canada, who had still retained their German citizenship, or, had not become American or Canadian citizens.[1]

The massive statistical profiles created by the AO in 1937, indicated that the U.S.-Canada office (AO Amt VI) figures revealed considerable contrasts between the Germans in that region of the world, and those who lived abroad elsewhere. A disappointment for Bohle was the relatively few Nazi Party members among the large German population, a clear indication that the majority of the residents had a reluctance to be identified with National Socialism. The AO files listed only eighteen party members in the United States before 1930, and it was only after the Reichstag elections in September when the Nazis made a strong showing (12 seats to 107), that there was a small increase in membership in the United States. Between the end of 1931 until Hitler's appointment as chancellor in January 1933, the Party membership increased from 36 to 115. The 1937 AO-Statistics listed 569 members in the United States, and 88 members in Canada.[2]

The 1937 data on the United States provided some interesting detail profiling the Party membership. Almost all of the members were male, and between twenty-seven and forty-four years of age (indicating that they were men of the post-war generation who had migrated after 1919). The majority (345) was almost equally divided among those who worked in some aspect of business (either independently owned, or employed), and those who worked as skilled craftsmen. There was a handful of professionals (engineers, physicians, academics), and a few farmers. Fifteen female party members were described as housewives.[3]

The relationship of Bohle and the Auslandsorganisation to the United States was a complicated one. There is no denying, that in the first years of the Hitler regime, the potential for developing a following of some kind was there, but it was mired in endless arguments over leadership and direction. Long before young Ernst Bohle appeared on the scene, there were a few faithful Hitler supporters preaching the virtues of National Socialism on American soil. A leading Hitler advocate was a German immigrant named Arno Friedrich (Fritz) Gissibl, who had arrived in the United States after the First World War. His initial effort was to organize a group that called itself the "Freie Vereinigung Teutonia" (Free Association of Teutonia), which occurred in Chicago in 1924. He was born in Nuremberg in 1903, and had entered the United States in 1923, but had already made contact with the Hitler movement the year before, when he joined a branch of the NSDAP in Hamburg. During some of the darkest days of Hitler's political career in the 1920s, when the party was at it lowest ebb, Gissibl sent him some modest sums of money. He kept a careful record of the gifts, the first was for twenty dollars on the occasion of Hitler's thirty-sixth birthday in April 1925, for which he received a personal note of thanks; by 1932, he had sent the party money on seven occasions.[4]

Because of his early membership in the Party, Gissibl held one of the very coveted low numbers (45,000), and unlike many of the first followers of Hitler, he was fairly well educated, having attended the University of Hamburg, and while in the United States, worked as a journalist, largely for the German language press. In the decade before Hitler assumed power, the Teutonia was not a branch of the Nazi Party, and it is doubtful if Hitler, with his struggle to take control of Germany, devoted much thought to a handful of German supporters in faraway America, although their financial gifts were welcome. According to Gissibl's later account, the relationship became more positive when, in 1932, at the urging of the Foreign Section of the NSDAP (Dr. Nieland), an official group was formed in Chicago (Ortsgruppe Chicago).[5]

Although some correspondence in the AO files referred to the "Landesgruppe USA" in 1929, Bohle contended that there had never been any official designation given to Gissibl's group in the U.S., and that Gissibl was never a party representative. Bohle said that when he assumed the leadership of the AO, the party representative in the United States was a man named Heinz Spanknoebel, who had joined the party in 1929, and organized a branch in Detroit, where he was employed by the Ford Motor Company. Later, after returning to Germany in 1935, Spanknoebel described his role in America as "Country leader [of the NSDAP] in the U.S.A."[6]

Actually, as a challenger to Gissibl in this Detroit versus Chicago struggle, Spanknoebel had succeeded in replacing the Teutonia with an organization that called itself "The Friends of New Germany" (Bund der Freunde des Neuen Deutschlands). As the confusion mounted, Hess ordered that German citizens were not to participate in the functions of the groups in America, and while Bohle could have forced both Gissibl and Spanknoebel to return to Germany, he did not do so, and the two continued to disseminate Nazi propaganda. While this may have seemed contrary to the spirit of the Hess order, it had become a familiar pattern of publicly dampening any rising concern in host countries concerning Nazi activity on their soil, while continuing to support Party members' efforts to establish a front group. This was a pattern that Bohle was prepared to follow in the United States, but there were unanticipated problems.

To a number of National Socialists, the United States always appeared to have the potential for a strong, active party branch. There was a large German population that could provide financial support, and enough party sympathizers that could constitute a following. It was a situation that attracted not only Gissibl and Spanknoebel, but other followers of Hitler, who felt that their credentials entitled them a leadership position. The line of authority between Bohle's office and party members in the United States had always been somewhat murky, in that people like Gissibl and Spanknoebel went back to the earlier days of the Hitler movement, and they had close contacts with individuals from that time who had climbed to positions of influence in the party at home. This allowed them to circumvent AO directives if they did not agree with them, and Bohle was not always in a position to enforce his orders against an individual who not only held a low Party number, but was personally acquainted with Hitler since the early days of the struggle for power.

At times, there were other reasons party members in America did not immediately respond to one of Bohle's requests. A U.S. Congressional committee, led by John McCormack, had become curious about the activities of certain groups that they labeled subversive, and individuals from these groups were being called before the investigative body. One such individual, who wanted to avoid any involvement with U.S. government authorities, was a party member named Friedrich Mensing, a sea captain employed by the German ship lines North German Lloyd in New York. He had been asked by Bohle, when the connection between party members in the United States and the AO, became difficult, to maintain contact and collect the party dues, but before agreeing, Mensing took the precaution of contacting the German Ambassador to the United States, Hans Luther. The sea captain wanted to know if he could run afoul of the American State Department position for such activity, however, Luther assured him that there would be no objections raised if there was no organizational structure involved.[7]

In spite of his care to avoid becoming a target of the McCormack committee, Mensing was called to testify as the investigations continued, and when he appeared in July 1934, he denied that Bohle or anyone in the Auslandsorganisation der NSDAP directed a Nazi Party branch in the United States. He did admit, that the Gauleiter was in touch with individual party members from time to time, but this was in the form of personal correspondence, and Heinz Spanknoebel was not among them.[8] When asked about these events more than thirty years later, Mensing, now long settled in San Francisco, California, said only that he recalled that time "...with very mixed feelings."[9]

While Mensing had never been a serious contender for Bohle's job, or the leadership of the Auslandsorganisation, that could not be said about Kurt Lüdecke. As already noted, he was a man of unbounded ambition, and had made no secret of his desire to be recognized as the appointed leader of the German citizens who lived abroad, but his falling out with the party, and his flight from Germany ended any possibility of that. However, he continued to be a problem when he gained sensational press coverage in the United States for his book in 1937, *I Knew Hitler*. It purported to be a detailed account of his relationship with the Führer, and was highly critical of the Nazi leadership..

The interesting fact was, that despite his alienation from the party, it was discovered that when the book appeared he was still carried on the books as a member. In February 1938, Bohle was notified by the party headquarters in Munich that the rolls indicated that Lüdecke was listed as a member of the AO Ortsgruppe USA, and ordered his immediate dismissal. However, Bohle replied that when he discussed the matter with Rudolf Hess, the deputy Führer told him that Lüdecke had been dismissed from the party at the time that he had been imprisoned in the concentration camp in Germany, and further, a search of AO records produced no enrollment listing for him.[10]

At the time that Lüdecke was called before the McCormack committee, his book had not yet appeared in the United States, but he knew that as soon as it did, it would attract publishers in other countries. Well aware that this was not an event that the Hitler government would welcome, and never without a scheme, he went to the German embassy in Washington, D.C., and proposed a deal. He would sell Germany the copyrights, and this would ensure that the book would only appear in English. The offer was refused, and although Lüdecke continued to make news in the United States, his book did not have the impact that he hoped.[11]

Meanwhile, in spite of the Hess order to dissolve affairs in the United States, Heinz Spanknoebel claimed that the Deputy Führer did not object to him taking over the leadership of fellow Party members. Captain Mensing, who evidently maintained contact with him, said that Spanknoebel had a letter from an important party official, Rudolf Schmeer, that verified his claim of support from Hess. Spanknoebel was convinced that the Friends of New Germany would enlist the support of a large number of Germans in America, if the right kind of appeal was made. He visited the publisher of the German language newspaper, *New York Staats Zeitung*, which he knew many German Americans read, and made the point that the Friends had full backing from Germany, including Bohle's Auslandsorganisation. Next, he contacted German firms operating in the United States, and informed them that any employees holding German citizenship were required to join the Friends of New Germany.[12]

Spanknoebel's ambitious endeavors were alarming American authorities, however, and soon he was charged with working as an unregistered agent for a foreign government, and ordered deported. Before the deportation order could be executed, Spanknoebel left, but according to his private secretary, Frederick Kruppa, he did not do so willingly. A man from Germany's Propaganda Ministry, known only as Feldmann, appeared at the Friends' office, showed a gun, and personally escorted Spanknoebel by taxi to a waiting ship, the *Europa*, that was going to Germany. Obviously confused and upset by this turn of events, Captain Mensing made a trip back to Germany to discuss the whole situation. He said that both Hess and Bohle denied that they had given any authorization to Spanknoebel, but the AO leader insisted that German citizens residing in the United States could not be prevented from attending social functions sponsored by the Friends of New Germany.[13]

The German Foreign Office, however, was concerned by the rising anti-German feelings sweeping the United States, and placed much of the blame on the Friends. Of course, Bohle's refusal to issue a clear directive prohibiting all German citizens from participating in any of the Friends' activities, social or otherwise, was partially to blame. He knew that the impression in the United States was that the AO was directing matters, but he resented

Foreign Office interference. There is nothing to indicate that he took the growing public hostility toward Germans and the Hitler government seriously, although he was well aware of the publicity that the McCormack committee was generating throughout America.

Even if Bohle had wanted to take some decisive action to curtail all participation of the German citizens in the Friends' functions, he had to contend with other party stalwarts eager to establish a branch on U.S. soil. One such was an individual in Hitler's intimate circle who expressed an interest in possibly taking the leadership of the Germans in America. His name was Ernst F. S. Hanfstaengl, a man from a German-American family, who had attended Harvard University before World War I, but after a return to Germany in the 1920s, became friends with Hitler, and was instrumental in helping him regain his footing after his prison term for the failed putsch in 1923. After the Nazis gained power, Hanfstaengl worked in press relations for the Party, and kept in close touch with a number of Germans living in the United States. Because of his American education and business contacts in New York, he regarded himself as fully qualified to assume leadership there. However, when his relationship with Hitler became strained due to his less than enthusiastic support of some of the governments' programs, his candidacy for any further posts faded.[14]

Another figure clamoring for the leadership of the Friends was Walter Kappe, who had been in the United States since 1924, and had joined with Fritz Gissibl and his brother Peter, to create the Teutonia. Like Gissibl, he had joined the Nazi Party early, and sent Hitler some modest amounts of money during the lean years. As party member number 45,199, he was guaranteed special consideration after Hitler became chancellor, and therefore, Bohle had to take him seriously, but Kappe was too closely identified with the Nazi Party to be that useful on the American scene.[15]

What was needed, if party organization was to survive in the United States, was a total make-over. It had to be an organization that could withstand scrutiny by U.S. authorities, and avoid public arguments over the eligibility requirements. By June 1936, after a six month reorganization, a new leader and a new organization were announced. The new leader was an American citizen named Fritz Julius Kuhn, a veteran of the German army in World War I, and a resident of America since1924. The organization carried the all-embracing name of the German-American Bund (Amerika-Deutscher Volksbund), but neither Bohle nor the German Foreign Office were convinced, that this would still the American criticism, and thought it might even anger the public more because its was such an obvious subterfuge. Any reservations that Bohle may have had did not prevent him from maintaining a close connection with the Bund,[16] although his private opinion of Kuhn was that he was full of self importance, and tried too hard to impress everyone he met. Of course, this view came after Kuhn led a German-American delegation to the 1936 Olympics held in

Berlin, and presented Hitler personally with three-thousand dollars for the Winterhilfe charity.[17]

Bohle was, no doubt, irritated by news of Kuhn's boasting after his return to the United States, that he had been given a hearty welcome by Hitler personally during his Berlin visit, but the AO leader was not the only one upset by Kuhn's behavior. Hans Heinrich Dieckhoff, now the German ambassador to the United States, caballed the Foreign Office his concerns: "Nothing has resulted in so much hostility toward us in the last few months as the stupid and noisy activities of a handful of German Americans. I am referring to the efforts of the German-American Bund. Kuhn refers again and again to his close connections with Germany and his reception by the Führer...I know that the Auslandsorganisation has clearly disassociated itself from the German-American Bund, but I am not sure that all the agencies in Berlin are observing similar restraint."[18]

The "agencies in Berlin" that the ambassador was referring to was the Volksdeutsche Mittelstelle (VoMi), for he had received reliable information that it was in direct contact with Kuhn. Bohle also was aware of this, and therefore, was particularly incensed when a complaint came to the German Foreign Office from the American chargé d'affaires in Berlin, charging the Auslandsorganisation with supporting the German-American Bund. Bohle admitted that his office was in contact with some individual Party members living in the United States, and they were probably Bund members, but he denied any contact with Kuhn or support of the Bund itself.[19]

Again, this was a typical and oft repeated situation in the Nazi bureaucracy when influential members pursued their own agenda without regard to anyone else. Sometimes it was done deliberately to satisfy an old score, and the results were very often confusion and increased animosity among the Party membership. The episode with Kuhn and the German-American Bund was certainly an example. While the German Foreign Office was receiving complaints about Bohle's operations, the German-American Bund was receiving encouragement not only from VoMi, but Goebbels' Propaganda Ministry, as well. An agent working directly for Goebbels, named Ulrich von Gienanth, was attached to the German embassy in Washington, D.C., as a librarian, and was, among other things, funneling support (funds) to the German-American Bund.[20]

As diplomatic relations worsened between the United States and Germany, Dieckhoff, who was unaware of Gienanth's dealings with the German-American Bund, continued to warn Berlin of the growing damage. His analysis of the situation was clear and concise, and his comments accurately portrayed what was happening in America. He emphasized that the most serious danger was that Bund activity and Kuhn's speeches had convinced American governmental leaders and the public, that Germany was trying to actually create a National Socialist political movement in the United States. The ambassador did not think that the American people were actually anti-German, but he felt it was necessary to initiate some measures to stimulate feelings of good will toward Germany.[21]

Dieckhoff then posed some questions that he felt should be explored. For example, just how important was the German American population in terms of influencing the political situation in Germany? Was it possible to create a German-American organization that had a favorable view of Germany without arousing a hostile public opinion in America? Was there anything to be learned from studying the lessons of 1917, when German Americans suffered such sharp discrimination in the United States? The ambassador then proceeded to answer his own questions. He did not think that it was possible to create a German-American organization that could be effective in any meaningful way. In pointing out the obvious, Dieckhoff wrote that National Socialism had never found a significant following in the United States, and to prove his point, he used the German American community in the Chicago area. Estimating the German American population there at approximately 700,000 persons, the ambassador noted that while some 40,000 of this number belonged to various German clubs and organizations, only 450 people had actually joined the German-American Bund: "Also 700,000, 40,000, 450!"[22]

Dieckhoff warned that German-U.S. relations were nearing a crisis point, and a diplomatic break was a real possibility unless the Roosevelt government could be persuaded that the whole business of the German-American Bund and the Auslandsorganisation had no political significance in America. To do this, Dieckhoff continued, meant that it was necessary for Germany to issue a clear declaration severing any and all connections to the German-American Bund, and to announce that any German citizen residing in the United States who remained a member of that organization would immediately have his passport withdrawn. It was imperative, he concluded, to absolutely destroy the impression that the Party was in any way in contact with or directing the German-American Bund.[23] Obviously impressed by the Dieckhoff report, the German Foreign Office instructed the ambassador to explain to the American government that while Kuhn had rejected its admonitions and those of the Auslandsorganisation to curtail his offensive activities, all German citizens in the United States had been informed of the consequences of joining his organization.[24]

As part of the lengthy campaign of persuasion that the party was not meddling in the affairs of other nations, Bohle gave the *New York Times* an interview in September of 1938, in which he denied any interest in trying to increase the influence of the Auslandsorganisation der NSDAP abroad. He said that the AO's only concern was the welfare of German citizens living abroad who held valid passports (approximately 50,000 persons), and that no branch or office of his organization existed in the United States. He explained that those Germans who had chosen to immigrate to the United States, quickly assimilated, and therefore were not in need of any care from the AO. [25]

What Bohle carefully omitted from his interview was the fact that he maintained regular contact with Party members living in the United States. He knew very well that this encouraged Bundist activity, since most of these members were in the German American Bund. He also knew that American public opinion was convinced that the AO der NSDAP secretly directed the Bund. Still unaware of some of the full extent of this intrigue, the German Foreign Office continued to receive complaints from its diplomatic personnel in the United States, who apparently received information from various sources in the German communities there, that Bohle was definitely connected to the German American Bund.[26] Incredibly, Dieckhoff still did not know of Gienanth's secret association with Goebbels, even though he continued to be employed in the German embassy in Washington, D.C. Gienanth's party file showed that he had joined the NSDAP in 1930, and had been working in the embassy in Washington, D.C., since 1935. In a postwar interrogation, Gienanth admitted that while employed there, he had supplied German Abwehr (intelligence) agents with funds from time to time.[27]

The possibility should not be ruled out that Foreign Minister Ribbentrop was privy to much of what was happening in the United States, including the Gienanth activity, and simply did not share it with Dieckhoff because he wanted Bohle and the AO to be blamed for the growing American animosity toward Germany. If this were so, then those concerned in the party leadership, including Hitler, would hold Bohle responsible for mishandling the Bundist affair. An additional factor was the amount of negative publicity directed at the AO in the American press during this time that made it appear to the public that Bohle was the mastermind behind a world wide Nazi spy network.

The AO leader obviously had mixed feelings about his unflattering reputation abroad as the director of a spy apparatus because most of it was untrue, however, in his fierce competition with Ribbentrop, he was not above garnering all the recognition he could, even if it was of a negative nature. Anything and everything that pointed to the importance of the AO der NSDAP in Germany's foreign affairs was part of the game he had been playing with the Foreign Office ever since he had become the designated leader of the "Foreign Section of the Nazi Party."

As for the American situation, Bohle did not regard it nearly as serious as Dieckhoff did. At one time, he told Martin Bormann that he did not think that the United States would take any action against the Bund, and that Germany should not openly disavow those German who were supporters of National Socialism. He felt that the United States had a high tolerance toward dissident political organizations, and the crisis would pass without long term consequences. In the meantime, the AO could continue to maintain contact.[28] Bohle was not oblivious to what was happening in America, however, and he knew that there had never been any widespread support for Hitler and National Socialism among the German American population there, and that a political movement had little or no chance to succeed. He also knew that those who had emerged as leaders in the Teutonia and the Bund were men who had left Germany after World War I, bitter and humiliated by the defeat, and were not acceptable as leaders in the mainstream German American communities. Many of them had retained their German citizenship, and some, like Gissibl, had actually joined the Nazi Party before entering the United States.

Knowing all of this, and personally never have taken any deep interest in the German American population, why did he persist in placing German-American relations in jeopardy over an issue that he could have defused ? It is true that some of the hardcore Bund members may have disputed any orders from Bohle about ending their activity and may have sought support from influential sources in Germany, but the AO leader had the ultimate authority to recall any German citizen back home, and if necessary, withdraw the passport. He almost certainly would have had the backing of the German Foreign Office and Dieckhoff in such an endeavor. Instead, he continued to try and extend his own influence and undermine Ribbentrop's position as much as possible, even at the expense of damaging foreign relations with the United States.

By 1939, however, the beginning of World War II would change the shape of international relations so profoundly that the role the Auslandsorganisation der NSDAP had occupied for the past six years would no longer have the same function, and Bohle would face challenges that he could never have anticipated.

11 The Outbreak of War

Nineteen-thirty-nine was a decisive year for Europe, as Hitler's demands for more living space (Lebensraum) for the German people continued to dominate the European diplomatic arena. German expansion had already absorbed Austria and the Sudetenland, and the remainder of the Czech state would only enjoy a temporary independence after Poland and Hungary assisted in its dissection. The fate of Czechoslovakia had been sealed at the Munich Conference in September 1938, when Great Britain and France, in the face of Hitler's blunt warning that Germany was prepared to take action, agreed to its dismantling. Encouraged by his success, and fully cognizant that the world depression and the fear of communism had weakened the capabilities of the two major western European powers to deal with a crisis that might demand a military response, Hitler seized upon the appeasement sentiment in certain political circles in Great Britain, to move to his next agenda: The Free City of Danzig and the Polish Corridor. However, no longer could the dictator's arguments that he was only revising the injustices visited upon Germany by the Versailles Treaty be defended, and finally, in March 1939, Great Britain and France promised to defend Polish independence against all aggressors.

Meanwhile, although not oblivious to the ominous direction that world events were going, Bohle was still deeply involved in his repugnant relationship with Ribbentrop, and was subject to the whims of the foreign minister's ego, such as required appearances in full dress uniform on every possible occasion.[1] After one of these events, Propaganda Minister Goebbels noted that Ribbentrop's behavior did not endear him to the people around him: "He has pushed Bohle to the wall. He wants to build a city within a state, where he rules."[2]

Always anxious to present his Gau as aggressively supporting the Third Reich, Bohle exhorted his people to show a greater enthusiasm for public causes, and specifically named a Nazi welfare organization (NSV, or Volkswohlfahrt). It had a membership in the millions and was praised every year at the party congress for its good work among the needy. In a note to his employees, Bohle complained that too few of the AO people belonged, and cited the importance of such work not only among the Germans at home, but those abroad as well. He urged that each and everyone subscribe to a monthly sum for the NSV, and become a model for other agencies.[3]

He could have added that he wanted his AO to be a model in other ways, too. One idea he initiated was the creation of a leadership program that would prepare younger people to assume more responsible positions within the organization. In a daily communiqué to his people in May 1939, he explained that when he had come to his post in 1933, he already had certain goals in mind, and now, with new challenges facing the nation, he had decided the time was right to develop a group of selected young party members to receive special training under his personal direction. There were no formal training sessions. Instead, from time to time, he would provide the group with certain directives to fulfill that would, hopefully, bring out the creativeness that he knew resided there.[4] Actually, in practice, the Gauleiter had been doing something along these lines for some time. He had always shown an interest in promoting more youthful members of the party with a better education than the older rank and file, such as his longtime assistant, Emil Ehrich. Although a faithful party member himself, Bohle never emphasized this as a requirement for promotion to his employees.

As the international situation worsened, however, and the government concentrated more and more funds on armaments, Bohle found financing his projects became increasingly difficult. In developing his arguments with Reichsschatzmeister Schwarz for more funding, Bohle emphasized the mounting hostility against Germany in many countries around the world, and the need to mount programs to counter these feelings. The Gauleiter insisted that Schwarz's contention that the AO was doing the same thing in some instances that the Foreign Office was doing, was wrong, and that the needs of the Germans abroad were not being met by the Foreign Office. In his plea for more money, Bohle cited the growing crisis of thousands of German citizens who were clamoring to return home, and the huge costs involved in providing adequate transport. Among those eligible for return were approximately thirty thousand party members.[5]

The discussion with the Nazi Party Schatzmeister occurred shortly after Hitler's demands upon Poland for the Corridor and Danzig, and this may well have prompted Bohle's request for more money, for he knew that any territorial changes would bring more Germans into the Reich, and more resettlement responsibilities for the AO. He was already aware that there might be a possible move by Hitler into the Polish Corridor and Danzig, and the previous October ordered the development of evacuation plans for the Germans living in the Baltic region in the event of war. At the very date of his talk with Schwarz, Bohle's office was busily drafting plans for the evacuation of all German citizens from Poland.[6]

On June first, Bohle received a secret message from Goebbels's Propaganda Ministry directing that all the German citizens currently in Poland be advised through the AO representatives there that an attack upon that country was possible. The message emphasized that this information was to be passed by word-of-mouth only. Actually, only two months previously, Bohle had begun investigating the problem of providing gas masks for German citizens living on Germany's borders, but the process had stalled in attempting to estimate the numbers involved and exactly where they would be needed first. Just how such equipment could pass through border customs, if at all, and not bring instant political repercussions, was not answered. Although Bohle was worried that he would be unable to keep such an operation secret very long, neither could he ignore Goebbels's advisory, and plans proceeded apace.[7]

By this time the AO leader was obviously aware of Hitler's plan to attack Poland, although he may not have known the exact date. He admitted that a major worry was the possibility of widespread panic among the Germans there as soon as word circulated that Germany was preparing an evacuation of its citizens. This could cause all the roads and rail lines leading to Germany to become filled with fleeing refugees, and block the passage of German troops into Poland. He suggested that the best way to proceed was to warn all Germans in Poland by radio of certain border cross points when the invasion was launched.[8]

In the meantime, and under the utmost secrecy, the plan to provide gas masks to the German citizens in Poland had been abandoned, and instead the decision was made that they should be told orally through the AO leaders there that they should prepare for an evacuation. They should also be warned not to seek refuge in the German embassy in Warsaw, for the city would be under attack. Once the invasion began, the Germans were cautioned to stay off the streets, and if possible, take refuge in a foreign consulate, such as the Dutch. On August 25, Bohle notified the German embassy in Warsaw that all of the German citizens residing in Poland were prepared for evacuation, and at the same time he contacted the German embassies in London and Paris, and advised that all of the German citizens in those two nations leave for Germany by the fastest means available to them.[9]

Although the messages and correspondence relating to these unfolding events were transmitted in the strictest of secrecy, it was clear to most observers that Germany was moving toward military action, and Bohle's advisories were coming after the fact, because most of the German citizens who were affected had already departed for home. The documentation does establish, however, that Bohle knew well in advance that Hitler planned to go to war against Poland, and was preparing accordingly for his changing role.[10]

Shortly before the invasion plan for Poland (Case White) was executed, the world was astonished by the joint announcement of the governments of Germany and the Soviet Union that a non-aggression pact had been signed. A secret protocol called for the division of Poland, and territorial changes in the Baltic states that surrendered control to Russia. Soon after the launching of the invasion on September 1, both Great Britain and France, in responding to their pledge to preserve Polish independence, declared war against Germany, although neither nation was capable of preventing the German aggression nor the ultimate defeat of Poland. Thus began the Second World War.

A major responsibility for the Auslandsorganisation became the management and directing of massive integration and relocation programs as millions of Germans, both citizens and non-citizens, who resided in the conquered areas now were absorbed into a greater Germany. The multiple tasks for the AO involved resettlement, clarifying citizenship status, arranging employment and providing housing for these people. Whether Bohle instantly recognized that all of these new duties would place limitations upon his ability to pursue his ambitions in the diplomatic field is difficult to ascertain from his correspondence at the time, however, the sheer volume of work on matters little connected to foreign policy must have caused him moments of reflection about the future of the Auslandsorganisation. The war also brought changes to the ruling Nazi hierarchy that was disturbing to the AO leader. His mentor and longtime protector, Deputy Führer Rudolf Hess, seemed to be moving further and further away from the center of decision making in the circle of people around Hitler. Of course, Bohle could not exert any influence on the situation, but considering the amount of interaction that his office had with the Deputy Führer, he certainly must have been aware of the concern Hess had in searching for a peace with Great Britain.

A matter of great importance for Germany was just how the war was viewed in neutral countries, and judging public opinion was crucial in determining that. In addition to monitoring the news media, the really in depth reports had to come from the German diplomatic service and the members of the AO. Bohle recognized the vital role that his organization could play in the process, and knew that not only could his people provide valuable insights, but could be central to the distribution of propaganda materials that presented the German side of the war. In this connection, one of his first proposals was to give widespread exposure to a document compiled by the German Foreign Office called the "Whitebook" (Weissbuch, Zweites). It contained copies of some of notes exchanged with France and Great Britain between 1 and 3 September, 1939, with the object of establishing Germany's innocence in the start of the conflict. Bohle wrote that he regarded it as very important that Germans living in the neutral countries receive copies, and that the document be printed in other languages as well. Armed with the information in the Whitebook, Bohle felt that the Germans abroad would have a basis for discussing Germany's role in the war with the people among whom they lived, and could even provide copies to those who were interested. Ribbentrop's office agreed with Bohle's suggestion and offered to provide copies of the Weissbuch for the AO Landesgruppen to distribute.[11] It was an offer that Ribbentrop could not deny to the AO, even though the document had originated with the Foreign

Office, but the idea had come from Bohle, and he still held the position of a state secretary.

At the same time, Bohle issued instructions to all AO and Foreign Office personnel concerning any contact in those countries that were regarded as unfriendly. Always defend the standpoint, he wrote, that Germany was forced into the war. Do not unnecessarily socialize with the citizens of these nations, and if an invitation is received from a neutral and guests from an unfriendly nation are going to be present, do not attend. In the event of encounters with persons known to be from unfriendly nations, do not greet them first. Above, he cautioned, be careful that your actions do not arouse suspicion that you are engaged in any illegal activities.[12]

As soon the outbreak of war was announced, the Auslandsorganisation's Berlin headquarters was inundated with telephone calls and telegrams from Germans around the world, both citizens and non-citizens alike. The immediate concern was fear that the funds they were receiving from Germany would be interrupted. Bohle was already hearing from some of his Landesgruppenleiter that an emergency fund was needed, and several of them had started soliciting money from the German communities in which they resided. Following upon this, Bohle telegraphed the German consuls throughout the United States to spread the word among the hundreds of thousands of German Americans living there that a small donation would help sustain the German citizens in their communities until they could be transported back to Germany.[13]

Bohle knew that his organization was responsible for providing the major share of help needed by Germany's citizens abroad, but he also knew that it would require resources well beyond his own budget, and therefore, he called upon the Foreign Office to work together with his people in providing the necessary assistance. In his role as state secretary, Bohle informed the Foreign Office diplomatic mission heads and office supervisors abroad that they would be held personally responsible for seeing that the help was provided.. It is expected, he wrote, that advice and assistance be given those Germans seeking it, and that offices be open night and day.[14]

The content of Bohle's messages during these first days of war, and the proposals he was making, indicated a new assurance in his position as AO leader and state secretary in the Foreign Office. He felt, no doubt, that with the new responsibilities placed on the AO that this gave him sufficient reason to exert his authority, and if necessary, challenge Ribbentrop on certain issues. Bohle was secure in his knowledge that as the party champion for the care and concern for the Germans living abroad, he was in a strong position to suggest measures that Ribbentrop would have vetoed just weeks before. The Auslandsorganisation as a listening post with eyes and ears around the world, constituted an extremely valuable asset for a country at war. There were AO Landesgruppen in virtually every important neutral nation on the globe, and each was fully capable of compiling reports on almost any subject that was of interest to Germany's intelligence organizations, not the least of which was public opinion. During the second week of the war, Bohle dispatched a secret message to all Foreign Office personnel abroad informing them that it was also important for them to aid in the monitoring of public opinion, and requested information on how German citizens were being treated in the neutral states. He asked that special attention be given to the attitudes exhibited by officials toward the Germans, and suggested that it might be a good idea to coordinate reports with the local AO party member.[15]

As early as April of 1939, the German government had ordered that all German citizens abroad who were eligible for military service, return home as soon as possible in the event of war. At news of war's outbreak, the Auslandsorganisation was immediately contacted by hundreds of men who fell into this category, and who requested assistance to return home. They needed not only money, but some mode of transportation as well. While the Foreign Office offered its cooperation, Bohle was informed that available funds were very limited. This was not an answer that the Gauleiter was willing to accept, and he immediately notified all concerned diplomatic personnel that he wanted them to submit as soon as possible a monthly accounting of their expenses. He suspected that some of the older veteran diplomats were putting funds into foreign investments, and asked that everyone who was required to fill out the sworn monthly statements to list all assets they owned abroad: "I believe," he wrote, "that it is only natural that in these difficult times that the employees make all possible wealth available to the Reich."[16]

Even as the war proceeded, Bohle continued to prepare his recommendations for the list of speakers the AO would send to German communities abroad to commemorate Hitler's November 1923 march on the Feldherrnhalle in Munich. This was regarded as one of the most important dates in the party's history, even though the attempted putsch was a failure and Hitler went to prison. Bohle was convinced that there would be no problem with the commemoration in Denmark, Sweden, Norway, Spain, Portugal, Italy, Yugoslavia, Bulgaria, and Rumania. Greece, Switzerland, Holland, and Belgium he listed as question marks. Without explaining why, he decided that no speakers would be dispatched to Luxemburg, Hungary, or Turkey.[17]

Meanwhile, he had the problem of assisting in the evacuation of German citizens from the Baltic region. This had been agreed upon in the secret protocol signed by Germany and the Soviet Union in August: "It is understood that this resettlement requested by Germany will be undertaken by Germany in cooperation with local authorities, and will thereby protect the property rights of the emigrant. Germany agrees to a like responsibility in her areas of interest for resident persons of Ukranian or White Russian descent."[18] Actually, while the Baltic states did not welcome Russian occupation, there was also a history there of anti-German domination, and this had increased since the beginning of the war.

It now became the task of the AO to implement the secret protocol, but the job was not made easy by the absence of AO Landesgruppen in the Soviet Union, so Bohle had to make do with German citizens in the area who volunteered. This was a large undertaking considering that the region consisted of Lithuania, Latvia, Estonia, and even parts of the Soviet Union and Poland. As for the non-German citizens in the area, who wished to go to Germany, that job was left to the Volksdeutsche Mittelstelle (VoMi). The Auslandsorganisation had a list of 648 names of German citizens living in Latvia, including 154 who were Jewish, but all of them opted to return to Germany. Estonia had over 1,000 German citizens and Latvia had some 3,000, who desired to return to Germany. VoMi was inundated with requests from almost 80,000 persons of German origin or descent, who wanted relocation to Germany.[19]

By early October, the AO was ready to start the evacuations, and Bohle knew that it had to go rapidly because the Russians were preparing for their occupation. The Gauleiter needed ships and enlisted the cooperation of the Foreign Office to secure them, and he requested armed guards to be aboard because he knew that some of the evacuees would try to bring goods with them that could not be accommodated. He also suggested that medical supplies and personnel be aboard the ships. Within hours after the receipt of Bohle's requests, the Foreign Office informed him that a naval force was in the process of assembling at Danzig with the express mission of transporting the German citizens from Latvia and Estonia. Other vessels were being dispatched to Memel and Pillau for use as needed. In addition, all diplomatic personnel in the legations at Riga and Rival were standing by to process all of the departure documents . It was suggested to Bohle that he designate people from the AO to remain behind to safeguard Germany's financial interests until a final settlement was arranged.[20]

Wasting no time, the people Bohle had designated to remain behind were already busily liquidating all of Germany's available assets. All the proceeds were to be deposited with Germany's embassies, and transactions processed through a specially created company, the German Resettlement Trustee Co., or D.U.T. Bohle called the entire affair a delicate matter, and faulted VoMi for trying to favor the ethnic Germans over the German citizens: "For this reason", he wrote, "and in order to safeguard the interests of those Germans for whom I am responsible, namely the German nationals, I put one of my men in an honorary capacity on the supervisory board of the D.T.U., exclusively for the purpose of safeguarding the financial interests of those returnees who were German citizens."

The evacuation of the Germans from the Baltic region was not the only assignment Bohle had to deal with, because he had to oversee the removal of German citizens from Russia, as well. On the eve of the First World War, there were approximately 21,000 German citizens living there, and the majority of them held responsible positions in mining and land management, and enjoyed considerable prestige and respect. This had all changed with the Russian Revolution, and by the time of Bohle's mission, there were only some ten thousand German citizens there. In Bohle's opinion, most of these people would opt to return to Germany, however, his inquires had revealed that some four hundred of these persons languished in Russian jails, but he could not verify this.[21]

When he delved deeper into the reasons some of these German citizens were incarcerated, Bohle found that they were charged with crimes such as espionage, encouraging acts of terrorism, and spreading fascist propaganda. Many of them had resided in the Soviet Union since the 1920s, and Count Friedrich von Schulenburg, the German ambassador there, had supplied Bohle with most of the information on the prisoners. Schulenburg told Bohle that there were exactly 484 German citizens being held, and of that number, 378 of the prisoners were still being investigated, and 106 of them had already received sentences for up to eight years. He said that some of the men had been in custody for over two years without any charges being made, and it was his opinion that the moment had arrived when Germany could secure the release of all of its citizens in the Soviet Union. The ambassador had also worked in behalf of the Russian wives (154) of some of the German citizens, and had had meetings with Foreign Minister Molotov, and had secured a promise that they could leave with their husbands.[22]

Evacuating German citizens from the Baltic and Soviet Russia, was only part of the picture. Bohle had to contend with the clamor from German citizens around the world who wanted to return home. It began almost immediately after the attack upon Poland, and Bohle was informed by his own Landesgruppenleiter and German diplomatic missions there. Aside from the logistical nightmare and financial burden, the immediate concern of the Auslandsorganisation was the impact upon the German citizens in the neutral lands, plus the reactions from those governments about it. Any number of questions regarding these people were raised, such as what restrictions would be placed upon their movements? Were their properties safe from confiscation? What about discrimination in public?

The concerns of the Germans abroad were not uniform because some of them lived in countries that had already shown open disdain for the Hitler government, and then there were states that took no position on the war, or openly supported the Nazis. National attitudes were somewhat predictable depending upon their proximity to Germany. Therefore, smaller states in western and central Europe anxious about Hitler's expansion plans, were far more accommodating toward their German residents, both citizens and non-citizens, than national states elsewhere. In the early period of the war, many of the Germans living in these neighboring states, informed Bohle of conditions and the AO received lengthy reports from their own people, and the German Foreign Office, too.

A German diplomat employed in the embassy in Budapest wrote to Bohle in September: "In certain sections of the population", he wrote, "there is a distinct sympathy for the Poles and, stemming from the fear that a powerful German Reich can one day shrink Hungary's independence, an unfriendly stance toward Germany." However, he added that in the capitol city, where some 15,000 German citizens reside, the posture of the government and the civilians is very correct.[23] A somewhat similar report came from a German diplomat serving in Belgrade ("The treatment of German citizens in Yugoslavia has not changed since the beginning of the European conflict"). Another diplomat in Bucharest wrote that the German citizens in Rumania had no reason to complain about their treatment by the authorities or the civilian population. A third German diplomat, employed in the embassy in Sofia, also informed Bohle, that since the outbreak of war the attitude of both the authorities and the civilians in Bulgaria had not changed noticeably.[24]

The reports that came to the AO from the smaller border states was not as uniformly reassuring, and while their attitude toward Germany was not unfriendly, understandably, they did not wish to give Hitler a reason for launching an attack. It was no secret that Holland, Belgium, Switzerland, and the Scandinavian states had long since viewed the actions of the Auslandsorganisation der NSDAP as undesirable. This fact was known to the German Foreign Office, and the diplomatic corps kept its distance on the internal politics of those states, although it continued to monitor attitudes and opinions, and inform the AO. Of course, there were people from the AO who were employed in the Foreign Office.

One such was Dr. Otto Butting, Bohle's man in Holland, who was on the German diplomatic staff in the Hague. He notified that while the Dutch official attitude toward the German citizens there was correct, they had recently announced that the flying of a foreign flag was forbidden. He had noticed, Butting wrote, that while the behavior of the upper class Dutch was reserved, there was a very distinct hostility coming from the lower classes. The entire lower class has been quite outspoken since the beginning of the war. They are very open in their criticism of the Germans and the Führer. To date, he concluded, there have been no real outbursts of anger. Butting did complain, however, that while the German Foreign Office was increasing its staff in Holland, his own promotion to consul general was stalled. He hinted that he could be far more effective in the AO if the promotion came through.[25]

A report on conditions in Belgium that came from the German embassy in Brussels stated that since war's begin, the officials and citizens have conducted themselves quite correctly toward the German citizens. Insults, daily attacks, or violence have not happened here, the report read, but the situation is different in the Limburger mining area where the communists have made life quite difficult for the Germans living there. When the Auslandsorganisation assisted some of the Germans to leave, the Belgium border police and the custom officials were quite rude.[26]

In early October, the German General Consul in Zurich described the treatment that the German citizens were receiving in Switzerland as correct, although in some instances the police had exhibited an unfriendly attitude. Usually, this was in the form of insulting words, and this was replied to in formal complaints to the higher authorities. It should be understood, of course, that such complaints were weighed on the basis of their seriousness, and this varied from canton to canton, the report continued. Those with strong social democratic parties were often the most stringent in enforcing any fractions against German citizens, but in other cantons the hostility was evident as Germans were dismissed from their jobs.[27]

In the case of Sweden, where the AO still had a functioning unit, although the Landesgruppenleiter, Heinrich Bartels, had been expelled before the war began, Bohle was concerned about the strong negative tone of the press. In November, he registered a formal complaint through the German Foreign Office, and warned the Swedish government that continued attacks in the press could damage relations between the two countries. When the Swedish press continued to criticize the presence of the Auslandsorganisation, Bohle initiated a new tactic to register his displeasure by demanding that Sweden hand over the Germans who had taken refuge there from the Third Reich. In reply, the Swedes pretended complete innocence and said that a camp had been established for all kinds of European refugees, and that just who came from where, had not yet been determined. Bohle immediately recognized this as a stalling tactic and wired the German embassy in Stockholm that he would not accept it as an explanation. He stated that as the Gauleiter of the AO der NSDAP, he had the responsibility to look after the safety of all German citizens residing abroad, and he fully intended to do so. He knew that some of the Germans in the camp still held German citizenship, and he demanded their names, and the details of how they came to be in the camp.[28] No mention was made of the fact that Bohle, and other authorities in the Reich, regarded the interned refugees as having secured some protection from the Swedish government because they opposed the Hitler regime.

In reply, the Swedish government finally admitted that there were about fifty persons in the camp that were of German "origin," but assured Bohle that they was no reason for concern because they were adequately guarded. Bohle answered that he had received confidential information that some of these Germans were enemies of the Reich, and that the security was very lax. The Gauleiter threatened that if these individuals were not surrendered to Germany, then the refusal would have to be interpreted as an unfriendly act. Retreating under the pressure, Swedish authorities promised a thorough investigation of the problem, and implied a friendly solution.[29]

The early war reports from the German diplomats in Denmark and Norway, to the AO, were written with the same platitudes that their fellow diplomats in the other neutral countries had employed. Officially, everything looked correct in the capitol cities of Oslo and Copenhagen, although German citizens were treated with reserve by the more educated persons there. In both countries popular opinion seemed to favor the English over the Germans, it was reported.[30]

As might be anticipated, German consular reports that came in the early days of the war from Spain and Italy were fully supportive of Hitler's actions. In fact, the German consul in Tetuan informed Berlin that he was receiving inquiries from young Spanish men about the possibility of joining the German army. A November report from Madrid described conditions as very friendly toward Germany, although it noted that a group of Spanish communists near the northern border by France refused to recognize the friendship agreement that had been signed by Ribbentrop and Molotov last August.[31]

An interesting note from the German consul in Genoa, Italy, on the conditions there stated that he was working very closely with the local AO Ortsgruppe to handle large numbers of German citizens who were pouring in from France, Spain, Portugal, North Africa, and even Brazil. Unfortunately, the consul wrote Bohle, most of them did not have enough money to get to the German border, and they come to the consulate and beg for funds to catch a ship to Germany. The AO Ortsgruppe is working side by side with the consulate to assist them as much as possible.[32]

From the numerous communications that came into the Foreign Office in Berlin from around the world, very few reported any instances of open hostility toward the German communities. The main problem for both Bohle and the Foreign Office was the lack of funds to deal with the huge number of German citizens who wanted to return home. In the case of those men eligible for military service, both agencies had an obligation to transport them back without delay. It meant that there was a necessity to cooperate closely, a situation that each leader tried to capitalize upon, but Bohle had the advantage because it allowed the AO to exert an authority that Ribbentrop would surely have resisted if it had not been wartime. Many of the messages that came into the Foreign Office, however, expressed some gratitude that the AO people in the field were proving so helpful, and not leaving the logistics to the diplomats alone. One problem that cropped up stemmed from the number of complaints that poured in from Holland, Greece, Italy, and Portugal, regarding the number of German domestics who were "good time girls." Since all of them had valid passports, and many of them worked in port cities, the concern was that they would fall prey to an enemy of Germany, and provide information that would be helpful. Bohle immediately issued instructions that all of the women born since 1900 were to return home.[33]

The fall of 1939, had proven a busy one for Ernst Wilhelm Bohle, and had witnessed dramatic changes for the Auslandsorganisation. For most Germans, the entrance into the war against Poland and the declaration of war toward Germany from Great Britain and France had not resulted in such drastic measures on the home front. To all appearances, the war, now dubbed the Sitzkrieg, looked like it would be mediated to a peaceful resolution. Both Great Britain and France would ultimately have to admit that they could not preserve Poland's independence, and accept the situation as it was. To many observers it was a vindication of Hitler's expansionist policy. As for Bohle, those final months of 1939 seemed to open a new avenue for the Gauleiter in presenting opportunities to exert his authority in enlarging the role of the AO at the expense of the Ribbentrop and Foreign Office.

12 New Responsibilities

The European states that had assumed a position of neutrality when Germany invaded Poland in September 1939, soon found themselves unable to maintain that status very long. After a winter of little action in the west Sitzkrieg), German forces suddenly invaded Denmark, Norway, Holland, Luxemburg, and Belgium in April–May of 1940. France, next on the list, agreed to an armistice that permitted the southern portion of the state to remain virtually unoccupied as the Paris government took up its function in the town of Vichy. With all of western and northern Europe under German domination, and now with plans to incorporate it into a greater Germany, and place some of the administration under military authorities, the functions of the AO in that entire area became somewhat superfluous.

The war was also making it increasingly difficult for the AO to maintain its contacts worldwide, and Bohle had to continually devise new ways to communicate with his Landesgruppen. Even in the neutral states, life was becoming more difficult for the German communities, and hostilities were mounting as more and more details of the German occupations became public. Even as the role of the AO was diminishing abroad as a factor in the lives of the Germans who lived outside of Europe, Bohle was being given a new role that promised more of the responsibilities that heretofore had been the province of the Foreign Office. This was certainly not the choice of Ribbentrop, but as the volume of work increased, the Foreign Office could not do it without the assistance of the AO. In fact, Bohle boasted in 1940, that the Auslandsorganisation now occupied some three hundred rooms in central Berlin (Westfälischenstrasse) and had a staff of over six hundred.[1]

The AO was given a wide variety of tasks covering some unusual situations. For example, a list of dos and don'ts regarding visiting Soviet seamen in German ports to supplying passports for the German sailors stranded in South American ports. Bohle decided that current policy on the treatment of the Soviet seamen was sufficient, however, he cautioned that there should be no reasons for any complaints. The Gauleiter also decided that the order that he forward all reports from his office on the conduct of the Soviet seamen to Hitler be ignored. His rationale was that a communist was a communist, and their behavior did not really change.[2]

During that first year 1939–1940, there was a conflict between the Soviet Union and Finland (Winter War), and Bohle found one of his tasks to be the evacuation of all German citizens from Finland in March 1940. He was cautioned by Ribbentrop that the operation had to be done very carefully, and above all, not to arouse too much attention abroad. Ribbentrop was, of course, concerned that Russia not be offended by anything in the process, and insisted that the AO not issue any instructions to their people in Finland. The German foreign minister was adamant that there be no press coverage concerning the affair, and that the German citizens who were going to be relocated, be individuals who had expressed the desire to return home to the Reich.[3] Apparently the evacuation was successful, although it can be assumed that Bohle was not enthusiastic about receiving any orders from Ribbentrop.

In his next assignment, the Gauleiter was able to flex some of his diplomatic muscle. By the spring of 1940 Germany had more than two thousand British citizens interned, most of them having been in the Third Reich since before the war began. As the "expert" on British life, Bohle was consulted by the Foreign Office with a request that he advise on their care. Bohle suggested that for diet, mail, etc., that Germany copy the manner in which German interned citizens were being treated by those nations at war with the Third Reich.[4] Although Bohle appeared pleased to participate in the assignment, it did not mean any softening of relations between him and the foreign minister. In fact, a note from a young diplomat in Ribbentrop's office at the time, stated that he was told by his superior that the foreign minister was intent on ridding the Foreign Office of the party influence, as it had become too strong: "Especially the removal of the leader of the AO, State Secretary Bohle."[5]

Actually, Bohle's first involvement with war prisoners occurred when the AO negotiated to free German citizens interned by the Dutch authorities in the East Indies, which happened after the German invasion of Holland in May 1940. When word came that the German citizens, including the consular staff at Batavia, had been arrested, Bohle immediately responded by threatening to take some Dutch citizens as hostages, and subject them to the same conditions. He said that the Dutch in the East Indies who were responsible must have relatives in Holland, and these individuals can be interned.[6] Bohle had already made it clear to all of the AO personnel abroad, that they must take a strong stand against any abuse of German citizens, and warn those authorities concerned that their citizens would become targets of the same treatment. Never forget, he directed, that Germany is at war, and when delivering your responses, make sure it is done with alacrity and energy.[7]

The German Reichskomissar for occupied Holland, Artur von Seyss-Inquart, informed Bohle that 400 Dutch citizens had already been arrested, although 500 of them had been released for heath reasons, 259 of them were sent to the Buchenwald concentration camp, and the remainder awaited transport elsewhere. Seyss-Inquart said that he intended to wait a week before arresting some more Dutch people, and that the previous action had already created a wide sensation in Holland. He suggested that perhaps it was time to select a prominent Dutchman, and have him telephone the authorities in the Dutch East Indies, and inform them of the happenings at home.[8]

In providing Ribbentrop with a report on the living conditions of the German citizens interned in the East Indies, Bohle said that informants in both Japan and the Philippines had notified the AO that some 1,500 of them were not receiving adequate food nor decent sanitary facilities. The German foreign minister replied that there must be more stringent measures taken in Holland, and no warnings given when arrests were to be made. Women and children should be arrested , and no one of prominence should be spared. Thereupon, Bohle asked Seyss-Inquart to compile a list of the most influential Dutchmen with Far East connections, and who had relatives in the Dutch East Indies. The Gauleiter expressed some doubt, however, that since Germany already had almost one thousand Dutch people interned in Germany, that the arrest of an additional five hundred Dutchmen could have serious consequences for the economy in Holland. The doubt quickly vanished though when a Swiss diplomat serving in the Dutch East Indies reported that the German citizens had been moved to the island of Onrust in the Bay of Batavia, where the living quarters were damp, and the food and medical care woefully inadequate. As a result of this turn of events, Bohle secured a Führer order to have the additional Dutchmen arrested, and brought to Germany for internment.[9]

Meanwhile, Seyss-Inquart supplied Bohle with the names of several Dutch collaborators, with the suggestion that they be sent to Switzerland and open telephone negotiations with the authorities in the Dutch East Indies. His idea was that the interned German citizens be moved to better quarters, and placed under the control of a neutral commission. Bohle rejected all of this absolutely, however, replying that Holland was a country under German occupation, and there was no need to bargain. He demanded that all of the German citizens be released unconditionally and given all the necessary emergency services required, as well as immediate access to German diplomatic personnel.[10]

Bohle's tough stance was immediately endorsed by Hitler, who authorized the taking of Dutch hostages at a ratio of 10 to 1, and since the AO leader said that there was reliable information that some three thousand German citizens had been arrested, this meant that at least thirty thousand Dutch were now subject to arrest and deportation to Germany. This new development, however, created a rift between the Gauleiter and Seyss-Inquart, who protested that this would present him with serious problems in trying to administer the occupation of Holland, but Bohle could not be persuaded to back off, and was convinced that the quick arrests that he advocated would bring fast results.[11]

Unable to convince the Gauleiter to change his mind, Seyss-Inquart appealed directly to Hitler, who obviously accepted the Reichskommissar's argument, for he ordered Bohle to cease all activity in Holland immediately. It was obviously a setback for the Gauleiter, and remained a bitter memory for years to come, as evidenced by a postwar statement: "That was a decision taken by and at the instigation of Seyss-Inquart at a meeting of Hitler's, and I was told afterward that it had been decided to withdraw the AO."[12]

In an attempt to preserve the appearance of party harmony, it was decided that Bohle would go to Holland personally to preside over the dissolution of AO operations there. When he appeared in Utrecht in October, he told the assembled AO people that it had become necessary to place the country under a separate occupational authority for administrative reasons, and that all party members would be transferred to AO jurisdiction. He praised the group for their loyal service and named them one of the best units of the Auslands-Organisation. Their conduct, he said, had brought great credit to the Third Reich, and they had upheld the highest traditions of National Socialism.[13]

The pressures were mounting for Bohle and the AO, as increasing numbers of requests for travel home were pouring into his Berlin office from German citizens around the world. The process was dubbed the "Heimschaffungsaktion" (Operation: Assistance to Return Home), and had become largely Bohle's responsibility. The expenses were heavy, and for 1940 the AO leader had requested over RM 300,000, although this did not appear adequate to handle the demands. Although the Foreign Office agreed to pay some of the costs, the German citizens who applied for travel funds were advised to use their own resources.[14]

Ultimately, it was left to Bohle to decide who would receive the available aid and who would not. He did so on the basis of who had the strongest party record, and empowered his Landesgruppenleitern to make the decisions, and reminded them that they should be guided by the people who reflected the best spirit of National Socialism It was a big responsibility, because the initial costs had to come from the respective Landesgruppe and the local German consul. Every applicant was required to have a request on file with the AO Rückwandereramt, and the local German consul. All travel permits had to be signed by an authorized party member.[15]

Bohle was also confronted with another travel problem, and one that was unusual, even for war time. In December 1939, the German battleship *Admiral Graf Spee* had taken refuge in the harbor of Montevideo, Uruguay, to escape British cruisers. The problem was that the vessel could not remain for too long. Under orders from Hitler, the captain was directed to scuttle the ship rather than allow it to fall into British hands. It had a crew of over one thousand sailors, who were set ashore. Some of them were interned in Uruguay, but others fled to Argentina and Brazil with the assistance of AO people. In an effort to return the escaped seamen to Germany, Bohle contacted the Italian Ambassador Zamloni in Berlin with a plan. The Gauleiter told the ambassador that some of the seamen were in Rio de Janeiro, and since Italy had not yet entered the war, he suggested that perhaps the Italian airline Lati, still operating in Latin America, could transport the Germans, a few at a time, on a mail flight to Rome.[16]

Bohle was soon informed that Graf Ciano, Italy's foreign minister, had approved the plan, and Lati had been ordered to stand by to accept the German seamen. Since there was concern about what the governments of Argentina and Brazil might say if news of the plan leaked out, it was decided that each of the German seamen be given a new name and passport. Bohle instantly agreed, and knew that he had to work fast and get the documents into the seamen's hands as quickly as possible. Before the end of October 1940, all of the seamen in question had reached home, and Bohle said it had only been possible with the good work of the AO Landegruppe in Argentina.[17] The AO leader had managed a very difficult assignment, for both Uruguay and Argentina were under heavy pressure from the United States to outlaw all activity of the German government in their respective countries. In fact, in anticipation of Uruguay deporting members of the AO Landegruppe there, Bohle had already notified the Landesgeruppenleiter that all party functions should cease because relations with Germany were at the breaking point.[18]

Conditions were just as precarious in Argentina, where charges of spying and sabotage had been lodged against some members of the AO Landesgruppe there. Even though Bohle had ordered the Landesgruppe dissolved, several of the members were jailed while awaiting deportation proceedings. Using the same tactics that he had employed in the situation Holland, Bohle directed that a list be compiled of all of the Argentine citizens residing in Germany, and indicated that they would be held as hostages until the German citizens in Argentina were freed The AO leader knew that relations could not have been worse, and recognized that the work of his organization was finished in Latin America, at least, for the time being. However, as he confided to a friend, the return of all of the German citizens to the Reich would only provide people to settle the new regions that had been acquired in Europe.[19]

Bohle did keep the Foreign Office informed of the measures that were being taken against German citizens in other neutral areas of the world, and he was frank in his appraisal of the situation. In April of 1940, he informed all diplomatic personnel that the hostility toward German citizens abroad had increased measurably in the neutral nations since the beginning of the war. This was calculated by the number of cancellations in work and residence permits, and even a few arrests. While the violation of local law may have been the reason in certain instances, Bohle wrote, it was really an outgrowth of the growing hostile attitude toward Germany. When such incidents are encountered, he continued, it is the duty of every German diplomat to react in the strongest manner possible in providing the individual in question with all the protection available. The central authorities are to be made aware that their citizens in Germany are now vulnerable to similar treatment, and serious social and economic measures may result. No consideration was to be given the fact that some of these neutral states had very few citizens residing in Germany, and that there were many German citizens in the country under question. The main point is, he emphasized, was quick and decisive action from the German representative on the scene, who must work in concert with the AO person locally. The deciding factor is to show foreign governments that Germany will act in an energetic and resolute manner. [20]

In spite of Bohle's tough-sounding talk, there were some neutrals who were not to be bluffed by his threats, For example, in Sweden, where the interned Germans had still not been released as late as October 1940, the question had been referred back to the German ambassador. He was told by the Swedish government that while some of the Germans did not have proper papers, there were others with expired visas, and some who were claiming asylum as political refugees. None of these individuals were being prevented from leaving Sweden, or visiting the offices of the German ambassador in Stockholm. In fact, each of these persons had been fully informed of their rights, but not one of them had requested permission to see the German ambassador. If Germany presented evidence that any one of these persons had committed a crime, then that individual would be turned over to German authorities. In conclusion, the Swedish government suggested that all of the people in the interment camp remain under Sweden's control. [21]

This was not a satisfactory answer for Bohle, and he soon let the German ambassador in Stockholm know. In a message headed the "Swedish concentration camp," Bohle complained that the answer was far too vague, and the excuse that there were people there of German origin whose background had not yet been determined, was not good enough. The Swedish government knew exactly who they were and why they had taken refuge in Sweden. The Gauleiter also challenged Sweden on their definition of the right of asylum as applying to those individuals who still held German citizenship. He urged that these views be communicated to the Swedish government as quickly as possible, and with the request that the German government be allowed to examine all cases in question and make the final judgment. [22]

This was not an unusual tactic for Germany to utilize when searching for German citizens abroad who were wanted for their anti-Nazi activities. The hunt was especially vigorous when any of them engaged in campaigning against the Nazi regime. Bohle knew only too well that the Swedish government understood the game he was playing, but they were not easily intimidated, even though the game continued. Working through the German diplomatic representatives in Stockholm, Bohle ordered that all of the German internees that could be identified as citizens of Germany be stripped of their citizenship. [23] Of course, this did not alter the situation for the Germans in the camp, and they remained under the protection of the Swedish government throughout the war period.

These negotiations with Sweden were suddenly swept aside when Bohle heard that his mentor, and party leader, Rudolf Hess had flown by himself to Great Britain. This bizarre event even pushed the war news from the front pages of the world's press, and sent shock waves through the Nazi hierarchy. Josef Goebbels wrote: "One simply can't grasp what has happened. I was called to the Berghof, and the Führer is absolutely shattered. What a view for the world: a mentally ruined man...horrible and unthinkable...at the moment I don't know any way out."[24]

The significance of the Hess flight to Bohle's subsequent career can not be exaggerated. The AO leader may well have been the only ranking Nazi to have known in advance of Hess's intention to leave Germany for the purpose of making contact with the English to discuss a peace arrangement. Sometime in October of 1940, Hess had summoned Bohle to his office in Berlin, and informed him that he had been at work on the idea of ending the war with Great Britain. Because Bohle was regarded as the English expert in Nazi circles, Hess requested his assistance in translating some relevant material. He was aware that Hess had been considering something, because after the surrender of France in June 1940, Hess was convinced that this would persuade England to seek an armistice.[25] According to a postwar account, Bohle explained: "I was suddenly called to the office of Hess in the Wilhelmstrasse late at night where he received me alone and told me that he had some special work for me to do. He then revealed to me that he wished to contract the Duke of Hamilton, whose acquaintance he had made at the Olympic Games in 1936, with the object of terminating the war...and asked me whether I was prepared to collaborate wholeheartedly with him in this...and especially help him set up a letter in English to the Duke of Hamiliton."[26]

Bohle was instantly aware of the highly secret nature of what the Deputy Führer had told him, and understood the warning that none of the information be leaked. From the very beginning Bohle had assumed that Hess was planning a meeting with the Duke of Hamilton in Switzerland, and hoped to go along. The Gauleiter also assumed that Hess had discussed his plan with Hitler. While the plan may have appeared bizarre to some, it was not entirely beyond a possibility, for Hitler's successes by this point were astounding. Hess also viewed himself as a spokesman for those around Hitler, who found the stubborn resistance of the English frustrating. No doubt, Hess thought of being the catalyst that would bring all parties to the peace table, and open the road to an armistice. Very important to Hess was the fact that the Duke of Hamiliton served as Lord Steward to the King, which gave him ready access to the monarch. This was an essential point in Hess's mind. Although Bohle thought he was fully involved in the Hess plan, there is some evidence indicating that he was not at the center of the planning.[27]

Hess informed Bohle that the letter for the Duke had to contain an out-line of Germany's position, and points for discussion. According to Bohle's account Hess said: "You are the only man I trust enough and you speak English." The Gauleiter began work on a draft of the letter, and by January 1941, had a satisfactory translation that Hess carried on his flight. It consisted of twelve pages of single-spaced English text. Essentially, it stated that Hitler had no designs on England, but wanted a free hand in Europe. There would be no negotiations with Prime Minister Winston Churchill.[28]

Meanwhile, Hess had already acquired an airplane (Messerschmitt 110), and had been practicing his flying skills from a field in Augsburg. Although his actual plan was to fly to Lord Hamilton's estate near Glasgow, Scot-land, Hess told Bohle that he was to meet the Duke in Switzerland, and "...if he were to take anybody along with him, it would be only I. After January 1941, I heard nothing more about the whole matter, and was taken completely by surprise on May 12, 1941 when I heard that he had flown to England two days before."[29]

The exact location of Hess's landing was near the village of Eaglesham, some nineteen miles south of Glasgow. A farmer found him limping from an injury received when he parachuted from his plane, but did not recognize Hess. He was taken to a local military installation, where he identified him-self as Captain Alfred Horn. After his true identity was verified, the British government released a statement that he was in custody. Lord Hamilton, when told of the affair, denied that he had ever met the Deputy Führer.

Now, of course, everyone even remotely connected with Hess in Ger-many found themselves the focus of an investigation ordered by Hitler. Two of his adjutants, Alfred Leitgen and Karlheinz Pinsch, were immediately arrested, and his brother, Alfred, was dismissed from the Auslands-Organ-isation. Bohle said: "After he [Hess] left all the leaders of the Party and the Government were called to Hitler, and naturally disavowed Hess...it was then I reported to Hitler and told him that I had helped Hess in this matter, but that I had always been of the opinion that Hess was carrying out this proposal with Hitler's personal consent."[30]

There is no hard evidence that contradicts Bohle's version, and the Brit-ish have maintained a careful silence surrounding any official documenta-tion, however, given certain facts, it is difficult to accept it at face value. Bohle was an intelligent young man who had worked closely with Rudolf Hess for the entire time he had been the Gauleiter of the AO, and while it can only be speculated as to what his thoughts were during the meetings with Hess, he could not have been as uninformed as he pretended to be after the war. Some vital questions remain unanswered. What were Bohle's own views about a negotiated peace with England? Did he detect any prob-lems in Hess's mental condition? What role did Bohle see for himself, if Hess succeeded in arranging a peace?

After the failure of the Hess flight, Bohle fully expected to lose his posi-tion too, and knew that he had lost what small favor he had previously enjoyed with Hitler. A major concern for Hitler was the possibility that Hess, in trying to gain English support for his proposal, had revealed Germany's plan to attack the Soviet Union (code name "Barbarossa") in June 1941. While this information continues to elude historians, Bohle's papers and interrogations provide no hint that the Gauleiter knew more than what Hess had told him.

Bohle thought that Hitler did not remove him from head of the AO because he did not want to create the impression that the Hess departure had left serious problems, nor sow confusion among the German communities abroad. Additionally, Hitler was on the verge of an attack upon Soviet Russia, and wanted no distractions from the planning, however, this did not mean that Bohle suffered no consequences. Party leaders were of the opinion that Hess was a traitor to the cause of National Socialism, and had betrayed Hitler. It was Bohle's view that he too, was regarded as a traitor for his assistance to Hess, although Goebbels and Bormann continued to work with him in a cooperative fashion.[31]

One influential party leader who was not going to let the AO leader off easy was the German Foreign Minister Ribbentrop. He was determined to use the opportunity to rid himself of Bohle once and for all, and reduce the AO to an appendage of the Foreign Office. The news of the Hess departure was the signal for the Foreign Minister to ask Hitler to dismiss the Gauleiter, and transfer all functions of the AO to the Foreign Ministry. However, Martin Bormann, who had already assumed most of Hess's functions, informed Ribbentrop that he had already spoken with the Führer about the situation, and was told that the AO was very definitely a party office and should remain quite distinct from the Foreign Office. The only concession made was the "retirement" of Bohle from his position as a state secretary in the Foreign Office. Any future problem involving the AO leader's intrusion into foreign policy was to be reported to Bormann's office. To cover any appearance of dissension, Bohle was permitted to request retirement from the Foreign Office, but none of this became public. Thus, he continued to use the title on official stationary, but received no salary except from the party funds.[32]

The fact that Bohle escaped a more severe fate probably did not lessen his disappointment that his days of aspiring to greater influence in Germany's foreign affairs were definitely over. He knew that although Bormann had rebuffed Ribbentrop's efforts to relegate him to obscurity, it had also ended his influence over Foreign Office personnel. Afterwards, he had virtually no contact with the foreign minister, and only encountered him rarely at social functions, but there was no person to person involvement. All necessary business was handled by a liaison person, and Bohle never attended any more meetings in the Foreign Office.[33]

A fascinating dimension to the Bohle-Hess relationship unfolded after the war. Bohle was an allied prisoner awaiting his sentencing, and Hess was in England, where he had been confined since landing in Scotland in May of 1941, except for the time spent on trial in Nuremberg. Bohle was able to speak with Hess there, and asked him if he remembered the translation he did of the letter to the Duke of Hamilton. To Bohle's astonishment, Hess denied having any recollection of the incident. "That is flabbergasting!" Bohle said, because "Hess was the only man I knew personally in the German government who was definitely opposed to war of any kind."[34]

Despite the giant shadow that the Hess affair cast over Bohle's future, he still had some support from Propaganda Minister Josef Goebbels. At one time, when Bohle complained to Goebbels about Ribbentrop, the Propaganda Minister told him to just ignore him. Afterwards, Goebbels wrote in his diary: "He [Bohle] has a fear that the Führer will place the AO under the Foreign Office. That will not even come into question. The state does not rule the Party. Bohle is looking someplace for protection after the departure of Hess. I will take him somewhat under my wing."[35]

While there is no question but that the Hess flight probably represents the most traumatic event in Bohle's career as Gauleiter of the Auslands-Organisation, some questions remain unanswered. Beyond the many interrogations and testimony of Ernst Wilhelm Bohle, there exists no known really in-depth account of the experience by him. His relationship with Hess was of extreme importance to him as a young and unknown party member. He had no connections, no experience, and no qualifications for the job beyond having been born in England, and speaking the language. It was only with the help of the Deputy Führer that Bohle had a future, and could hope, one day, to play a larger role in Germany's diplomatic affairs.

Another puzzling factor is the silence regarding Hess's mental condition. Bohle had discussed various matters with him numerous times before the Duke of Hamilton matter emerged, but seems to have ignored any signs of deterioration. Of course, it is entirely possible that the AO leader may have remarked about it to someone on his staff, or even his wife, however, there is no record of it. Nor did Bohle have anything to say about the possibility that Hess had indicated that he would take the AO leader along with him.

The AO leader never indicated whether or not he and Hess had ever discussed the nature of English government. After all, Bohle had been born there, attended school, and knew the language, so he must have been exposed to some of its history. He was certainly aware that the king and British royalty did not control government, and that any agreement to a peace settlement required the consent of parliament and the prime minister. As one of the few high officials in Hitler's government, Bohle understood the workings of the British system, and yet he assisted Hess in translating a letter that made totally unrealistic demands. To have sought the support of a member of the house of lords would have accomplished nothing, and to ask to see the king, and demand the resignation of the prime minister, revealed a complete ignorance of the structure of English government. Even if their relationship was such that Hess would not listen to him, Bohle's papers contain no hint of his own doubts about the approach the Deputy Führer was taking.

After Hess's departure, his duties were largely assumed by Martin Bormann, who then became Bohle's boss. This was not the most desirable result from Bohle's standpoint, even though Bormann had not been exactly unfriendly in past dealings. According to Bohle's version, in a description that reflected his prejudice against all Germans who had never lived abroad, Bormann was a very impolite individual: "With him it was very difficult to get on. It wasn't worthwhile seeing him because he didn't understand anything about my work at all, he was a typical inland German who hadn't grasped it. He saw things with the spectacles of an inland German."[36]

It was clear that since the beginning of the war, and especially in 1941, the functions of the Auslands-Organisation had been declining, as well as Bohle's importance. Many of the AO Landesgruppen in other nations had ceased to operate, communications were growing more and more difficult, and many men of military age were being drafted into the armed forces or assigned to pressing duties elsewhere. All of this had a depressing effect upon the AO leader, because he saw no immediate future that permitted a recovery. The only promise was the possibility of a Hitler victory, but in the meantime, he had to shoulder the tasks given him, and hope that his organization would survive. [37]

13 The Eclipse of the Auslands-Organisation der NSDAP

By 1942, the war had assumed global proportions. The United States, after an attack by Japan, had entered the conflict in December 1941. Together with Great Britain and the Soviet Union, a coalition was formed with the purpose of defeating Germany as the first priority. Up to this point, Hitler's successes had been dramatic and impressive. To many of the conquered peoples of Europe, it truly appeared as if the Third Reich was going to last a thousand years. Now, however, with the formation of the Allied crusade, new hope was born. The decision to defeat Germany first was a momentous one, for it meant the concentration of major Allied resources upon that country, and during 1942–1943 Hitler began to suffer severe reversals. Although the war continued until 1945, the potential of Allied power to determine the military outcome of the conflict was clear.

It was not long before Ernst Wilhelm Bohle had to confront a new reality, too. In early 1942, his superior, Martin Bormann, informed him that he was no longer to use the title of "Chef der AO im Auswärtigen Amt" but could continue to retain the diplomatic rank of "Statssekretär," which carried the responsibility of promoting National Socialism among the Germans abroad. This could best be achieved, Bormann wrote, by working in a cooperative manner with the Foreign Office, and focusing upon German citizens abroad only. All reference to any political situations were to pass through the Foreign Office first, and any guests that the AO invited to any function abroad were to be cleared by the Foreign Office.[1]

With his services restricted largely to Europe, Bohle turned more and more to activities that contributed to the general war effort. For example, with the German army spread around the continent, and north Africa, the AO, through the efforts of Emil Ehrich, now Landesgruppenleiter in Italy, helped establish recreation centers and rest homes in various cities, and distribute thousands of food packages to the German Afrika-Korps. Meanwhile, the AO Berlin office had compiled a list of luxury hotels throughout occupied Europe that were reserved for German soldiers recuperating from injuries.[2]

Of significance to the war effort was the return of German citizens who provided skilled labor. This was a activity undertaken by the Auslands-Organisation, and which Bohle described as a vital aspect in the German economy. Large numbers of Germans were escorted back to Germany to border stations and facilities prepared by the AO, where they were processed for employment in the armaments and munitions industries. While other agencies, such as the Deutsches Ausland Institut (DAI), Volksdeutsche Mittelstelle(VoMi), and the Volksbund (Verein) für das Deutschtum im Ausland (VDA) also solicited Germans with labor skills to return home, the actual processing remained the work of the AO. An important part of the processing was the issuance of an identity card (Rückwandererausweiss) to each person accepted for employment, and a permit to reside in Germany.[3]

Actually, the return of Germans from various parts of the world was an aspect of the history of the Third Reich that began with the economic success of the first Four Year Plan that started in 1933. Designed to reduce the massive unemployment, the plan focused on government sponsored projects that soon had people back to work. The great success of Hitler's government in overcoming the unemployment malaise characterizing the nations of the industrial world did not go unnoticed by the Germans living abroad. By the mid-1930s, with the introduction of the second Four Year Plan, Germany was already experiencing a labor shortage. The scheme to increase the number of Germans from abroad who possessed desired labor skills on a "return to the Reich" (Heim ins Reich) program, was already widely publicized in the German communities, with the promise to subsidize the transportation costs.

Although business and farming had been the areas of greatest interest to Germans who left home prior to the turn of the century, that pattern had changed during the twentieth century, as industrial development surged ahead. By the time of the Third Reich, the nation with the largest body of skilled, unemployed Germans outside of the European continent, was the United States. It was there that a significant number of Germans, still relatively young and many with German citizenship, faced the massive unemployment situation of the Great Depression. The call to return home held the lure not only of National Socialism, but the promise of real employment. People like Fritz Gissibl and Walter Kappe, early leaders in the German-American movement, had focused attention on the available opportunities, and had worked closely with Bohle's AO in spreading the word. In fact, after Gissibl returned to Germany, and began working for the Deutsches Ausland Institut, he founded a social club in October 1938, especially for those fellow Germans who had returned from the United States. It was called the "Kameradschaft USA." By this time, thousands of German Americans had returned (at least seven thousand of them were listed in a 1936 survey).[4]

To organize the club, Gissibl had to secure permission from Willy Grothe, a longtime AO employee and America specialist, who discussed the proposal with Bohle. The idea was to organize discussion sessions that took up the problems of assimilation, and produce a monthly newsletter. The emphasis was to be upon the social aspects of returning to Germany, with a headquarters in the city of Stuttgart. Bohle had no objections so long as the returnees who did not have German citizenship, applied for it as soon as possible, and its activities did not infringe upon those of the AO Rückwandereramt. Thus, the program began enlisting members in Stuttgart and Munich in January 1939.[5]

Gissibl was somewhat typical of older party members who had lived abroad and obviously regarded Bohle, and the AO, with a certain amount of skepticism when they returned to Germany, and did not always take Bohle's instructions as the last word. At one point, when it was reported that Gissibl was going to Bremerhaven to meet the ships bringing some of the German Americans back, he received a note from AO headquarters with the invitation to visit Berlin and become acquainted with the workings of the Rückwandereramt, although Gissibl had already succeeded in establishing offices in Berlin, Hamburg, and Hannover, as well as Stuttgart and Munich. The essential documentation that a returning German needed to secure a resident permit, housing and employment, however, was only issued by the AO, and for this express purpose, the AO had opened offices throughout Germany's major cities.[6]

While Germans were encouraged to return to Germany, and were promised every means of assistance for resettlement, the ultimate picture was far from ideal. Instead of being welcomed with open arms by local authorities, they encountered innumerable difficulties in trying to obtain all the necessary documents for residence and work. Part of the problem was the fact that although Gissibl had assured Bohle that he only encouraged German citizens to return, and become members of the Kameradschaft USA, the truth was that many of the returnees had either never held German citizenship, or had lost it while living abroad. Many of these people now found themselves directed into employment that had virtually no relationship to the skills they possessed, and assigned inadequate housing. This was beginning to present Bohle with a difficult problem, but he found some relief as German forces advanced further eastward, and large areas of eastern Poland, and later, western Russia fell before the Wehrmacht's onslaught. This inspired a plan to resettle all of the returned Germans in conquered territories.

The idea had actually originated as part of Himmler's Reichskommissariat für die Festigung des Deutschen Volkstum (RKFDV), which was a project for the development of Germany's new eastern territories. Although the AO had been responsible for processing the settlers through their facilities by providing the necessary residence documentation, the responsibilities were enlarged as it became evident that the transfer of large numbers of people had to be processed according to the needed skills. The German Americans in the Kameradschaft were held up as an example of people with a pioneer spirit who were now ready to move eastward, and create new German-dominated regions. The entire project proved a horrendous disaster, however, as the tides of war shifted, and the thousands of Germans who had moved eastward, found themselves swept up in the movement of massive armies struggling against each other for supremacy. By 1944, virtually all of the civilian Germans, who had been resettled in 1941–42, had been evacuated back to Germany.[7]

No doubt, as many of Germany's leaders must have recognized, the war was a colossal mistake, but there was no way out beyond a humiliating surrender. It was also extremely dangerous to sound defeatists and face arrest, or worse. Bohle continued to praise the contribution of the Germans who had lived abroad, and pointed to the more than fifty thousand who were serving in the army: "Numerous of them have shown their loyalty to Greater Germany by joining the military. Many have exhibited the highest bravery in acts of heroism. After the war, these Germans [Auslandsdeutsche] who have become hardened in the heat of battle, will become the leaders in strengthening the unity throughout the world among the communities abroad." He also raised the specter of a Communist Europe if the war was lost: "One thing is certain", the AO leader said, "it is only due to the Germans and their allies that the true Europe remains free from Bolshevism."[8]

As the demands of war drained off AO personnel for military service, Bohle was regularly providing letters of recommendation for his people. Many of them had already served in the reservist ranks, largely the SS, and wanted to receive higher army ranks or officers' commissions. Bohle stressed their services to the National Socialist cause abroad before the war, and wrote strong letters of support. He too, held an SS rank, but was not liable for military service because of near blindness in one eye. He had been appointed a Brigadeführer in September 1936, and was advanced to a Gruppenführer less than a year later. With the start of the war in 1939, Bohle began including his rank in all correspondence. By 1943, he was a SS Obergruppenführer (lieutenant general in the Waffen SS), and on one occasion, when receiving congratulations from Himmler, replied: "I thank you sincerely for your good wishes, and for the renewed show of confidence. I will do everything I can to justify this confidence in the future." He later thanked the Reichsführer for sending him the SS insignia for his uniform.[9]

During one of his postwar interrogations, Bohle insisted that all of the decorations and SS rank were only routine for a person in his position. He said he did not take them seriously because Hitler and Himmler bestowed them upon every other Gauleiter as well, and no duties were attached to them. In support of Bohle's defense, the former SS General Karl Wolff, who was the individual who had informed Bohle that he had been inducted in the SS in 1936, confirmed that there were no responsibilities connected to it. He added that the Gauleiter could not have refused the honor, nor relinquished it later: "This would have provoked a wrath by Himmler against a person who attempted to resign, and the same if a routine promotion in the SS had been refused."[10]

By this time, it was apparent that the AO had lost its most important function in Hitler's Germany — serving as the unofficial eyes and ears abroad. Although it was never the super spy apparatus that was portrayed in the foreign press, it had provided the government and party offices with invaluable opinion and report service that was only possible through thousands of letters and visitors from around the world. Admittedly, some of the huge quantity of material that came into Bohle's office from abroad was worthless, but much of it was not. When properly evaluated, it gave an accurate picture on a wide variety of subjects that were of interest to the Nazi government. The subject matter ranged from details on foreign affairs, business matters, and certainly, attitudes toward the regime, and its policies. Any portion of the world where a German community resided was a source that could supply data that was virtually impossible to secure any other way. However, as the war continued beyond 1941, all of these valuable contacts began to disappear, and Bohle said that very little material came in to his Berlin office after this date. Occasionally, a German might come by who was late in returning home, and provide some bit of information, or a telephone call revealed some news, but nothing too important, according to Bohle.[11]

Under repeated questioning, Bohle admitted that in 1942, one of his employees was involved in a sabotage attempt against the United States, but he insisted that he had only loaned the individual in question to the Abwehr because he had been requested by Walter Kappe, Bohle said that he was only told that the mission was secret. "I consider it natural enough that some individual Germans abroad had secret missions for their fatherland, but the Auslands Organisation was certainly not the giver of such assignments nor the intermediary for such agents."[12]

One aspect of Bohle's behavior that never wavered through the war was his complaining about Ribbentrop and the handling of the German Foreign Office. He knew that he would find receptive ears among certain high ranking Nazis like Goebbels, Bormann, and Himmler, who all harbored feelings of resentment toward the foreign minister. In one instance, Bohle contacted Himmler about Franz von Papen, Germany's ambassador to Turkey, who had given a speech to the German community there. Bohle's complaint was that von Papen, a devout Catholic, had make frequent references to Christianity as a guiding force in life, and that this should not be tolerated. Interestingly, Himmler replied that this was typical von Papen, and had to be accepted because he could not be changed.[13]

Apparently Bohle was not put off by the negative tone of Himmler's answer, because he continued to pursue the theme that the Foreign Office was never fully supportive of National Socialism. To prove his point, the AO leader sent Himmler some statistics indicating that the older and more high ranking Foreign Office employees still retained their original religious preferences. For example, 506 of the members were Evangelical, 119 were Catholic, and 64 of them listed their position as non-Christian theism (a modern German cult described as "Gottgläubig"). Bohle emphasized that the non-Christian members were largely the younger people who had served in the Hitler Youth, and had only been hired by the Foreign Office in recent years. It was his contention that those people in the Foreign Office who had retained their orthodoxy Christian faith, had always been reluctant to accept the National Socialist state. It is an undisputed fact, he wrote, that this connection has worked against these people promoting National Socialism abroad.

Bohle's comments did not go unnoticed, even though Himmler's initial reaction was lukewarm. Both Goebbels and Bormann supported his position, and the Foreign Office had been informed that even though the war had changed the Auslands-Organisation's ability to pursue a full program abroad, Gauleiter Bohle still had the responsibility of keeping up the loyalty to National Socialism among the Germans who lived abroad. Bormann sent a personal message to all Foreign Office employees who held party membership that they had a duty to support Bohle in his efforts. In fact, the party treasurer provided the AO with additional funds to conduct their propaganda campaign. Ribbentrop agreed that more close cooperation was needed.[14]

Although these were essentially petty affairs in time of war, Bohle was, no doubt, elated that he had was able to bring some influence to bear at a time when he obviously felt his usefulness as the Gauleiter of the AO was weakening. Fully aware of the changing conditions, he had already started concentrating upon more areas of service to the war effort. There was no lack of shortages there, for the list was long. Beginning with holiday dinners for the soldiers serving in occupied Europe, arranging emergency leaves, providing travel funds, and assisting the wives of soldiers who had married in Norway, Belgium, Holland, and France, although many of these women met sharp discrimination for marrying Germans, and conditions for some of them proved intolerable when the husbands were transferred away.[15]

Although some situations must have proved annoying to the Gauleiter, these were the days when Germany reigned supreme on the European Continent, and the hard times were still ahead. However, the course of the war was slowly turning against Germany, and some of the huge territories that had been easily overrun, now began to face evacuation. This meant not only the German Wehrmacht, but the entire civilian apparatus that had been created upon occupation. It was a more extensive operation in the west, but also involved groups like the Kameradschaft USA in the east. Thus, began an exodus that placed important responsibilities upon the AO, and Bohle, to provide printed instructions for the massive retreat back to German territory. Much of the emphasis was placed on attempting to determine the exact time for departure, as the war drew ever closer. It was highly important not to create panic in the process, but to convey the possible danger of remaining in a combat zone in a manner that would not impact upon an orderly withdrawal. The AO leader referred to the bombings that Germany was suffering, and said that only hardened the resolve to resist more, and hang on until final victory. He acknowledged, however, that an invasion into some of the territories held by Germany was inevitable, and Germans must prepare themselves for it.[16]

There is no indication in Bohle's official correspondence that he had doubts about the war's outcome, but hinted at sinister forces within party ranks that were using Hitler's preoccupation with the war to turn Germany into a terrorist state. "I thought that Bormann especially, and possibly Himmler, were taking advantage of this almost total seclusion of Hitler, in order to form Germany into a terrorist state, and it was the hope that I had that at the close of the war Hitler would use the broom." Interestingly, during this same interrogation session, Bohle admitted that he had begun to doubt as early as 1943 that Germany could win the war.[17]

As Allied bombings intensified, Berlin was a prime target, and the offices of the Auslands Organisation were affected, as more and more structures were destroyed or damaged. Bohle ordered some of the offices moved to Bad Schandau and Komotau in the Sudeten region. In describing the worsening situation, he said: "I had several what you call emergency offices outside of Berlin. I personally lived in Bad Schandau with my wife and boy. I was there three days a week and the other three days in Berlin. When the Russians moved on Bad Schandau, we moved further south." This routine began in 1943, and involved traveling by train or car for the five hour trip to Berlin, which Bohle continued doing until almost the end of the war.[18]

A few weeks before the war ended, Bohle left Berlin completely, and soon after he heard about Hitler's demise. Another radio announcement on May 2, 1945, brought him the news that Ribbentrop had been replaced by Count Schwerin von Krosigk, and that Admiral Dönitz was forming a government in Flensburg. In one of his final acts, Hitler had named the Grand Admiral as his successor, and in the first days of May, Dönitz had started setting up a government in Flensburg with the intent of negotiating a peace with the western Allies. In what can only be described as an extraordinary act, Bohle managed to secure a ride on a German plane headed over the Russian lines to Flensburg in the north, where he planned to present himself to von Krosigk for service. Obviously, the departure of Ribbentrop had motivated him to embark on this bizarre venture in the hope that Dönitz might actually succeed in concluding a peace, and he could play some role in a new foreign policy structure. Illusions among the surviving Nazi hierarchy must have run rampant during these final days when they labored under the rumor that a negotiated peace was entirely possible.

After Bohle's arrival in Flensburg, he met with von Krosigk, who asked him to meet with Heinrich Himmler, who had also arrived seeking a high level post, and convey Dönitz's rejection. Bohle agreed, but wanted to talk with the Grand Admiral first. He recalled the meeting vividly: "The Admiral was of the opinion that any government he formed and which included the name of Himmler, didn't stand the ghost of a chance of ever being able to negotiate with the allies...a view which Count Schwerin and I shared. The Admiral, therefore, suggested that it might be useful if I too, would tell Himmler that he couldn't possibly remain a member of the government." When Bohle told Himmler that his request to join was absolutely unacceptable, the former Reichsführer said: "Give me half an hour's talk with General Eisenhower, and I'll come to terms with him because he needs me as the element of order in Germany." When Bohle refused again, he said: "Himmler gave me a vicious stare, spoke a few words to Count Schwerin, and abruptly left the room....that was the last I saw of him."[19]

Since the Allies had no intention of permitting the continued existence of a German government in any form, Dönitz and his band of hopefuls were soon interned as potential war criminals. For Bohle this meant the prospect of a trial as a war criminal himself and possibly a long prison sentence. He said later that he had thought about going into hiding or committing suicide, but decided against such actions. Instead, he presented himself to an American detachment at Falkenau on May 12, several days after the formal German surrender, and informed them of his identity. He was completely surprised when he was not arrested, but told to come back later. This occurred three times over the next two weeks because no one seemed to be able to find his name on a wanted list. Finally, he was arrested.

In retrospect such a thing appears astounding, but it really was not so unusual in the closing days of the war, and the immediate aftermath. The Allies did not have records to either confirm or deny the status of the individuals encountered in the chaos of a shattered Germany, and it was obvious that many people in prominent party positions had taken the precaution of arming themselves with false identity papers.

Virtually everything Bohle related about this period, Germany's collapse and surrender, came in statements given after the war in interrogations, and at a trial. This means that he had a time interval to reflect and collect his thoughts thoroughly and to recall events from a perspective. While most of the interrogations came first, the trial had the advantage of introducing witness testimony.

14 Trial and Judgment

Nineteen-forty-five will always remain the year that World War II ended. It will also be remembered as the period when there was still hope that the victorious Allies would continue their cooperation, and pursue the peace goals that had been enunciated in the wartime conferences. A paramount agreement was the promise to prosecute the leaders and organizations proven responsible for the war in accordance with international law.

Ernst Wilhelm Bohle and the Auslands Organisation der NSDAP now faced the scrutiny of an Allied court, which would determine the degree of guilt, or innocence, according to principles already agreed upon. Actually, two and one-half years elapsed before the trial began. It was officially designated *United States of America vs. Ernst von Weizsäcker, et al.,* and lasted longer than any of the other thirteen trials conducted at Nuremberg's Palace of Justice. It started on November 4, 1947, and ended on April 13, 1949. Bohle was tried together with twenty other individuals. He was charged with preparing and initiating wars of aggression (Count I), conspiring to commit crimes against the peace (Count II), crimes against German nationals between 1933 and 1937 (Count IV), crimes against humanity between 1938 and 1945 (Count V), plunder and spoliation (Count VI), and membership in the SS and political leadership corps (Count VIII).[1]

Prior to his trial, Bohle underwent a number of interrogations, and he knew that he could be adding incriminating evidence to the case against him, but he made no attempt to hide his membership in various Nazi organizations, and, at one instance, requested to examine a list of the National Socialist organizations in order to point out the ones to which he had belonged. As he told his interrogators: "I was in all sorts of things." He readily agreed that it was stupid to deny participation when it was so easily documented: "No, I don't understand that at all," he remarked, "I believe that when a man goes down, he should at least go down with some dignity."[2]

The willingness of Bohle to cooperate did not mean, however, that he intended to plead guilty to all of the charges against him. He refused to acknowledge guilt to Counts I and II that charged him with conducting extensive propaganda and espionage work in Poland, Yugoslavia, Russia, and the Western hemisphere. He also rejected the Allied assumption that the Auslands Organisation was a cover for activities conducted by Germany's spy services. It was Bohle's contention that if this had been true, and proof was produced, his organization would have been immediately banned in virtually all of the countries concerned.[3]

Of course, Bohle was still awaiting his sentence when such statements were made, and he was, no doubt, aware that he could face a lengthy prison sentence, but he was not evasive with the prosecution, and readily admitted that he knew of many of the spy operations that Germany undertook. However, he said that he was very firm that the people employed by the AO should not participate in any spy operations while still in the organization, and made it known to the intelligence chiefs that he should be informed if they had an interest in any particular individual.[4] When asked why he ordered all AO records destroyed at war's end, if he had nothing to hide, the former Gauleiter replied that this was normal procedure at that time, and was going on all over Germany.[5]

Rudolf Hess's brother, Alfred, supported Bohle's statements in his own testimony before the tribunal in Nuremberg, and stated that the foreign press accounts of the AO being a German spy apparatus were completely wrong. In fact, he said, there was much amusement when such stories appeared. He did admit, however, that there were Germans living abroad who were recruited for secret missions, but not by the Auslands Organisation, nor was the organization an intermediary for any agent activity.[6]

Although Bohle denied any direct spy activity, he could not explain away the actions of many of the members of the AO in certain countries who facilitated a German invasion. There was solid evidence that AO members engaged in spying and through acts of sabotage, assisted German forces to enter certain countries conquered by Germany. When questioned on this point, Bohle admitted that some of the AO people had been helpful to the German army at times, but insisted that this only occurred after the start of an invasion operation. An example he cited was the attack upon Greece, where a number of German citizens were interned, and were subsequently liberated by a spontaneous action directed by the AO Landesgruppenleiter there. It was not a preconceived plan, however, he said, and at no time did the AO people there engage in any combat operations.[7]

The actual role of the Auslands Organisation in espionage activities can not be eliminated on the basis of Bohle's testimony, however. He may have pretended ignorance of the details, but he had years of mutual undertakings with people like Heinrich Himmler, the Gestapo chief, and he offered the services of the AO to other Nazi Party leaders, when he saw a career advantage. Nor could it be ignored that the AO had some of the most fanatic Hitler followers who had no difficulties betraying their adopted lands in the name of National Socialism. To what extent that Bohle recognized this, and gave support to various schemes proposed by Germany's intelligence community, remained undocumented, but the prosecution eventually accepted his plea of innocence to the charge.

In regard to Count IV, offenses and atrocities committed against Jews before 1937, Bohle was charged with supporting police measures carried out according to the Nuremberg Laws. Specifically, this meant working with German authorities in order to take reprisal action against the relatives in Germany of German citizens living abroad. Before the presentation of this charge was complete, however, Bohle's lawyer, a very competent woman named Dr. Elizabeth Gombel (whom Bohle later married), filed a change of motion plea changing his earlier not guilty plea to Count V, to guilty to paragraphs 38 and 40, and Count VIII only. The motion was accepted by the prosecution. Immediately thereafter, Gombel asked for the dismissal of Count V, arguing that the former AO leader had held the position only because he was a Gauleiter, and that this constituted guilt by association with no supporting evidence: "The basic theory underlying the contention of the prosecution would seem to be as follows: The defendant Bohle is guilty of having committed crimes against humanity and war crimes with respect to Count V of the indictment because he held a high office within the political and governmental structure of the Third Reich."[8]

Gombel's argument was rejected, however. The Tribunal replied that Bohle was punishable within the framework Allied Control Council Law No. 10 because "...he participated in the mechanism of depriving German and Austrian Jews of their citizenship;...thus making them subject to the hand of the Nazi hangman whenever the country was overrun...he caused the economic strangulation of German stateless and foreign Jews...he participated in the expropriation of Jewish business employees and agents by causing their dismissal from jobs in Nazi-controlled or influenced firms."[9]

Gombel was not going to accept the Tribunal's judgment without a rebuttal, however. She challenged their conclusions by stating that by their own admission they had not been able to prove a single instance of AO involvement in a case of Jews being deprived of their identity papers in occupied France. She also denied that canceling passports of Jews was a crime against humanity, as the prosecution charged, and that it was an undisputed right under international law that nations could revoke citizenship for whatever reason they desired. Further, she stated, the prosecution had failed to establish a criminal intent on Bohle's part, even though he may have bypassed certain legal procedures: "On the contrary" she continued, "the Prosecution have introduced abundant evidence showing that Jews were deprived of life and liberty without any regard at all to their national status, which clearly demonstrates that a German passport gave a Jew not the slightest protection against prosecution."[10]

As for the charges in Count V that accused Bohle of "economic strangulation of German stateless and foreign Jews," Gombel said that this had already been included in Count IV, and had been dismissed. On the dismissal accusations, Gombel denied that the prosecution had made a successful case: "...I wish to emphasize once more that no breaches of contracts or application of expropriation laws were involved, but that all contracts were lawfully terminated in accordance with the civil laws applicable in the various cases. I deduct therefrom that actions in conformity with the civil laws of the countries where the dismissals were effected cannot violate penal law, let alone be a crime against humanity according to Control Council law No. 10."[11] Her arguments were successful, and Bohle was acquitted on Count V. The only remaining charge against him was that of membership in a criminal organization (Count VIII).

Among the almost two hundred defendants on trial at Nuremberg, Ernst W. Bohle had the dubious distinction of being the single individual who entered a guilty plea to membership in a criminal organization (SS), but his resourceful lawyer again accused the prosecution of attempting to find the former AO leader of guilt by association. Gombel argued that the prosecution had relied too much upon the opinion of the Soviet legal expert at the trial, Professor An. Tranin, but the prosecution rejected her effort to exploit the changing relationship between the western Allies and Russia, and ruled that Bohle was guilty.[12]

Before the final judgment was rendered, the prosecution delved into the question of Bohle's exact place in the larger structure of the Nazi leadership, and examined the nature of his territorial jurisdiction under the authority of the Party. The intent was to determine if Bohle was linked to any other criminal activities. Specifically, since the Nazi Leadership Corps had been declared a criminal organization for the mistreatment of Jews, prisoners of war, and the use of slave labor, and since all Gauleiters were members, it was to be assumed that Bohle was just as responsible as all of the others. Lawyer Gombel denied that this applied to Bohle, however, and proceeded to detail just why the Auslands Organisation was quite different from all of the other forty-two regional Gaue. She carefully explained that the AO der NSDAP never had any territorial sovereignty like the others did, and had only been elevated to Gau status in 1935 because it was an administrative convenience. At the time of this change, Bohle was then given the Gauleiter title for economic purposes.[13]

In the second week of April 1949, however, Allied Military Tribunal IV, found Bohle guilty of membership in the Nazi Leadership Corps and the SS, and in ten brief lines sentenced him to five years imprisonment. Dr. Gombel immediately filed a motion requesting the Tribunal to reduce the sentence to time already served, but this was rejected. She then proceeded to submit petitions for clemency based upon several supportive letters from a U.S. Army major and two sergeants, who attested to Bohle's helpful assistance as an interpreter during the time of his detention, and his behavior as a model prisoner. Meanwhile, Gombel had become acquainted with Roger Baldwin, the director of the American Civil Liberties Union, and had succeeded in interesting him, and the counsel for the ACLU, Arthur G. Hays, in Bohle's case. This was highly unusual, because the ACLU generally only concerned itself with cases involving U.S. citizens, but they agreed to examine the case.[14]

After looking at the documentation in the case, the first thing that Hays did was to write to General Lucius D. Clay, the American military governor for the American Zone in occupied Germany, and requested the general to give some consideration to the fact that Bohle was only found guilty of SS membership after September 1, 1939. He pointed out that the former AO leader pled guilty, which constituted the only plea of this kind made during the Nuremberg trials. Hays explained that neither he nor Baldwin had been eager to talk with Bohle initially, but after some discussion with Gombel, had agreed to such a conversation. "We both formed the very strong impression, however, that Bohle was much interested in persuading the Germans of their guilt, and that he felt that was the first step towards regeneration," Hays wrote, "This attitude of his together with his plea of guilt naturally aroused a hostile attitude among other defendants, a consequence which must be difficult for him to bear. The man has already served four years of the five....It seems to me, in view of the considerations stated above, that it would be advisable to reduce his sentence to at least four years, and Roger Baldwin has the same feeling about the case."[15]

Hays was personally acquainted with the general and knew that he respected the work of the ACLU, but when he received no answer, he found that Clay had left for the United States, and had been succeeded by General Clarence R. Huebner. Continuing his crusade on Bohle's behalf, Hay then proceeded to write Huebner, and enclosed a copy of his letter to Clay. Hays also added that Gombel had informed him that the clemency appeal had been denied, and Bohle was scheduled to be sent to Landsberg prison. Included in the communication from Gombel, was a letter signed by two of the prosecutors (Dr. Kempner and Mr. Caming) in the case against Bohle, urging that he not be placed in Landsberg prison, the implication being that because of his stand at the trial, he would not be safe from the other prisoners.[16]

When a quick answer was not forthcoming from General Huebner, Hays contacted the Acting Secretary of the Army, Gordon Gray, and forwarded the growing correspondence on Bohle. He made the request that the former AO leader be removed from Landsberg, where he had recently been sent, and placed in another jail. Rather than making any decision, and in a period when public anger at the release of any accused Nazi criminal was running high, Gray stalled Hays by replying that the case rested with the jurisdiction of the military governor in Germany, and assured the Washington lawyer that his letters would receive every consideration from Clay and Huebner.[17]

By late June, and still no replies from either Clay or Huebner, Hays wrote directly to the Office of Military Government, United States, in Germany (OMGUS). He addressed the letter to Major General George P. Hays (no relation), and again requested that Bohle be moved to a safer place of confinement. He explained that he had been informed by reliable sources that the former AO head was being constantly threatened, and feared for his life. Although Bohle had been held in solitary confinement, he had recently signed a statement that he was not simply inventing the threats as a means to get out of his cell for some exercise. Hays stressed the urgency of his request to permit Bohle to finish his sentence elsewhere. Roger Baldwin also contacted Secretary Gordon Gray, and informed him of Hay's letter.[18]

Although Hays never received a reply from OMGUS, his actions obviously prompted some action by the military. A Lt. Col. Frederick A. Sturm, acting judge advocate for OMGUS, sent a lengthy report of the Bohle case to the Office of the Judge Advocate General in Washington, D.C. He wrote that when the first petition had been received back in April requesting special consideration for Bohle, the case had been thoroughly reviewed with the U.S. Deputy Governor for Germany, and the decision was that no exceptions should be made. Sturm continued that Gombel had come to Berlin with additional petitions requesting that Bohle be placed in a German prison for Nazis, presumably because they were not considered hard-core prisoners. She also requested that Bohle's plea for clemency be given priority when reviewing his case. Sturm pointed out that this last request was already under review by the OMGUS office in Berlin. He also explained that Gombel was misinformed about the details of Bohle's confinement. It was true that he was held in a single cell at night, but it was located under a guard tower. During the day, however, he worked in the prison mail room, and had voluntarily signed a statement that he had no fear for his personal safety. In conclusion, Sturm said that it would be "impracticable and legally impossible" to transfer Bohle to a German prison. In mid-September, both Hays and Baldwin received identical letters from Secretary of the Army Gray that was brief and to the point: "I have now received a communication from the Office of the Military Governor, Berlin, Germany, which reports that the matter of confining Bohle in a place other than Landsberg has been considered, and that it has been decided that no exception can be made in this case."[19]

This ended all efforts to secure a transfer for Bohle to a German prison for the remainder of his sentence. There is no record of any act of violence being committed against him before he was released in 1949. The entire episode was rather extraordinary, however, considering the strong public feelings about the treatment of Nazis who were placed on trial as war criminals. Bohle had become quite friendly with several of his interrogators, but there is no indication that he ever said that National Socialism was an evil system, although he expressed some disgust about a few of the Nazi leaders confined in jail with him. He stated at one time, that these individuals, while displaying unsavory characteristics, were not war criminals, just as he was not.[20]

Some of the details of Bohle's past life that became evident during the interrogations and trial, pointed to an individual that had not enriched himself while in the service of the Third Reich, as many of his colleagues had. He had shown little interest in ostentatious displays and material wealth, and he and his family always lived in rented quarters in a Berlin suburb with no household help. According to a former acquaintance for the Foreign Office, the Bohles "...always maintained their hospitality within middle class bounds—even when foreigners were present." Court records showed that Bohle never owned any real property, and at the end of the war, his cash and securities amounted to RM 60,000, with a postal account of RM 5,000.[21] Obviously not the estate of a person who had become a rich man while heading the AO as a Nazi Gauleiter.

While these facts reveal a man who lived modestly under the circumstances, he was not without ambition. He wanted to play a major role in the making of German foreign policy, and possibly become the foreign minister of the Third Reich. He readily admitted that a major influence in his life was his English upbringing, and by his own account, his school, his friends, and his recreations as a boy were all English. This began to change with the coming of the First World War, however, when he became the object of ridicule, and was nicknamed "Kaiser Bill." When the newspapers carried stories about German atrocities, he was sometimes beaten by boys at school, he said. Meanwhile, at home, life was strictly German in all aspects. The father did not permit any English to be spoken.[22]

These experiences did not sour him on England, however, quite the contrary. He said that as he matured and studied history, he admired the manner in which the British held a vast empire. "I mean the Boers. The way the British handled this question is undoubtedly one of the most magnificent achievements of British colonial policy." He felt that Germany, with many more people than England, and spread around the world, could do even a better job.[23]

When asked how he viewed the modern history of Germany, and the rise of National Socialism, Bohle said that it was the Nazi movement that brought the dynamic changes to Germandom. It infused Germans everywhere with a political awareness and the people became conscious of the importance of blood and race. The mistakes of the past were explained, and the question of living space was explored against the backdrop of Germany's lost colonies as a result of the Versailles Treaty. English history provided him a valuable lesson, and nowhere was it a better place than in a English school to become familiar with the English mentality, Bohle said.[24]

He remembered that it was in December of 1931 that he first decided that the National Socialist movement offered the best solution for Germany's recovery from the economic and political chaos that engulfed the country. He could recall the date, because he answered an add for a job advertised in a Hamburg newspaper that was to change his life, and ultimately propel him into the leadership of the Auslands Organisation der NSDAP. In a statement somewhat exaggerated in scope, Bohle said: "The one big guiding principle I had was my firm determination to unify our German communities abroad in the same spirit of national solidarity which I knew prevailed among Britishers abroad, and which I tried to copy."[25]

Bohle denied that he was interested in the racial or ideological aspects of National Socialism, but recognized the importance of instilling the nationalistic spirit, for this was essential to organizing the Germans living abroad. He said that these people had never supported the Weimar Republic, but always had strong feelings for the deposed monarchy of Kaiser Wilhelm II. One had to understand, he continued, that there had been great pride in the Imperial Germany, when possessing a German passport meant something, and this pride had returned with the Hitler government. He recalled with some nostalgia, the few times he had participated in some high level function when Hitler was present, and actually felt a part of the inner circle. One such occasion was Hitler's state visit to Italy in May 1938, and Bohle was included in the delegation. He had to admit, however, that he never had easy access to Hitler, and never had a discussion of any substance with him. When pressed for the number of times that he had actually talked with the Nazi dictator, Bohle answered: "I believe four or five times for a talk on general matters, but only in the presence of others. He never displayed any special interest in our work. In fact, he was always politically uninterested."[26]

Bohle's explanation for Hitler's lack of interest was the old argument put forth by Germans who lived abroad, and that was the Germans who stayed at home could never understand the experience of living abroad. Other languages and other cultures provided a dimension to life that could only be acquired by living in other countries, and this had not been Hitler's background. Bohle included many of the Nazi leaders in this category, and expressed some bitterness that they did not appreciate what the AO was doing. In fact, he not only encountered general indifference, but, at times, outright hostility.[27]

Despite the frictions at home, Bohle stated, there was no lack of enthusiasm among the Germans abroad to participate in Party affairs, when the opportunity presented itself. He felt that this was related strongly to German emigration patterns, and noted that while the AO was world wide in scope, its contacts and influence varied from place to place, and was not uniform in nature. Distance also played a role in terms of the party interest in a particular community of Germans abroad, and this was often connected to current political affairs. For example, the three thousand German citizens living in England in 1933 were of more concern to the party than a similar number living in Australia. Time also was a factor in evaluating the importance of a German community. Those Germans who migrated before the outbreak of World War I were far less receptive to National Socialism than those who did so later, although there are exceptions, such as the former German colony of South West Africa. Actually, the desire of all former German colonies to return to German rule was strong, and they found new hope with the rise of National Socialism. Even in this situation, however, the most strident voices came from those who had arrived in 1920s.

It is important that German nationalism and National Socialism not be confused when surveying the sentiments of the Germans abroad. While many did not support Hitler, and did not take an active role during the Third Reich period, they were, never-the-less, proud of the recognition and respect that Germany had achieved since 1933. The German business men living abroad understood the importance of good relations with the fatherland, and how vital it was to their business interests to be on a good footing with the AO Landesgruppenleiter. Of course, most of the German communities had their own political factions, and the degree of cooperation with the local AO representative depended upon several things. Most important, was his background in and relationship to the community in question. It made a difference if he was sent out from Berlin or had developed his reputation as a leader in the community first. Bohle preferred making all appointments, but he understood the value of having someone represent the AO that the community knew and trusted.

The history of a community obviously played a large role in terms of its relationship to the Third Reich. In most areas of the world where a German community emerged, the Germans had arrived with some capital, and enjoyed some standing in the business community almost immediately. They were usually better educated, and brought with them useful skills that were welcome in the country chosen. This meant that, for the most part, they avoided assimilation since their continued well being depended upon occupying a certain status. This pattern was followed in eastern Europe, the Balkans, Russia, the Baltic, Latin America, and elsewhere. The one important exception was in the United States, where German immigration was strong. In the beginning, the German communities maintained their ethnicity for a time, but over a generation or so, they assimilated into the American population.[28] The major reason for this was the availability of economic opportunity that encouraged assimilation. The pattern was broken somewhat with the onset of the Great Depression, and many Germans who had arrived in the twentieth century found themselves unemployed. The offer of jobs in Germany stimulated a reverse migration, and it was here that the AO played a helpful role.

The real importance of Bohle's career unfolded before the outbreak of World War II, and rested with a potential that was never realized. His strongest possibility of becoming more than a high level functionary in Nazi Germany occurred before Ribbentrop's appointment as foreign minister in 1938. The strongly held opinion of the older party faithful was that their concept of the state overrode the traditional institutions, and leadership was earned through loyalty and service, and not necessarily ability. Therefore, it was not too unreasonable for Bohle to hope that one day the AO could replace the German Foreign Office. Unfortunately, his most important avenue was his friendship with Rudolf Hess, but once he was out of the picture, Bohle was relegated to the role of a secondary official, and his hopes were dashed of ever playing a larger role. The fact that Hitler did not take any overt action against him was, no doubt, a great relief, and the responsibilities of the AO during the first years of the war obscured worries about the future. Just when he decided the war was lost is not clear, but by 1943, he must have certainly sensed the outcome.

Bohle completed his prison sentence in December 1949, and was released into a divided Germany, a land that had become the center of the ideological struggle between the United States and the Soviet Union, and would dominate the world for the next forty years as the Cold War. His Nazi past made it difficult for him to secure employment, either because he was too closely identified with the Hitler regime, or because he had acknowledged that the leadership was guilty of many misdeeds. Eventually, he got a position in sales, but remained out of the public eye as much as possible. When he died of a heart attack in Düsseldorf in November 1960, he was fifty-seven years old. In an epitaph that would surely have amazed him, the *New York Times* devoted a full column to his obituary, which was headed: "Ernst Bohle Dies: Top Nazi Official Organized Fifth Column Was Jailed for Being a Member of SS...In 1940, Herr Bohle was reported to be the man Hitler had selected as ruler of Great Britain when the Nazis won the war."[29]

Notes

INTRODUCTION

1. The Foreign Office ranks were filled with individuals from some of Germany's most distinguished families. They were people who had wealth and influence in society before the advent of the Hitler government, and were generally conservative in their politics. Although they usually supported a government on the political right, this did not mean the endorsement of a dictatorship, and especially not one led by people like Hitler and his followers. However, these were difficult times, and they did favor a strong hand. Thus, most of the career diplomats remained at their posts.
2. Reichsdeutsche meant full citizenship, which could be retained while living abroad. However, these people were still referred to as Auslandsdeutsche and, while subject to the authority of the German Foreign Office, increasingly came under the influence of Bohle's AO. Volksdeutsche were Germans who were either former citizens or of German extraction, and resided abroad. Germans who lived on the borders outside of Germany, especially after the First World War, were known as Grenzlanddeutsche, or border Germans. There were also designations for German-speaking communities located in other states, such as Inseldeutschen, Volksinseln or Sprachinseln.
3. Das Bundesarchiv, Slg. Jacobsen 19, Bd. 5, Bohle Lebenslauf, 29/3/36. Hereafter BA.
4. Under the National Socialist government, party administration was divided into regional districts throughout Germany called Gaue. Each was head by a district leader, or Gauleiter, who was appointed by Hitler. In turn, the district was divided into counties or Kreise, and led by a Kreisleiter. Branches of the AO abroad were led by a Landesgruppenleiter with a staff that paralleled the Gaue structure at home.

CHAPTER 1

1. The word Nazi is an acronym created from the first syllable of National, and the second syllable of Sozialistische. The initials NS were also often used to identify followers of Hitler.
2. BA, Friedrich Gissibl file, Hitler to Gissibl, 20.5.25 (ehem. Berlin Document Center).
3. Gissibl had emigrated to the United States in 1923, No doubt, he had had some contact with Hitler before that date, for he already considered himself

a National Socialist upon his arrival in America. His AO file contains the following note: "Gissibl, who founded a National Socialist organization in Chicago in 1924, could well be the oldest of all Party members abroad." BA, Ernst Wilhelm Bohle file, 18.2.43 (ehem. BDC).

4. Ibid., Gissibl file, Strasser letter, 22.2.28.
5. Ibid.
6. Ibid., Fricke file, Propaganda Abteilung to Fricke, 8.3.29.
7. Ibid., 12.3.29.
8. Bundesarchiv, Slg. Jacobsen 56, Bd.1, Bruno Fricke Denkschrift Nr. 1, 23.2.30, pp. 1–2.
9. Ibid., p. 3.
10. BA, NS 22/1049, Strasser to Löpelmann, 11.11.30. Ficke was later expelled from the party, and went to Buenos Aires where he became the editor of an anti-Hitler publication.
11. BA, Martin Löpelmann file, "In Sachen des. Pg. Dr. Martin Löpelmann," 30.3.38 (ehem.BDC). In 1937 he was removed from his school administrator's job because he was accused of not providing the proper support to the Hitler Jugend.
12. BA, Slg. Jacobsen 56, Bd. 1, Löpelmann to Jacobsen, 1.3.1967.
13. Depending upon the source, his name was also spelled Ludecke or Luedecke.
14. Kurt G. W. Ludecke, *I Knew Hitler, The Story of a Nazi Who Exposed the Blood Purge* (New York: Charle Scribner's Sons, 1937), p. 23.
15. Arthur L. Smith, Jr., "Kurt Lüdecke: The Man Who Knew Hitler," *German Studies Review* XXVI (October 2003); p. 598.
16. Ibid. It was Lüdecke's claim that he had persuaded Hitler that the party lacked some badly needed prestige, and therefore an approach was made to enlist the support of General Erich Ludendorff, the well known World War I figure still prominent in certain German political circles. It was thought that this would also impress Mussolini. Ludecke, *I Knew Hitler*, pp. 66–67.
17. Ibid., pp. 190–191.
18. Ibid., p. 304.
19. Smith, "Kurt Lüdecke," p. 600.
20. Ludecke, *I Knew Hitler*, pp. 318–319.
21. Ibid., p. 411.
22. Ibid., p. 412.
23. Ernst Wilhelm Bohle, "Die Auslandsorganisation der NSDAP," in Wihelm Kube, Hrsg., *Almanach der nationalsozialistischen Revolution* (Berlin: Brunnen Verlag, 1934), p. 34. In a postwar interrogation referring to Nieland, Bohle said that it was his opinion that the Reichstag deputy took the job out of sheer opportunism. NA, RG 238, World War II Crimes Records. Interrogations of Ernst Wilhelm Bohle, 1945 and 1947. Interrogation by John Martin, Sept. 5–9, 1945. Hereafter NA, RG 238, Bohle interrogations. To some extent, Nieland represented a young and better educated NS follower then those who had initially supported Hitler. He had earned a doctor's degree in political science, and had joined the party in 1926. Later, as a functionary in the Gau Hamburg, he was placed on the elections list for 1930, and won a seat in the Reichstag. BA, Hans Nieland file, Lebenslauf, 22.12.37.
24. Ibid., Slg. Schumacher 292, Strasser Anordung 28.4.31.
25. Ibid., Rundverfügung Nr. 1, p. 2.
26. Europa und die Levante, Pg. [Parteigenosse or Party member] Lange; Afrika, Pg. Grothe; Nordamerika (Vereingte Staaten, Mexico, Kanada), Pg. Lahts; Südamerika, West Indien, and Zentral Amerika, Pg. Ruehte; Australien

(Neuseeland), Pg. Ewald; Indien (British-Indien, Ceylon, Niederl. Indien, Kl. Sunda-Ins.), Pg. Droessler; Ostasien (China, Manchurei, Japan, Philippinen), Pg. Droessler. Ibid.

27. Ibid., p. 3.
28. Ibid., p. 4.
29. There was an existing network of party members in various countries around the world, and while it was impressive geographically, their number was actually small.
30. BA, Slg. Jacobsen 56, Bd. 1, Org. Abtlg. 1, 10.8.31, pp. 1–3.
31. Ibid., Slg. Schumacher 292, Nieland to Reichsorganisationsleiter.
32. Ibid., pp. 2–3.
33. Ibid., p. 4. Strasser had rejected Nieland's earlier suggestion that party members who resided abroad be accorded the same status as those at home.
34. Ibid., Dienstanweisung Nr. 1, 28.9.31.
35. NA, T-580, BDC reels 57, Ord. 296a, and 54, Ord.291-292.
36. Ibid., reel 58, Ord. 298.
37. Ibid.

CHAPTER 2

1. BA, Slg. Schumacher 292, Nieland to Strasser, 15.2.32.
2. Ibid., Nieland to Strasser, 23.3.32.
3. Ibid.
4. Ibid., Strasser to Nieland, 25.3.32.
5. Adolf Hitler, *Mein Kampf* (Munich: Zentralverlag der NSDAP, 1939), p. 437.
6. NA, T-580, BDC, r.59, Ord.301, Nieland to Strasser, 5.3.32. Although Nieland's language sounded forceful, it did not deter further efforts at circumventing his authority both in Holland and elsewhere. The incidents almost always involved petty complaints and charges, many of which were either ignored by the Reichsleitung, or went to the party court for resolution.
7. BA, Slg. Schumacher 292, "Vertrauliche nationalsozialistische Auslandsbriefe Nr. 1," p. 2.
8. Ibid., pp. 4–6. The newsletter also contained a variety of comments, presumably sent in to Nieland's office by Germans living abroad. One from Chicago read: "The arrogant Jewish secretary in the consulate won't be there in the Third Reich." Ibid., p. 8. The newsletter was soon supplanted by a new publication in pamphlet form, "Der Auslandsdeutsche Beobachter," which instructed all party members abroad to identify themselves openly as National Socialists who belonged to the NSDAP, and not to mix in local politics. Ibid., pp. 8–15. These instructions are interesting considering that the biggest complaint of host countries was that Nazi Party people were involving themselves in the local politics.
9. BA, Slg. Schumacher 292, Nieland to Reichsleitung, 3.9.32.
10. NA, German Records Microfilmed at Alexandria, VA, T-81, No.3, reel 134, frames 168755-56. Hereafter NA, German Records. An interesting fact about the identity cards issued to Germans living abroad by Nieland's office was the absence of any reference to citizenship, only the birth date was listed. German men married to foreign women were regarded as an asset by Nieland, because it meant that they had strong local contacts which could prove helpful. To return to Germany with a foreign wife was a different question, however. Ibid.

11. BA, Slg, Jacobsen 56, Bd. 1, Nieland to Reichsleitung, 16.9.32. According to a later statement by Ernst Bohle, the financial picture of the Gau Ausland painted by Nieland in 1932 was not as positive as he made it sound. There had been periods during the year when the office was quite desperate for funds, and Nieland had sent out frantic messages asking for support. NA, RG 238, World War II Crimes Records, Transcripts of Interrogations of Ernst Wilhelm Bohle, 1945 and 1947. Martin, Nov. 13, 1945. Washington, D.C.: NA, 1964. Hereafter NA, RG, WW II Crimes Records, Bohle interrogations.
12. BA, Slg. Schumacher 292, Nieland to Strasser, 15.2.32.
13. Ibid., pp. 17–22.
14. Ibid., pp. 23–41.
15. Ibid., pp. 33–34.
16. Ibid., pp. 51–62.
17. Nieland interview by Hans-Adolf Jacobsen, Hamburg, Dec. 7, 1966. A few years after leaving his police position in Hamburg, Nieland became mayor of Dresden. After the disastrous Allied bombing of the city in February 1945, he was removed from his office for failure of having provided proper leadership during the aftermath of the terrible catastrophe. BA, BDC, Nieland file, Mutschmann to Nieland, 19.2.45.
18. NA, RG 238, WWII Crimes Records, Bohle interrogation, Martin III, p. 10.
19. Ibid.
20. Ibid., Brundage V, pp. 19–20.
21. Ibid., Martin III, p. 10–11.
22. Among the Auslandsdeutsche were a number of people who could never seem to settle permanently either in Germany or abroad. Often they exhausted their resources in moving back and forth every few years. See the interesting study by Alfred Vagts, *Deutsch-Amerikanische Rückwanderung* (Heidelberg: Carl Winter Universitäts Verlag, 1960).
23. *Trials of the War Criminals Before the Nuremberg Military Tribunals* (Washington, D.C.: 1952) XII, p.1197. Hereafter *TWC*. Bohle renounced his British citizenship in August 1937.
24. NA, BDC, r.58, Ord. 298.
25. Ibid.
26. BA, Slg. Jacobsen 57, Bd. 2, Dok. E.W. Bohle, Nr.37, pp. 71 and 73.
27. BA, Bohle file; and, NA, RG 238, WWII Crimes Records, Bohle interrogations, Brundage VI, p.1, and Lewis XIV, p. 70.
28. Bohle interrogations, Martin I, p. 3.
29. Ibid., Martin III, pp. 3–11.

CHAPTER 3

1. BA, Slg. Jacobsen 57, Bd.2, Dok. E. W. Bohle Nr. 67.
2. NA, RG 238, WWII Crimes Records, Bohle interrogation, Martin II, pp. 11–12.
3. BA, Slg. Jacobsen 57, Bd. 2, Dok. E. W. Bohle Nr. 42.
4. Jacobsen interview with Gertrud Bohle, 16.12.65.
5. Ibid.
6. BA, Slg. Jacobsen 57, Bd. 2, Dok. E. W. Bohle, Nr. 38.
7. Ibid., Dok. E. W. Bohle Nr. 42.
8. NA, RG 238, WWII Crimes Records, Bohle interrogation, Blancke, p. 3.

9. Ibid., Brundage VI, p. 5.
10. NA, German records, T-81, 419/5165490-97.
11. Ibid.
12. Ibid.
13. NA, RG 238, WW II War Crimes Records, Bohle interrogation, Brundage VI, p. 5.
14. NA, German Records, T-81, 419/5165490-97, and *Trials of the Major War Criminals before the Nuremberg Military Tribunal* (Nuremberg, 1947), v.10, pp.12–13. Hereafter *I.M.T.*
15. BA, Slg. Schumacher 293, "Zukunftsaugaben der Auslands-Abteilung der NSDAP," pp. 3–6.
16. NA, German Records, T-81, 419/5165490-97. Of course, the other side of the coin was that after Hitler's victory thousands of persons clamored to become party members, and it was not possible.
17. NA. BDC, T-580, r.56, Ord.295, and *Die Auslands-Organisation der NSDAP* (Berlin, 1937), p. 7.
18. NA, RG 59, Dept. of State, Bohle interrogation, Smith I, p. 4.
19. British Foreign Office Library Microfilm, German Auswärtiges Amt, Büro des Chef der Auslands-Organisation, Serial 81, 60165. Hereafter F.O. Lib.
20. NA, RG 59, Dept.of State, Bohle interrogation, Blanke, p. 18.
21. BA, Slg. Schumacher 293, Bohle letter to Schwarz, 12.5.33.
22. BA, Slg. Jacobsen, Bd. 3, Bohle to Stellvertreter des Führers, 4.12.33.
23. Ibid.
24. NA, RG 59, Dept. Of State, Bohle interrogation, Smith I, p. 17.
25. Jacobsen interview with Emil Ehrich, 13.9.1965.
26. NA, RG 238, WW II War Crimes, Bohle interrogation, Brundage V, p. 24.
27. British F.O., ser. 837, fr. 281485-86.
28. NA, RG 238, WW II War Crimes, Bohle interrogation, Martin II, p. 9.
29. Hans Steinacher notes, 7.12.34. Hereafter Steinacher notes. See also Hans-Adolf Jacobsen, ed., *Hans Steinacher, Bundesleiter des VDA 1933–1934. Erinnerungen und Dokumente*(Boppard: Schriften des Bundesarchivs 19 , 1970).
30. NA, RG 59, Dept. of State, Bohle interrogation, Blancke, p. 14.
31. For a history of the DAI, see Arthur L. Smith, Jr., *The Deutschtum of Nazi Germany and the United States* (The Hague: Martinus Nijhoff, 1965).
32. NA, RG 59, Dept. of State, Strölin interrogation, Blancke, p. 6.
33. NA, German Records, T-81, 21/404/5147395-97 and 5147278-79.
34. These involved organizations like the Hitlerjugend, National Socialist Women's Group (NS Frauenschaft), National Socialist People's Welfare Organization (NS Volkswohlfahrt), etc.
35. U.S. Military Tribunal, Nuremberg Trials, Case XI, Von Weizsäcker. Nuremberg, Germany, 1948. Document 51, Bohle Bk.III, No. 55, pp.44–45. Hereafter U.S. Military Tribunal, Case XI, Von Weizsäcker.
36. Ibid., Testimony, 23.7.48, pp.13486–87.
37. NA, RG 238, WWII Crimes Records, Bohle interrogation, Lewis XIV, p. 107.
38. U.S. Military Tribunal, Case XI, Von Weizsäcker, Testimony, 23.6.48, p. 13486.
39. Ibid., Testimony, 16.2.48, p.1163, and 12.2.48, p. 1825.
40. NA, T-580, BDC, r.533, Ord. 301.
41. F.O. Lib., AA records, ser. 269, 174738-43.
42. NA, RG 59, Dept. of State, Bohle interrogation, Blancke, p. 7.
43. Ibid., Bohle interrogation, Smith I, p. 12.

44. BA, BDC, Franz Xaver Schwarz file.
45. NA, RG 59, Dept. of State, Bohle interrogation, Blancke, p. 7. It was on Bohle's orders that most of the financial records of the Auslandsorganisation were destroyed at the close of World War II F.O. Lib., AA records, ser. 102, 110847-67.

CHAPTER 4

1. NA, T-580, r.55, Ord.293.
2. BA, BDC, Alfred Hess file.
3. Ibid., and BA, Slg. Jacobsen, 19, Bd. 5, A. Hess to Rudolf, 19.3.34. In 1937, when recommending Alfred for a party honor (Goldenen Ehrenzeichen), Bohle wrote that "Party member Hess is a fanatical National Socialist with extraordinary energy, and is untiring in his work ." Ibid., 3.4.1937.
4. Reuth, Hrsg., *Goebbels Tagebücher*, Bd. 3, p. 905.
5. NA, RG 59, Dept. of State, Bohle interrogation, Smith I, p. 10.
6. Ibid. Additionally, the AO distributed news about party happenings and news items relating to NS affairs in Germany. This appeared regularly in an information bulletin (Mitteilungsblatt der AO), and was received by seamen as well. Bohle communicated with his staff on a daily basis with "orders of the day", and with office memorandums.
7. NA, RG 59, Dept. of State, Bohle interrogation, Smith I, p. 11.
8. Ibid.
9. F.O., AA, Büro des Chef der AO, ser.81, 59904-07.
10. NA, RG 238, World War II Crimes Records, Bohle interrogations, Brundage VI, p. 4, and NA, RG 59, Dept. of State, Bohle interrogations, Blancke, p. 5. Bohle said that about twenty of the thirty-four leaders usually attended, but that the AO did not always pay the travel expenses because many of the men were well off and could easily absorb the costs. Those who attended most often were from countries closest to Germany. Ibid.
11. Ibid., RG 238, Martin II, pp.14–15, 28–29.
12. Ibid., RG 59, Blancke, p. 8.
13. Ibid., RG 238, Martin II, p. 29.
14. Ibid., German Records, T-89, 3/135/176388.
15. Ibid., RG 238, Martin II, pp. 31–32, and RG 59, Blancke, p. 6.
16. AA, PA Inland II, A/B, 82-04, Bd. 1.
17. Jacobsen interview with Ehrich,13.9.65, p. 18.
18. Ibid., p. 22.
19. NA, German Records, T-81, 21/404/5147571.
20. AA, PA, Inland II, A/B. Bd. 1, Kempff to AA Berlin, 15.1.34, pp. 1–2. The membership card for the league stated that the bearer swore that he/she was of German Aryan stock with no Jewish or colored blood. After promising to support the league with all of their strength, members agreed to pay a one dollar entry fee, and one dollar per month. Ibid..
21. Ibid., Kempff to Hackett, 4.4.34, and Hackett to Kempff, 8.1.34.
22. BA, Slg. Jacobsen, 59, Bd. 4, AA Berlin, 5.7.34.
23. AA, PA, Inland II, A/B, 82-02, AA Erlass 120-11, 7.2.34.
24. Ibid. Membership was still restricted in Germany.
25. BA, Slg. Jacobsen, 57, Bd. 2, Dok. E. W. Bohle, Nr.42; Nr.38; Nr.66.
26. AA, PA, Inland II, A/B, 82-02, Bd. 1, Bülow an Missionen, 8.12.34.

CHAPTER 5

1. NA, Microfilm Publication, M942, Roll 1, Records of the United States Nuremberg War Crimes Trials, NP 019, Dec. 5, 1936. Hereafter NA, MP, M942, r.1, NP no., date.
2. AA, PA, Inland II, A/B, 82-02, Bd. 4, Schluze to Berlin, 6.5.35.
3. NA, German Records, T-81, 21/404, 5147192.
4. NA, RG 238, WW II Crimes Records, Bohle interrogations, Martin II, p. 35.
5. Ibid., Lewis XIII, pp. 2–3.
6. NA, German Records, T-81, 3/27/23988 and 24116.
7. *Documents on German Foreign Policy*, ser. C, v. II (Washington, D.C.: U.S. Gov't. Print. Off. 1959), pp. 758–759.
8. United States Congress, House, *Investigation of Nazi Propaganda Activities and the Investigation of Certain Other Propaganda Activities*, 73rd Cong., 2nd Session, June 5–6, and July 9–12, 1934 (Washington, D.C.: U.S. Gov't. Print. Off., 1935), pp. 112–113 and 241–244. Hereafter U.S. Cong., H.R. Hearings.
9. U.S. Cong., H.R. Hearings, Oct. 16–17, 1934, pp. 5–13 and 101.
10. *Docs. On Ger. For. Pol.*, C III, pp. 1115–1116.
11. Ibid., pp. 1120–1121.
12. NA, German Records, T-81, 3/146/0185108-110. It was not always the best situation for a party member to be separated from his membership, even temporarily, because he rarely received the same number again. Some of the members that were in America had very low party numbers, a valuable asset in Germany, but upon reinstatement received new, and much higher, numbers. BDC, Gissibl file, "Parteigenossen in USA, welche aus der NSDAP austraten, um in Bunde 'Freunde des Neuen Deutschland' weiterhin tätig sein zu können."
13. NA, RG 238, WW II Crimes Records, Bohle interrogation, Martin II, p. 35.
14. Steinacher notes, 28.12.34.
15. Ibid., 12.2.35.
16. British F.O., ser. 81, frs. 60086-88.
17. Steinacher notes, 26.9.35.
18. AA, PA, Inland II, A/B, 82-02, Bd. 3, Rohland to AA, 18.3.35.
19. Ibid., Von Bülow-Schwante to Deutsche Botschaft in London, Paris, usw., 30.3.35.
20. Ibid., Hess to Neurath, 6.12.35.
21. Ibid., Neurath "An alle diplomatischen Missionen und berufskonsularischen Vetretungen," 1.5.35.
22. Ibid., Bülow-Schwante, 31.5.35
23. AA, PA, Inland II, A/B, 82-02, Bd. 4, Erythropel to AA, 8.5.35. The German consuls also began to express surprise to Berlin about the increase in the number of Germans who were showing up for their functions when the AO was active in a community. Ibid., Freyling to AA, 27.5.35.
24. BA, Slg. Schumacher, Akte 293, Anordnung 66/35, 15.4.35.
25. British F.O., ser. 2769, fr. D536372-79.
26. NA, MP, M942, r.1, NP 009, 2.27.36.
27. Ibid., Hess to AA, 19.3.36.
28. Ibid., Abschrift, Gezantschap der Nederlanden, 26.6.36.
29. BA, BDC, Wilhelm Gustloff file, "Wiener Enthüllungen über Gustloff".
30. AA, PA, Inland II, A/B, 82-02, Bd. 4, Weizsäcker telegram, Bern, 18.4.35.

31. Ibid., Weizsäcker to Berlin, 28.9.35.
32. Ibid.
33. Hitler personally spoke at Gustloff's funeral, which was held in Schwerin.
34. British F.O., ser. 6048, E44613 and E446173-74.
35. NA, MP, M942, r.1, NP, Neurath telegram, 20.2.36.
36. Ibid., Antwort der Schweizerischen Regierung, 28.2.36.

CHAPTER 6

1. Soon after the appointment, Bohle recommended Gustloff's wife, Hedwig, for a party decoration for assisting her husband in his work in Switzerland. AA, PA, Inland II, A/B, Chef AO, Bd.47, Bohle 1936–1940, Vorschlag Nr. 1, 3.4.37. In response to a friend, who wrote to congratulate Bohle on his appointment, the Gauleiter answered: "You are the first AO-man that I am writing [after the appointment] on my new stationary, and you can see what the letterhead looks like." Ibid., Persönliche Korrrespondenz, 1936–1940, Bohle letter, 1.3.37.
2. Ibid., Bd. 1, 1937–1938, Führer und Reichskanzler Erlass, 30.1.37.
3. Ibid., Neurath to staff, 19.2.37.
4. Ibid., 82-00A, Der Chef AO, Nr. AO 1, 1.3.37.
5. Ibid., Chef AO, 42, Beamte des AA, 1937-1939, Bohle letter, 13.4.37.
6. BA, BDC, Emil Ehrich file. Ehrich's place in Bohle's Berlin office was filled by a young lawyer from the AO legal department named Rudolf Tesmann. He was twenty-seven years old. Ibid., Rudolf Tesmann file.
7. AA, PA, Inland II, A/B, 82-00A, Chef AO, 47, Persönliche Korrespondenz, 1936–1940, Bohle letter, 1.3.37; and Chef AO, 48, 1937-1941, Ehrich letter, 9.6.37.
8. Jacobsen interviews with Fritz Grobba, 2.4.66, and Werner von Schmieden, 19.4.66.
9. NA, German Records, T-81, 3/220/274653.
10. Ibid., and NA, RG 238, WW II Crimes Records, Bohle interrogations, Martin III, p. 18.
11. Ibid., Martin III, pp. 19–25.
12. *Nazi Conspiracy and Aggression* (Washington, D.C., 1948), Supplement B, p. 1490.
13. NA, RG 238, WW II Crimes Records, Bohle interrogations, Martin III, pp. 19–25.
14. Ibid.
15. Ibid.
16. Bülow-Schwante letter to John L. Heineman, 5.9.63, p. 8. Copy provided by H.-A. Jacobsen.
17. AA, PA, Inland II, A/B, 8200A, Bülow-Schwanrte letter, 10.12.36.
18. U.S. Military Tribunal, Nuremberg Trials, Nuremberg, Germany, 1948. Ernst Freiherr von Weizsäcker Case XI, Testimony, 23.7.1948, pp. 13510–13511.
19. Ibid., p. 13509.
20. NA, RG 238, WW II Crimes Records, Bohle interrogation, Martin III, p. 12.
21. Weizsäcker Case XI, Documents 51, Bohle Doc. Bk. II, No.39, pp. 81–82.
22. Ibid., No. 41, p. 89.
23. BA, BDC, Konstantin von Neurath file, n.d.
24. Ibid., copy of *Berliner Tageblatt*, 19.9.37.
25. Von Bülow-Schwante letter to John Heineman, 5.9.63, p. 7.

26. No doubt feeling he could be generous about the turn of events, Bohle directed an assistant to send Frau von Neurath a floral arrangement for Christmas, noting that it should be "extra nice". AA, PA, Inland II, A/B, Chief AO, Bd. 47, Bohle note, 22.12.37.
27. Ibid., Bd. 72, Bohle Erlass Nr. 6, 11.10.37.
28. BA, BDC, Bohle file, Himmler/Hitler notes, 16.4.37. At his postwar trial, Bohle said that he received similar rank in the SA, but characterized it all as "...pure chance." *T.W.C.*, v.XIII, pp. 1201–1202.
29. NA, RG 238, WW II Crimes Records, Bohle interrogation, Fanta-Lewis, pp. 20–21, and declaration, 7.11.47, p.3.
30. F.O., 257, 168732-33.
31. Weizsäcker Case XI, 23.7.48, pp. 13475–13476.
32. BA, BDC, Bohle file, Bohle to Himmler, 17.8.37. Interestingly, Bohle's note was not written on his AO stationary, but on stationary that only carried his title as a major general in the SS.
33. AA, PA, Inland II, A/B, Chef AO, Bd.47, Bohle to Lammers, 18.8.37.
34. BA, Slg. Jacobsen, 19, Bd. 5, Bohle Vorschlag Nr. 4, 3.4.37. Bohle then recommended Bene for the position of German general consul in Milan, Italy, which he received, and he departed England in 1937.
35. The *New York Times*, Sept. 1, 1937, 1:4.
36. NA, MP, M942, r.1, Winston Churchill in "Tidens Tegn," 27.8.37.
37. *I.M.T.*, v.10, p. 13.
38. Ibid., p. 14.
39. NA, RG 59, Dept. of State, Bohle interrogation, Blancke, p. 9.
40. Ibid., p. 15.
41. BA, BDC, Erich Schnauss file.
42. NA, RG 238, WW II Crimes Records, Bohle interrogation, Martin III, pp. 34–35.
43. Ibid., Lewis XIII, p. 13, and Brundage, VI, p. 15.
44. F.O., ser. 81/59953-54.

CHAPTER 7

1. BA, Slg. Schumacher, 294, *Völkischer Beobachter*, 30.8.37.
2. Ibid.
3. F.O., ser. 81, 60145-165, AO Statistics.
4. AA, PA, 88, Chef A/O, Terminologie Auslandsdeutscher, 24.11.37, p. 1.
5. NA, RG 59, Dept. of State, Special Interrogation Mission, Wellington interrogation of Steengracht v. Moyland, p. 5.
6. *Verplictendes Erb e* (Kiel: Ferdinand Hirt, 1954), p. 44.
7. NA, RG 59, Dept. of Sate, Bohle interrogations, Martin II, p. 8, and RG 238, WW II Crimes Records, Bohle interrogation, Rodell IX, p. 8.
8. Another challenger for Bohle was Alfred Rosenberg, who headed a Foreign Political Office (Aussenpolitischen Amt, or APA), that dabbled in a certain amount of foreign intrigue. He had considerable influence with Hitler, and was recognized as the party theorist and ideologue The APA had pretensions toward guiding some aspects of Hitler's policies, however, it never emerged as a serious competitor to the Foreign Office.
9. AA, PA, 147, Chef A/O, Persönliche Korrespondez Gauleiter Bohle, 1936–1940, Bohle to Karlova, 17.9.37.
10. Jacobsen interview with Fritz Grobba, Bad Godesberg, 2.4.66.
11. Ibid., interview with Werner von Schmieden, Baden Baden, 19.4.66.

12. BA, Slg. Jacobsen, 19, Bd. 5, v. Bülow-Schwante, Eidsstatliche Erklärung, Düsseldorf, 2.6.49.
13. NA, RG 238, WW II War Crimes Records, Bohle interrogations, Brundage, pp. 21–22.
14. Weizsäcker Case XI, mimeographed testimony, July 23, 1948, p. 13504. Von Ribbentrop wrote that it was Bohle's fault that he lost the friendship of Rudolf Hess, and described the young Gauleiter as difficult to work with. *The Ribbentrop Memiors* (London: Weidenfeld & Nicolson, 1954), p. 87.
15. NA, RG 238, WW II Crimes Records, Bohle interrogation, Martin II, p. 4.
16. Ibid.
17. Ibid., Brundage IV, pp. 3–4.
18. Weizsäcker was already a seasoned diplomat by this time, having been in the Foreign Office since 1920. He was a party member, and held SS rank. BA, BDC, Weizsäcker file.
19. NA, RG 238, WW II Crimes Records, Bohle interrogations, Martin III, p. 29.
20. NA, RG 59, Dept. of State, Spec. Interrogation Mission, Steengracht v. Moyland, Deutsch, p. 5.
21. AA, PA, Inland, A/B, Chef A/O, Erlasses des AA, 74, Bohle, 19.1.38, p. 1.
22. Ibid.
23. BA, Slg. Schumacher, 294, Tagesbefehl Nr. 33/38, 23.5.38.
24. NA, RG 238, WW II Crimes Records, Bohle interrogations, Brundage IV, pp. 3–4.
25. Reuth, hrsg. *Goebbels Tagebücher*, Bd. 4., p. 1431.
26. Weizsäcker Case XI, mimeographed testimony, July 23, 1948, p. 13514.
27. F.O., ser. 81/59766-71; 102/110847-67.
28. *D.G.F.P.*, ser.D, IV, p. 657.
29. NA, RG 59, Dept. of State, Spec. Interrogation Mission, Harnden, p. 11.
30. F.O., ser. 81/59778-79.
31. Ibid., 597780.
32. An interesting note in the Schwarz Party file is a copy of an order issued by a Munich court in 1925 sentencing him to one day in jail and a fine of five marks for soliciting money on the street for the NSDAP without a police permit. BA, BDC, Schwarz file, October 25, 1925.
33. F.O., ser. 81/59766-83.
34. AA, PA, Chef A/O, 74, Erlass des AA, Neurath, 20.3.35., and 30.6.37.
35. Ibid., Chef A/O, 95, Vertretungen deutscher Firmen im Ausland, Ehrich, 18.2.37.
36. NA, RG238, WW II Crimes Records, Bohle interrogations, Brundage VI, p. 8.
37. F.O., ser. 72/51604-17.
38. AA, PA, Chef A/O, 56, b)Auswanderer, 1937-1941, 30.10.37, pp. 4–6.
39. NA, RG 238, WW II Crimes Records, Bohle interrogation, Kempner X, p. 3.
40. BA, Slg. Jacobsen, 57, Bd. 2, Neurath secret telegram, 1.6.37.
41. Weizsäcker Case XI, mimeographed testimony, July 23, 1948, pp. 13516–13517.
42. Ibid., p.13518.
43. Ibid., mimeographed Documents 51, Bohle. Doc., Bk. II, no. 37, pp. 72–74.
44. Ibid., Bohle, Doc., Bk. III, no. 58, pp. 53–54.
45. AA, PA, 42, Chef A/O, AA Beamte, 1937–39, Bohle on PG. Rath, 9.11.38, and Fischer on Bohle, 11.11.38.
46. Weizsäcker Case XI, mimeographed testimony, July 23, 1948, p. 13521.

47. Ibid.
48. Ibid., mimeographed Documents 51, Bohle Doc. Bk. II, No. 27, p. 49.
49. Ibid.
50. Ibid.

CHAPTER 8

1. BA, BDC , Bohle file, Hitler to Bohle, 26.7.38.
2. F.O., Ser. 81, 60145, AO-Statistics.
3. Ibid.
4. Ibid. 60146-64.
5. AA, PA, Chef A/O. 55, a) Reichsdeutsche im Ausland, 1937–1942.
6. Ibid.
7. Ibid.
8. Ibid., Chef A/O, 88, d) Terminologie Auslandsdeutschen, 1937–1940; and, BA, BDC, Bohle files, *V.B.*, 25.1.38.
9. AA, PA, Chef A/O, 88, a) Reichsdeutsche im Ausland, 1937–1942; and, R. Reuth, hrsg., *Gobbels Tagebücher*, Bd. 3, p. 1182.
10. F.O., Ser. 81, D536380-83.
11. Ibid., D536417-19.
12. BA, BDC, Butting file.
13. F.O., Ser. 81, D536417-29.
14. Ibid., D536463-76.
15. Ibid. The fact that Graf von Zech-Burkersroda was the son-in-law of former German Chancellor Bethmann-Hollweg, afforded him a certain degree of immunity.
16. F.O., Ser. 81, 60159-65, AO Statistics, 30.6.37.
17. NA, RG 59, Dept. of State, Special Interrogation Mission, Blanke interrogation of Bohle, p.12.
18. Dr. Hans H. Völckers letter to Prof. Hans-Adolf Jacobsen, 16.5.66. Völckers also wrote that when the war first broke out in Spain, and the question of evacuating German citizens back home arose, the first to get in line were Bohle's AO people.
19. NA, R59, Dept. of State, Special Interrogation Mission, Bohle interrogation, Blancke, p. 13. At one point, while serving as ambassador to Spain, Faupel had some difficulty with a diplomatic embassy member, who was reprimanded by Bohle. However, the AO leader thought it was time that Faupel joined the party, and offered his sponsorship. After all, the Gauleiter wrote: "I certainly don't think that the Italians have any ambassadors who do not belong to the Fascist Party? Therefore, we would be pleased to have an old front line soldier like Wilhelm Faupel who, by joining the Party, demonstrates his unity with us." AA, PA, Chewf A/O, 47, Bohle (Persönliche Korrespondenz), Bohle to Faupel, 6.5.37.
20 AA, PA, Chef A/O, 47, Gauleiter Bohle(Persönliche Korrespondenz), 1936–1940, Faupel to Bohle, 8.1.37; Bohle to Faupel, 22.1.37.
21. Ibid., Köhn to Bohle, 12.2.37; Bohle to Köhn, 5.3.37.
22. Völckers to Jacobsen, 16.5.66.
23. F.O., Ser. 269, 174400, 177448, 174517-19.
24. AA, PA, Chef A/O, 47, Bohle (Persönliche Korrespondenz), Burbach to Bohle, 16.6.38. This view was also shared by Goebbels, who was critical of the new German ambassador to Spain, Eberhard von Stohrer, who had

recently replaced General Faupel, who was too Catholic. Reuth, hrsg., *Goebbels Tagebücher,* Bd.3, p.1263.
25. AA, PA, Chef A/O, 47, Ehrich to Bohle, 26.7.38.

CHAPTER 9

1. NA, RG 238, WW II Crimes Records, Bohle interrogations, Martin II, pp. 1–3.
2. NA, RG 238, WW II Crimes Records, Bohle interrogations, Lewis XIII, pp. 10–11.
3. F.O., Ser. 269, 175026-30.
4. Ibid., 175046-48.
5. Ibid.
6. Ibid., Ser. 996, 304734-35, and Ser. 269, 175212-222.
7. Ibid., Ser. 81, 60154.
8. NA, T-580, BDC, r.58, ord. 298. Prior to World War I, Germany's colonial empire included a part of the Cameroons, German East Africa, and South West Africa. Although these areas had not been profitable, they had provided the government with excuses to increase their naval expansion before 1914. The 1919 peace settlements stripped Germany of all of her colonial possessions.
9. F.O., Ser. 269, 174837-48.
10. Ibid. In the meantime, the AO sponsored a German youth group in South West Africa, and brought several hundred of them to Germany for schooling: "We will insure that these young people will have their education provided with a correct National Socialist base," Bohle said. NA. German Records, T-81, 21/404/5148425-26.
11. F.O., Ser. 269, 174738-39, and 174793-95.
12. Ibid., 174793-95.
13. Ibid., 174875.
14. BA, Slg. Jacobsen 56, Bd. 1, Nieland to ROL, 16.9.32.
15. F.O., Ser. 81, 60155.
16. N.A., RG 59, Dept. of State, Special Interrogation Mission, Bohle interrogationm, Blancke, pp. 2 and 12, and AA, PA, Chef A/O, 47, Gauleiter Bohle, Persönliche Korrespondenz, 1936–1940, Bohle to Staatssekretär Dr. Meissner, 19.10.36.
17. NA, RG 59, Bohle interrogation, Blancke, p. 26.
18. Ibid., p. 16.
19. F.O., Ser. 81, AO-Statistics, 60147.
20. NA, RG 59, Dept. of State, Special Interrogation Mission, Bohle interrogation, Blancke, pp. 26–30.
21. BA, BDC, v. Thermann file, 22.7.33, and SS Stamkarte.
22. F.O., Ser. 257, 168189 and 168749.
23. BA, BDC, Thermann file, copy of *Deutsche La Plata Zeitung,* 30.1.34.
24. F.O., Ser. 257, 168193-203.
25. Ibid., 168281-82.
26. Ibid., 168590.
27. Ibid., Ser. 2348, 487487-97.
28. Ibid., Ser. 257, 168293-94.
29. Ibid., 168296 and 168352.
30. Ibid., Ser. 263, 171229-31. The police exchange program was never started because of the outbreak of war in 1939.
31. Ibid., Ser. 263, 171229-31.

32. The Third Communist International, or Comintern, had been organized in 1919 and was dedicated to the overthrow of capitalism. It promoted the spread of communist propaganda throughout the world, and Communists in all nations were invited to attend the congresses held in Moscow.
33. F.O., Ser. 263, 170852-56.
34. Ibid., 170856.
35. Ibid., 170884-940
36. Ibid., 170973-78.
37. Ibid., 171032.
38. BA, Slg. Jacobsen 57, Bd. 2, Dok. E. W. Bohle Nr.38, s.55.
39. F.O., Ser. 263, 171247-52. Most of the nations in Latin America declared war against Germany within days of the entry of the United States in 1941. Argentina and Chile, did not declare war against Germany until early 1945.
40. F.O., Ser. 2348, 487498-503.
41. Ibid., 487500-503.
42. Ibid., 51574. Thermann advised that the job of keeping the German citizens separate from the Germans who were not citizens, was the responsibility of the Volksdeutschemittelstelle (VoMi).
43. Ibid.
44. Ibid.
45. In 1823, the U.S. President Monroe, in a message to Congress, warned the European nations against any intervention into South America. While the warning was aimed at Great Britain at the time, the Monroe Doctrine subsequently became a protective shield for the entire southern continent.
46. In spite of the pre-war feelings of some hostility toward the Germans, Latin America became the preferred refuge for Nazis fleeing post-war Germany.

CHAPTER 10

1. F.O., Ser. 81, AO-Statistics, 30.6.37.
2. Ibid. There are no exact figures for the number of Nazi Party members in the United States and Canada after 1937.
3. Ibid.
4. BA, BDC, Gissibl file, "Politischer Lebenslauf des Parteigenossen Fritz Gissibl", and BA, Slg. Jacobsen 19, Bd. 5, Gissibl, AO Schatzamt, 30.9.37.
5. Ibid., Gissibl file, "Polit. Lebenslauf."
6. Ibid., Spanknoebel file, 30.10.35.
7. *Docs. on Ger. For. Pol.*, Ser. C, vol. II, pp. 758–59. The McCormack committee was often referred to in the German press as the "Dickstein Ausschuss", because the initiation for the committee had come from a U.S. Congressman named Samuel Dickstein, who was Jewish.
8. U.S. Cong., H.R. Hearings, July 9–12, 1934, pp. 241-244.
9. Mensing letter to H.-A. Jacobsen, 11.4.67.
10. BA, BDC, Lüdecke file, Bohle to Reichsschatzmeister, 25.3.38. Lüdecke's NSDAP membership number was listed as 123,634, and dated from January 1, 1929. Ibid., Leonhardt letter, 26.2.38.
11. AA, PA, Inland II A/B, 8202, Lüdecke file, 1934–1941. Lüdecke tried to gain U.S. citizenship in 1939, after pleading before the naturalization court that he had become a new man and had found religion. He was interned as an enemy alien on Ellis Island during World War II, and eventually deported back to Germany in 1948, never to return. He died in Bavaria in 1960. See A. Smith,

"Kurt Lüdecke: The Man Who Knew Hitler," *German Studies Review* (Oct. 2003), pp. 595–606.

12. U.S. Cong., H.R. Hearings 73, pp. 237–38.
13. *Docs. on Ger. Foreign Pol.*, Ser. C, v.II, pp. 6–7.
14. Before the war started, Hanfstaengl came to the United States, but afterwards, returned to Germany. See Ernst Hanfstaegnl, *Hitler: The Missing Years* (London: Eyre & Spottiswoode, Ltd. 1957).
15. Kappe's party record showed that at one time in America, he had been accused by other party members of stealing money from the dues' fund. A party court in Germany (Uschla, or Untersuchungs-und Schlichtungsausschüsse) found him not guilty. BDC, BA, Walter Kappe file, "Der Uschla Beschluss, 29.6.32.
16. Shortly before the public emergence of the German-American Bund, Bohle had dispatched a former employee of the AO, to report on the situation. The former employee noted that the trip was taken with the purpose of gauging the feeling of the various German groups in the United States, and especially the German-American Bund. NA, German Records, T-81, 3/141/0179046.
17. NA, RG 238, WW II Crimes Records, Bohle interrogations, Martin II, pp 25–36.
18. *Docs. on Ger. Foreign Pol.*, Ser. D, v. I, p. 660.
19. Ibid., pp. 632–638, and NA, RG 238, WW II Crimes Records, Bohle Interrogations, Martin II, pp. 25–26.
20. NA, RG 59, Dept. of State, Special Interrogation Mission, Gienanth interrogation, p. 2, and BA, BDC Gienanth file, Lebenslauf und Fragebogen.
21. British F.O., Ser. 809, 276100.
22. Ibid.
23. Ibid., 276101-10.
24. *Docs. on Ger. Foreign Pol.*, Ser. D, v. I, pp. 685–686. Dieckhoff was not informed that back in Berlin there had been some speculation that Kuhn might return to Germany as events heated up in the U.S., and in that event, it had been agreed that he was not to receive any official reception. British F.O., Ser. 809, 2761133-116.
25. The *New York Times*, September 6, 1938, p. 7:2.
26. British F.O., Ser. 49, 32797-98.
27. NA, RG 59, Dept. of State, Special Interrogation Mission, Gienanth interrogation, pp. 3–4, and BA, BDC, Gienanth file, Lebenslauf und Fragebogen. Amazingly, Gienanth remained in the United States until 1942 — even though he was under suspicion by American authorities of engaging in espionage — when he was repatriated to Germany in an exchange of diplomatic personnel.
28. *Docs. On Ger. Foreign Pol.*, Ser. C, v. II, p. 1119.

CHAPTER 11

1. Bohle said that Ribbentrop even prescribed the correct uniform that was to be worn, down to the color of the gloves. AA, PA, Auswärtiges Amt, Chef AO, 100, Verschiedenes, vom 1937 bis 1939.
2. Reuth, Hrsg., *Goebbels Tagebücher*, Bd. 3, p. 1313.
3. BA, Slg. Schumacher, Akte 294, Tagesbefehl Nr. 46/39, 8.5.39.
4. Ibid. Tagesbefehl 47/39.
5. BA, BDC, Bohle file, 11.5.39, in den Amtsräumen des Reichsschatzmeisters.
6. British F.O., Ser. 102, 110994.

7. AA, PA, Chef A/O, 55, a)Reichsdeutsche im Ausland, 1937–1942, 4.4.39.
8. British F. O., Ser. 1494, 369885-86.
9. Ibid., Ser. 7969, E575044-46, and Ser. 2341, 487368.
10. Even though the Gauleiter was aware that war plans were in the offing, and Germany was literally on the brink of war, he decided to direct some of his resources to a publication (*Deutsches Wollen*) that would be sent to Germans overseas. The idea was that a sixty-page monthly would contain not only National Socialist propaganda, but have also some literary content that would presumably appeal to all German readers. He persuaded Rudolf Hess to write the introduction to the first issue, but the entire undertaking failed to take off and subscriptions were meager and the project was abandoned. Bohle was obviously disappointed because he said that it was an idea that he had hoped to realize from the very beginning of his career in the AO. NA, German Records, T-80, 3/141/0177213, 0177238, 0179188.
11. AA, PA, Chef A/O, 55, a)Reichsdeutsche im Ausland, 1937–42, Bohle to RAM, 18.9.39.
12. Ibid., Chef A/O, 72.
13. British F. O., Ser. 257, 168702-04, Ser. 49, 32878-97.
14. PA, AA, Chef A/O, 72, Erlasse A.O., 6/39, 30.9.39.
15. Ibid., Erlasse A.O., 5/39, 9.9.39.
16. Ibid., 41, Beamte. Allgemeines, 1937-1940, Aktennotiz, Chef A/O im AA, 24.10.39.
17. Ibid., Chef A/O, 91, b)NS-Feiertage im Ausland, 1935-1940, 24.10.39.
18. British F.O., Ser. 1272, 341892.
19. Ibid., 341936-42.
20. Von Weizsäcker Case XI, mimeographed documents 51, Bohle Doc. Bk. III, No. 31, p.11, and mimeographed testimony, Bohle Doc. 82, pp. 1–2.
21. British F. O., Ser. 1272, 341905-07, 342109-11.
22. Ibid., 342098-99, Ser. 1494, 370090.
23. PA, AA, Chef A/O, 71 Erlasse 1939, Erdmannsdorff, 20.9.39.
24. Ibid.
25. Ibid., Chef A/O 41, Allgemeines, 1937–1940, 31,10.39. After Holland was occupied by Germany in 1940, Bohle recommended Butting for a decoration for his services there: "Party member Dr. Butting carried out through directions from the Auslands-Organisation an order from the Supreme Commander of the Wehrmacht, to gather material about the Dutch army, the Dutch defense system and fortifications, and its intelligence network. He accomplished this task with the assistance of the Party members assigned to him." BA, BDC, Butting file, Bohle note, 7.11.40.
26. PA, AA, Chef A/O, 71, Deutsche Gesandtschaft, Brüssel, 14.10.39.
27. Ibid., Deutsches Generalkonsulat, Zurich, 4.10.39.
28. British F.O., Ser 3734, EO 37458-63, Ser. 3736, EO 37510-13.
29. Ibid., EO 3748092.
30. PA, AA, Chef A/O, 71, 1939, Deutsche Gesandtschaft, Oslo, 26.10.39, Deutsche Gesandtschaft, Kopenhagen, 28.9.39.
31. Ibid., Deutsche Botschaft, Madrid, 2.11.39.
32. Ibid., Deutsches Generalkonsulat, Genua, 9.10.39.
33. British F. O., Ser. 81, 59970-99.

CHAPTER 12

1. NA, RG 59, Dept. of State, Special Interrogation, Bohle interrogation, Smith I, p. 4.
2. British F.O., Ser 1494, 370083.
3. *Docs. on Ger. For. Pol.*, Ser. D, v. VIII, p. 893.
4. British F.O., Ser. 6986, E692910-16 and E692986-87.
5. BA Jacobsen, 57, Bd. 2, Dok. E.W. Bohle, Nr.20, Eidesstattliche Erklärung, Franz Rademacher.
6. British F.O.,Ser.2764, D535609-12 and Ser. 9828, E691848.
7. AA, PA, Chef A/O, 73, Erlasse AO, 1/40.
8. British F. O., Ser. 2764, E691844-45.
9. Ibid., D535629-42, and Ser. 98767, E692901-03.
10. Ibid., E692938-49.
11. Ibid., E692952-60.
12. NA, RG 238, WWII Crimes Records, Bohle interrogation, Lewis XIV, pp. 6–7.
13. NA, T-580, BDC, r.59, Ord. 301.
14. British F.O., Ser. 81, 59792 and 59991-92.
15. Ibid., 60062-63.
16. Ibid., Ser. 263, 171193-94.
17. Ibid., 171195-206.
18. Ibid., Ser. 200, 141078-83. Recent scholarship indicates that the United States put extensive and undue pressure upon the countries of Latin America to reject all Nazi contact, and, in some instances, arranged for the arrest of German citizens who were not deported back to Germany. Max Paul Friedman, *Nazis and Good Neighbors: The United States Campaign against the Germans in World War II* (Cambridge: Cambridge University Press, 2003).
19. British F.O., Ser.257,168481,and NA,German Records,T-81/3/142/9189679-80.
20. AA, PA, Chef A/O, AO Erlasse 73, 3/40, 12.4.40.
21. Ibid., Chef A/O 96, A.O. fremder Staaten, 1931–1941, Verbalnote, 19.10.40.
22 Ibid., Bohle to Deutsche Gesandtschaft, Stockholm, 28.1.41.
23. Ibid., 9.5.41. In one instance, a German soldier serving in the occupation of Norway, deserted to Sweden, and was placed in the camp there. Ibid., 15.5.41.2
24. Reuth, Hrsg.,*Goebbels Tagebücher*, Bd.4, pp. 1571–1572.
25. British F.O., Ser. 4199, E972923-24.
26. U.S. Military Tribunal Case XI, Von Weizsäcker, mimeographed testimony, July 23, 1948, p. 13497.
27. A recent study devoted to the Hess flight in May 1940, presents the view that Hitler and a professor named Albrecht Haushofer were far more informed about the plan. However, while the sources cited include those from the British Foreign Office, there are also some secondary sources included. See Martin Allen, *The Hitler/Hess Deception* (London: Harper Collins, 2003).
28. NA, RG 238, WWII Crimes Records, Bohle interrogation, Lewis XIV, pp. 39–41.
29. U.S. Military Tribunal XI, op. cit., p. 13498.
30. Ibid.
31. NA, RG 238, WWII Crimes Records, Bohle interrogation, Brundage, p. 6.
32. U.S. Military Tribunal, Case XI, Von Weiszäcker, mimeographed documents 51, Bohle Doc. Bk. V, No. 77, pp. 3–7.

33. NA, RG 238, WWII Crimes Records, Bohle interrogation, Kempner XVII, p. 3.
34. Ibid., Brundage VI, p. 3.
35. Reuth, Hrsg., *Goebbels Tagebücher*, Bd. 4, p. 1619.
36. NA, RG 238, WWII Crimes Records, Bohle interrogation, Brundage VI, p. 3.
37. BA, Slg. Jacobsen, 59, Bd.33, Dok. Nr. NG-3812, E.W. Bohle, 24.11.47.

CHAPTER 13

1. NA, German Records, T-81, 3/2/12388-91. At the same time, in a talk to some party members, Bohle stated that Germany was in a battle that could only result in the creation of a greater empire, or end in the complete destruction of the nation. BA, BDC, Ernst Wilhelm Bohle file, 16.4.42., "Berufung von führenden Luxemburgern in die Partei betreff," p. 4.
2. Ibid., Landesgruppe in Italien, 30.3.42, and 12.8.42.
3. NA, RG 59, Dept. of State, Special Interrogation Mission, Bohle interrogation, Bruce Smith, p.11.
4. NA, German Records, T-81, 2/15/386736. Exact figures were never established because of the partial destruction of the AO files at war's end, although the original idea for the club came from Sepp Schuster, who had brought some people together earlier, but it was Gissibl who organized the branches in several major German cities.
5. Ibid., 3/141/0178503-04.
6. Ibid., 3/140/0177201-05. Gissibl decided to create an archival exhibit of the struggle that German Americans endured during the 1930s in the United States, and take it on a tour of Germany. It was called "Amerikadeutschtum im Kampf," and consisted of photos and newspaper clippings that focused on the Bundist meetings and investigations by the U.S. government. It opened in Stuttgart in August 1939, and an estimated fifteen thousand persons attended. Before a tour could be organized, war was declared, and Gissibl was transferred to Poland. Ibid., 0183204.
7. See Arthur L. Smith, Jr., "The Kameradschaft USA," *The Journal of Modern History* (Vol. XXXIV, No. 4, December 1962), pp. 398–408.
8. BA, BDC, Bohle file, speech, Luxemburg, 16.4.43, pp. 29–36.
9. Ibid., Letter to the Reichsführer, 21.6.43.
10. Von Weizsäcker Case XI, mimeographed Documents 51, Bohle Doc. Bk. II, Nos. 28–33.
11. NA, RG 59, Dept. of State, Special Interrogation Mission, Bohle interrogation, Blanke, p. 8.
12. Ibid., RG 238, Rodell IX, p. 9.
13. BA, BDC, Bohle's file, letter to Himmler, 7.4.42, and Himmler reply, 9.5.42. Perhaps the fact that there had been a recent assassination attempt against von Papen and his wife in Ankara, accounted for the indulgent tone of Himmler's reply.
14. NA, T-580, BDC, r.55, Ord. 293.
15. German Records, T-81, 134/169276-77.
16. Ibid., 135/170576-78.
17. Von Weiszäcker Case XI, mimeographed testimony, July 23, 1948, pp. 13529–13530.
18. NA, RG 238, WWII Crimes Records, Bohle interrogation, Lewis, pp. 20–22.

19. Von Weiszäcker Case XI, mimeographed testimony, July 23, 1948, pp. 13515–13516. After his rejection, Himmler, disguised as a German soldier with shaved moustache and eye patch, was arrested in a small town near Bremen by British forces, but while undergoing a physical, he swallowed a vial of cyanide, and died almost instantly.

CHAPTER 14

1. Trials of War Criminals before the Nuremberg Military Tribunals, v.XII (Washington, D.C.: USGPO, 1952), pp. 2–3. Hereafter TWC.
2. NA, RG 238, WWII Crimes Records, Bohle interrogation, Beauvais XVIII, pp.1–2, and Kempner X, p. 6.
3. IMT, v.8, p.626ff., and v.7, p. 130ff.
4. Ibid., v.10, p. 15.
5. NA, RG 238, WWII Crimes Records, Bohle interrogation, Lewis XIV, p. 25.
6. IMT, v.10, p. 77.
7. NA, RG 238, WWII Crimes Records, Bohle interrogation, Lewis XIV, p. 107.
8. Von Weiszäcker Case XI, mimeographed testimony, July 23, 1948, p. 13463.
9. Ibid., November 15, 1948, p. 27544.
10. Ibid., pp. 27545–46.
11. Ibid., mimeographed Documents 51, Bohle Doc. Bk. II, Nos. 28, 29, 31, 32, 33.
12. Ibid.
13. Ibid.
14. Records of the Adjutant General's Office, Department of the Army, 1949 ACLU Correspondence concerning Ernst Wilhelm Bohle. Hereafter Dept. of Army ACLU correspondence, re. Bohle, and date.
15. Ibid.
16. Ibid., May 17, 1949.
17. Ibid., June 10, 1949.
18. Ibid., June 24, 1949.
19. Ibid., Sturm report, June 28, 1949, p.1, and Gray letter, September 17, 1949.
20. NA, RG 238, WWII Crimes Records, Bohle interrogation, Kempner XI, pp. 2–3.
21. Ibid., RG 59, Dept. of State, Special Interrogation Mission, Bohle interrogation, Smith, p.17, and Von Weizsäcker Case XI, mimeographed Documents 51, Bohle Dok. Bk. II, No. 38, p. 79.
22. Ibid., mimeographed testimony, July 23, 1948, p. 13477.
23. Ibid., p. 13478.
24. BA, BDC, Bohle files, 16.4.42.
25. Von Weizsäcker Case XI, mimeographed testimony, July 23, 1948, p. 13484.
26. Ibid., pp. 13485–86.
27. NA, RG 238, WWII Crimes Records, Bohle interrogation, Brundage VI, p. 11.
28. An exception to this rule were the so-called Pennsylvania Germans, who continued to maintain their rural and separate communities, and found no lure in the call of the new Germany.
29. New York Times, 13 November, 1960, p. 88.

Bibliography

When he was interrogated after the war, Ernst Wilhelm Bohle said that he received orders during the final days before Germany's collapse to destroy all the records of his office. He admitted, however, that he had not personally attended any burnings of the materials, but had entrusted the task to an aide named Erich Schnaus. He thought that this may not have been such an easy job because there were constant air raids upon Berlin at the time, and there were additional records that had been stored in several locations. Bohle recalled that when he later spoke to Schnaus about the records, the aide left the impression that the destruction had been carried out, but this was not true.

A most important portion of the AO records that survived are the personal files of many of the individuals who were either employed by Bohle, or worked with him in various capacities. The files constitute a small part of a massive collection of personal files of the members of the Nazi Party, and were, for many years, under the supervision of the U.S. State Department in Berlin. In 1994, the entire collection was taken over by the German Federal Archives (Bundesarchiv) in Koblenz, but the records remained in the Berlin depository, and carry the designation of the Berlin Document Center (BA, BDC).

Equally important for this study, are a number of interviews and interrogations conducted in connection with the prosecution of Bohle as a war criminal during the years immediately following the end of the Second World War. There were twenty-seven sessions of these that occurred between 1945 and 1947. They provide a wealth of information on the inner workings of the Auslands Organisation der NSDAP, as well as details on Bohle's life and career. His observations on a number of the leading figures of the Third Reich are particularly interesting. The material provided in this source, however, must be dealt with critically because it was obtained when Bohle was on trial, and awaiting his sentence. It was also secured in the immediate aftermath of a long and bloody war, and the emotions on all sides were running high as the demand for punishment of the Nazi leaders was at a fever pitch.

UNPUBLISHED SOURCES

Bundesarchiv (Koblenz)
Slg. Jacobsen (19 Bd. 5, 56 Bd. 1, 59 Bd. 4)\
Slg. Schumacher (292, 293, 294)
NS 22/1049
NL Rudolf Pechel (Akte 45/137)
Bundesarchiv (Berlin)
Individual files from the Berlin Document Center(BDC): Otto Bene, Ernst Wilhelm Bohle, Heinrich Bohle, Hermann Bohle, Martin Bormann, Vico von
 Bülow-Schwante, Friedrich Burbach, Otto Butting, Emil Ehrich, Bruno
 Fricke, Ulrich Frhr. Von Gienanth, Friedrich Gissibl, Willy Grothe, Wilhelm
 Gustloff, Alfred Hess, Rudolf Hess, Max Ilgner, Walter Kappe, Otto Karlowa, Karl Kaufmann, Robert Ley, Alfred Leitgen, Martin Löpelmann, Kurt
 Luedecke, Friedrich Carl Mensing, Gustav von Steengracht Moyland, Konstantin von Neurath, Hans Nieland, Franz von Papen, Joachim von Ribbentrop, Bernhard Ruberg, Erich Schnaus, Rudolf Schmeer, Heinz Spanknöbel,
 Hans Steinacher, Georg Strasser, Karl Strölin, Edmund Frhr. Von Thermann,
 Rudolf Tesmann, Ernst von Weizsäcker.
Auswärtiges Amt, Politisches Archiv (Berlin)
Inland II A/B(82-00A Partei und Staat, Bd. 1, 82-04 Aufnahme von Ausländern
 in die N.S.D.A.P., 82-02 NS Ortsg. Im Ausland, Bände 1,3,4,5,6, 82-00C
 Chef der AO im AA, Bd.1) Chef AO 41 Beamte: Allgemeines; 42 Beamte des
 AA; 47 Gauleiter Bohle, Persönliche Korrespondenz; 48 a.Reichsminister, b
 St. S. und Chef AO, c Persönlichkeiten im Ausland, d Besprechungen, e Reisen; 55 a Reichsdt. im Ausland, b Heiraten mit Ausländer, c Angehörige von
 Feindstaaten in Deutschland; 56 a Volksdt., b Auswanderer, c Rückwanderer,
 Heimschaffung-Unterstützung, d Doppelstaatler; 70 Erlasse A.O. 1, 2, 3, 4
 vom 1938; 71 Erlasse A.O. 1, 2, 3, 4, 5 vom 1939; 72 Erlasse A.O. 6, 7, 8, 9
 vom 1939; 73 Erlasse A.O. 1/40, 2/40, 3/40, 4/40, 5/40, 6/40 vom 1940; 74
 Erlasse A.A. 1936-1939; 81 Anträge Gesuche Auskünfte; 88 a Arbeitsdienst,
 b Austellungen, c Stadt der Auslandsdeutschen, d Terminologie Auslandsdeutscher, 91 a Vertretungen deutsche Firmen im Ausland, b Vermittlung
 von Arbeitsnehmer nach dem Ausland, c Kolonialgelegenheiten u.a.; 96 a
 Min.-Dir. Dr. Prüfer, b AO fremder Staaten, c Verfügungen an die Arbeitseinheiten, d Konsulangelegenheiten u.a.; 100 Verschiedenes vom 1937-1939;
 101 Verschiedenes vom 1940.
Personal interviews (oral and written), conducted in Germany by Prof. Hans-
 Adolf Jacobsen:
Gertrud Bohle, 16.12.65
Hans Nieland, 7.12.66
Emil Ehrich, 13.9.65
Fritz Grobba, 2.4.66
Werner von Schmieden, 19.4.66
Hans H. Völckers, 16.5.66
Friedrich C. Mensing, 11.4.67
British Foreign Office Library microfilm of German Auswärtiges Amt records of
 the Büro des Chef der Auslands-Organisation (serials 49, 59, 72, 81, 102,
 119, 200, 257, 261, 263, 269, 809, 996, 1016, 1494, 2341, 2348, 2617, 2764,
 2769, 3046, 3734, 3736, 4199, 6048, 6320, 6715, 6986, 7969 9828, 9867).
Hoover Institution and Archives. Collection title: Kurt Luedecke, Folder ID, Ts
 Germany P214a
U.S. National Archives. Microcopies: T-77, T-81, T-580.

Microfilm Publications M942, Records of the U.S. Nuremberg War Crimes Trials, NP Series 1934–1946.
Records of the Adjutant General's Office, U.S. Department of the Army, 1949. American Civil Liberties Union correspondence with the Dept. of the Army concerning Ernst Wilhelm Bohle.
Hans Steinacher notes provided by Prof. Hans-Adolf Jacobsen.
Transcripts of Bohle interrogations in Record Group 59, U.S. Dept. Of State Special Interrogation Mission (Dewitt C. Poole interrogations of Ernst Wilhelm Bohle, 1945).
Vicco von Bülow-Schwante letter to John L. Heineman, 5 Sept. 1963. Copy provided by Prof. Hans-Adolf Jacobsen.
U. S. Military Tribunal, Nuremberg Trials, Case XI Von Weizsäcker. Nuremberg, Germany, 1948. Mimeographed Testimony and Documents (n. 51).

PUBLISHED SOURCES

Documents on German Foreign Policy. Series C, vols. II, III. Series D, vols. IX, X. Washington, D.C.: USGPO, 1959.
Nazi Conspiracy and Aggression. Suppl. B. Washington, D.C.: USGPO, 1948.
Trials of the Major War Criminals before the Nuremberg Military Tribunal. Vols. VI, VIII, X. Nuremberg, Germany, 1947.
Trials of War Criminals before the Nuremberg Military Tribunals. Vol. XIII. Washington, D.C.: USGPO, 1952.
U.S. House of Representatives, 73rd Cong., 2nd Sess., Hearing no. 73. Washington, D.C.: USGPO, 1935.
U.S. House of Representatives, 76th Cong., 1st Sess., Hearing no. 76. Washington, D.C.: USGPO, 1939.

Books, pamphlets, articles, newspapers

Allen, Martin, *The Hitler/Hess Deception*, London: Harper Collins, 2004.
Die Auslands Organisation der NSDAP, Berlin, 1937.
Bohle, Ernst Wilhelm, "Die Auslandsorganisation der NSDAP," *Almanach der Nationalsozialistischen Revolution*, hrsg. Wilhelm Kube, Berlin: Brunnen Verlag, 1934.
Ehrich, Emil, *Die Auslands-Organisation der NSDAP*, Berlin: Junker u. Dünnhaupt, 1937.
Friedman, Max Paul, *Nazis and Good Neighbors, The United States Campaign against the Germans in World War II*, Cambridge, England: Cambridge University Press, 2003.
Hanfstaegnl, Ernst, *Hitler: The Missing Years*, London: Eyre Spottiswoode, 1957.
Hitler, Adolf, *Mein Kampf*, Munich: Zentralveralg der NSDAP, 1939.
Hüttenberger, Peter, *Die Gauleiter*, Stuttgart: Deutsche Verlags-Anstalt, 1969.
Jacobsen, Hans-Adolf, "Die Gründung der Auslandsabteilung der NSDAP (1931–1933)," *Gedenkschrift Martin Göhring*, Wiesbaden: Franz Steiner Verlag, 1968.
———, *Nationalsozialistische Aussenpolitik 1933–1938*, Frankfurt/M.: Metzner Verlag, 1968.
Jahrbuch der Auslands-Organisation der NSDAP, Berlin: 1942.
Kempner Robert M. W., *SS im Kreuzverhör*, Munich: Ruetten u. Loening Verlag, 1962.

Kube, Wilhelm, hrsg., *Almanach der Nationalsozialistischer Revolution*, Berlin: Brunnen Verlag, 1934.

Lilla, Joachim, *Die Stellvertretenden, Gauleiter und die Vertretung der Gauleiter der NSDAP im "Dritten Reich"*, Koblenz: Bundesarchiv, Heft 13, 2003.

Luedecke, Kurt, *I Knew Hitler, The Story of a Nazi Who Escaped the Blood Purge*, New York: Charles Scribner's Sons, 1937.

McKale, Donald M., *The Swastika Outside Germany*, Kent, Ohio: Kent State University Press, 1977.

The *New York Times*

Paechter, Heinz, *Nazi-Deutsch, A Glossary of Contemporary German Usage*, New York: Frederick Praeger, 1944.

Reuth, Ralf Georg, hrsg., *Joseph Goebbels Tagebücher 1924–1945* (5 vols.), Munich: Piper Verlag, 1992.

Ribbentrop, Joachim von, *The Ribbentrop Memoirs*, London: Weidenfeld and Nicolson, 1954.

Smith, Arthur L., Jr., *The Deutschtum of Nazi Germany and the United States*, The Hague: Nijhoff, 1965.

——, "The Foreign Organization of the Nazi Party and the United States," Hans Trefousse, *Germany and America*, New York: Brooklyn Press, 1980.

——, "Hitler's Gau Ausland," *Political Studies*, XIV (Feb. 1966).

——, "The Kameradschaft USA," *Journal of Modern History*, 34 (1962.)

——, "Kurt Luedecke: The Man Who Knew Hitler." *German Studies*, XXVI (Oct. 2003).

Verpflictendes Erbe, Kiel: Ferdinand Hirt, 1954.

Weizsäcker, Ernst von, *Memiors*, Chicago: Henry Regnery Co., 1951.

Index